"An utterly original memoir for our times, elegant, courageous, and deeply affecting."

—Philippe Sands,
author of *East West Street*

"Although she has written a searing book about the past, Schwarz's work is oriented toward the present and the future. . . . *Those Who Forget* is as readable as it is persuasive. Schwarz embeds her appeal to citizens and nations to do memory work in a gripping detective story centered on her own family's history. She has a gift for finding the single scene or exchange of dialogue that drives home her points. . . . Schwarz's book deserves to be read and discussed widely in the United States principally for all it has to teach us about the urgency of confronting the darkest dimensions of our own history. This is Schwarz's invaluable warning."

—Samantha Power,
The Washington Post

"Out of all the books I read this year—and I read many, stuck at home during 2020's endless quarantine—the one that resonated perhaps the most was *Those Who Forget,* an account by the French-German author Géraldine Schwarz of postwar Europe's, and her own family's, not entirely successful effort to reckon with the crimes of the Second World War. It made the very convincing case that, until and unless there is a full accounting for what happened with Donald Trump, 2020 is not over and never will be."

—Susan B. Glasser,
The New Yorker

"Schwarz's answer to the cultural amnesia of the last five or ten years has been this exacting and detailed memoir, a blend of personal and political history. . . . The stories are vital, and Schwarz is a meticulous, eloquent chronicler."

—*Los Angeles Review of Books*

"[A] riveting exploration of Germany's post–World War II reckoning with guilt and responsibility . . . With eloquence and passion, she demonstrates that we can never be reminded too often to never forget."

—Diane Cole,
The Wall Street Journal

"Schwarz's memoir is astonishing. It illustrates the human capacity to deny, forget, rationalize, and gloss over when we are face-to-face with the most unspeakable crimes against our fellow humans."

—Dannye Romine Powell,
The Charlotte Observer

"Among titles that are predicted to be the biggest books of 2020 . . . A Berlin journalist writes of her German and French grandparents, considered 'ordinary citizens' during World War II but whom she later learns may have had more complex roles."

—Jane Henderson,
St. Louis Post-Dispatch

"It took Europe arguably two generations to fully face up to its shameful Holocaust past. Books like this one are needed to make sure that future generations don't have any such guilt to deny."

—Fran Hawthorne,
New York Journal of Books

"The result of Schwarz's explorations and her determination to find answers to her questions is a work that,—as its subtitle indicates—is part memoir, part history, part warning. She has skillfully woven together 'the threads of major and minor history,' to offer us lessons for today."

—Jewish Book Council

"*Those Who Forget* is enlightening. . . . It's an absolutely excellent choice for anyone interested in history and current events, and for book groups, too, providing timely and important fodder for deep discussion."

—*BookBrowse*

"In this exceptionally timely and well-reasoned debut, Géraldine Schwarz, the granddaughter of a Nazi Party member, makes a powerful case that seeds of the recent resurgence of far-right nationalism in Europe were sown first by the denial and rationalizations of millions of people like her grandparents and then by postwar mythmaking that preempted the 'memory work' needed to correct faulty recollections of Nazism. A deserving winner of the European Book Prize, *Those Who Forget* shows clearly how a willful amnesia can poison nations that have sworn never to forget the Holocaust."

—*Kirkus Reviews* (starred review)

"In her debut, journalist and documentary filmmaker Schwarz offers a powerful and unflinching look at Germany during World War II and Europe's postwar reckoning with far-right nationalism, and calls for readers not to forget the painful lessons learned. . . . In searing yet engaging prose, Schwarz makes her case for the need for memory work in this highly recommended read."

—*Library Journal* (starred review)

"A timely must-read, this brutally honest memoir is also a smart historical analysis and a relevant warning for the future."

—*Booklist* (starred review)

"[An] astute debut . . . this timely memoir also serves as a perceptive look at the current rise of far-right nationalism throughout Europe and the U.S."

—*Publishers Weekly*

THOSE WHO FORGET

MY FAMILY'S STORY
IN NAZI EUROPE—

A MEMOIR,
A HISTORY,
A WARNING

GÉRALDINE SCHWARZ

Translated from the French by **Laura Marris**

SCRIBNER   New York   London   Toronto   Sydney   New Delhi

Scribner

An Imprint of Simon & Schuster, Inc.

1230 Avenue of the Americas

New York, NY 10020

First Scribner trade paperback edition September 2022

SCRIBNER and design are registered trademarks of The Gale Group, Inc.,
used under license by Simon & Schuster, Inc., the publisher of this work.

For information about special discounts for bulk purchases, please contact
Simon & Schuster Special Sales at 1-866-506-1949 or business@simonandschuster.com.

The Simon & Schuster Speakers Bureau can bring authors to your live event.
For more information or to book an event, contact
the Simon & Schuster Speakers Bureau at 1-866-248-3049
or visit our website at www.simonspeakers.com.

Interior design by Kyle Kabel

Photographs courtesy of the Schwarz family, except p. 37, courtesy of Lotte Kramer

Manufactured in the United States of America

1 3 5 7 9 10 8 6 4 2

Library of Congress Control Number: 2020004934

ISBN 978-1-5011-9908-0
ISBN 978-1-5011-9909-7 (pbk)
ISBN 978-1-5011-9910-3 (ebook)

To my parents

"Everything that needs to be said has already been said. But since no one is listening, everything must be said again."

—André Gide

Prologue to the Paperback Edition

I am a child of peace who has never known war. I owe this peace to Europe. I owe it to a promise made by Europeans after the Second World War: "Never again!" To keep this promise, we had to invent a new way to deal with the past. Using history not to glorify nations and to stir up revanchism, but to learn. Taking advantage of the experience of our ancestors to guide us through the complex labyrinth of humanity. Remembering what man is capable of, the best and the worst, to keep our balance on the narrow thread of justice, between trust and caution.

A decade or two ago, this memory began to unravel, abandoned by indifferent younger generations and mutilated by forgers of history intent on imposing nationalist narratives based on hatred. When memory fades, so does vigilance. We forget that peace, democracy, and freedom are legacies to be protected and nurtured tirelessly. We forget the countless sacrifices made by entire generations. Like the air we breathe, we think these achievements are immutable.

Then, one morning, we wake up to war. Not the war of Netflix series and video games, real war: scenes of bloodied young men; bullets tearing into jaws, hearts, brains; shells pulverizing a civilian shelter, despite the warning written in gigantic letters on the ground in the vain hope of dissuading Russian bombers: *CHILDREN*. In cities reduced to ashes, dazed grandmothers wander in the ruins, babies scream, women don't even have tears to cry. This is real war, with Russian soldiers parading around on their tanks, spreading terror and raping and torturing Ukrainian civilians, their bodies littering the street like trophies after a hunting party. Impunity is total. There are no borders, no national sovereignty, no international conventions anymore. Lies and cynicism have all the rights. Human dignity is nothing more than an old dream crushed by boots.

It is the return of barbarism to Europe. Why? Because of a leader's incapacity to come to terms with the past. Because Vladimir Putin, obsessed with history to the point of madness, believes himself to be invested with a sacred mission: reviving an idealized tsarist Russian empire, glorious, flawless, more powerful, more luminous than Europe. This past never existed, so he rewrites it, embellishes it, polishes it, purifies it, removes the shadows. Any criticism of Russian history is seen as a personal insult to Putin, as blasphemy. Even the abominations of Joseph Stalin are minimized. Stalin's Great Patriotic War against Nazism erases all his crimes; the Great Victory is a sacred myth used to attest to Russia's eternal moral superiority. Everywhere in Russia history is manipulated, distorted, and mutilated: in museums, schoolbooks, speeches, films, media. A law stipulates that the state guarantees "the protection of historical truth." Historians either collaborate or are finished.

In Putin's hands, history is not only an instrument for glorifying national identity but a weapon of mass destruction. He justifies violence with imperial nostalgia. Putin aims to unify all the Russian-speakers that belonged, at some point, to the tsardom, whether they like it or not. In his eyes, there are no Ukrainians, only Russians. Adolf Hitler also did not hesitate to swallow territories where "his people," German-speaking peoples, lived.

Putin has opened up a door that we thought we had closed after the Second World War. But this revival of old historical patterns clashes with the realities of the twenty-first century. European peoples, the Ukrainians among them, have tasted open and liberal societies. They no longer allow themselves to be divided. They resist. They have learned from the past that no ideology, no nationalism, no imperialism is worth sacrificing peace and freedom. And that no past, however glorious, is worth dying for.

—Géraldine Schwarz, Berlin, April 2022

THOSE WHO FORGET

To Be or Not to Be a Nazi

I wasn't particularly destined to take an interest in Nazis. My father's parents were neither on the victims' nor the executioners' side. They didn't distinguish themselves with acts of bravery, but neither did they commit the sin of excess zeal. They were simply *Mitläufer*, people who "followed the current." Simply, in the sense that their attitude was shared by the majority of the German people, an accumulation of little blindnesses and small acts of cowardice that, when combined, created the necessary conditions for the worst state-orchestrated crimes known to humanity. For many years after the defeat, my grandparents, like most Germans, lacked the hindsight to realize that though the impact of each *Mitläufer* was tiny on an individual level, it had a cumulative effect, since without their participation, Hitler would not have been able to commit crimes of such magnitude. The Führer himself sensed this and regularly took the measure of his people to see how far he could go, all the while inundating them with Nazi and anti-Semitic propaganda. The first massive deportation of Jews in Germany, which would test the general population's threshold of acceptance, took place in the exact same region where my grandparents lived. In October 1940, more than 6,500 Jews from the southwest of the country were deported to the Gurs camp in the south of France. To accustom their citizens to such a spectacle, German forces of law and order attempted to save face by avoiding violence and commissioning passenger cars—not the freight trains that were later used. But the Nazis wanted to know how much the people would be able to stomach. They didn't hesitate to operate in broad daylight, herding hundreds of Jews through the city center to reach the train station, with their heavy suitcases, their children in tears, and their exhausted elderly—all of this right before the eyes of apathetic citizens who were incapable of exercising their humanity. The next day, the *Gauleiter* (district chiefs) proudly announced to Berlin that their region was the first in Germany to be *judenrein* (purified of Jews). The Führer must have rejoiced to be so well understood by his people: the time was ripe for "following."

One episode, unfortunately one of the few, proved that the population had not been as powerless as it hoped to appear after the war. In 1941, protests by citizens and Catholic and Protestant bishops across Germany succeeded in disrupting the planned extermination of physically and mentally disabled people, or those judged as such, that had been ordered by Adolf Hitler in an effort to purge the Aryan race of "life unworthy of life." Although this secret operation, called Aktion T4, was in full swing, having already gassed 70,000 people in specialized centers in Germany and Austria, Hitler relented in the face of public indignation and called off his plan before it could be completed. The Führer understood the risk he would run if the population perceived him as too overtly cruel. This was also one of the reasons the Third Reich expended an insane amount of energy organizing an extremely complex and expensive system to transport Jews from all over Europe to isolated camps in Poland, where they were murdered far from the eyes of their fellow citizens.

But in the aftermath of the war, no one, or almost no one, in Germany asked themselves what might have happened if the majority of citizens had not followed the current, but instead turned *against* a politics that had revealed relatively early its intention to crush human dignity under its heel. Going along with these politics, like my grandpa, my *opa* did, was so widespread that this crime was mitigated by its banality, even in the eyes of the Allied forces who got it into their heads to denazify Germany. After their victory, Americans, French, British, and Soviets divided the country and Berlin into four zones of occupation where each engaged in eradicating the Nazi elements of society with the help of German arbitration hearings. They determined four degrees of implication in Nazi crimes, the first three of which theoretically justified the opening of a judicial investigation: the "major offenders" (*Hauptschuldige*); the "offenders" (*Belastete*); the "lesser offenders" (*Minderbelastete*); and the "followers" (*Mitläufer*). According to the official definition, this last term designated "those who did not participate more than nominally in National Socialism," in particular "the members of the National Socialist German Workers' Party (NSDAP) . . . who only went so far as to pay membership fees and attend required meetings."

In reality, among the 69 million inhabitants who lived within the borders of the Reich in 1937, the number of *Mitläufer* surpassed the 8 million members of the NSDAP. Millions of others had joined affiliated organizations, and still more had cheered National Socialism without belonging to a Nazi organization. For example, my grandmother, who was not an NSDAP member, was more devoted to Adolf Hitler than my grandfather, who was an official party member. But the Allies didn't have time to examine such nuances. They already had enough to handle with the offenders, both major and lesser: the multitude of high-level officials who had given criminal orders within the bureaucratic labyrinth of the Third Reich, and the many who had executed those orders, oftentimes with an infamous zeal.

People like my grandfather who were members of the Nazi Party emerged almost unscathed. His only punishment was to lose control of his small petroleum products business, Mineralölgesellschaft Schwarz & Co., which was consigned for several years to

an administrator appointed by the Allied authorities. He would probably have also found it difficult to get a job as a civil servant if he had
wanted one. His daughter, my aunt Ingrid, thinks she remembers
him being condemned to "break stones," but strangely, my father
has no memory of this and is sure that, in the unlikely event of such
a verdict, my grandfather, "clever as he was," would have arranged
to spare himself the task. He mainly remembers that his father's
business was never better than during that period of forced unemployment, as he turned out to be a much more resourceful businessman on the black market than on the regular one. He remembers
that there was always wine on the Schwarz table, as well as meat,
eggs, and apples—while many forgot the taste of these products in
the ruins of Germany after the war. This discrepancy between the
memories of Karl Schwarz's two children reflects the fact that one
was as devoted to her father as the other was estranged from him.

Of course, the Allies couldn't throw all 8 million members of
the NSDAP in prison, largely because there wasn't enough space
behind bars. From spring 1945 on, the Allies moved forward with
massive arrests of former party officials and members of the SS,
sending about 300,000 of them to prison. Among the Allies, the
Americans were by far the strictest in carrying out the denazification
of their zone, at least at the beginning. As one of the largest cities
of Baden-Württemberg, Mannheim, where my grandparents lived,
was just inside the southwestern American zone, which included
the north of Baden-Württemberg, Bavaria, and Hesse, along with
the southwest of Berlin and Bremerhaven to the north, with its
precious strategic location on the North Sea. The Americans had a
good reputation, and my aunt Ingrid remembers them "always with
a smile, healthy at the wheels of their Jeeps, adding a bit of cheer-
fulness" to the funerary atmosphere of postwar Germany. However,
their commander, the future president of the United States Dwight
D. Eisenhower, was quite pessimistic, estimating that it would take
at least fifty years of intensive reeducation to mold Germans to

democratic principles. The Americans were especially dependent on the media, which was under their control, to make the population feel the effects of crimes committed under the Third Reich and to convince the German people of democracy's charms. But above all, they had the titanic ambition to delve into the pasts of all Germans over eighteen by having them fill out questionnaires, each with about 130 questions designed to indicate their degree of complicity with the regime and their level of ideological indoctrination. With highly bureaucratic rigor, the Americans began to sift through the millions of forms on their desks, in the interest of punishing the guilty and removing the elements of society most deeply imbued with Nazism. They fired all the officials who had joined the NSDAP before May 1, 1937, and who were therefore suspected of belonging out of conviction. At the end of winter 1945–46, more than 40 percent of government officials in the American zone had been let go.

I couldn't find a copy of my grandfather's denazification questionnaire, but he must have filled one out, because a letter from the occupation authorities indicates that they knew very quickly of his party affiliation. After Karl Schwarz died in 1970, my father looked everywhere in his papers for traces of the card or for party insignia, without success. As soon as the Allies announced their entrance into Mannheim in March 1945, my grandfather, like many of his compatriots, must have thrown any compromising proof into the kitchen stove along with the Nazi flags that were flown from balconies on national holidays. Who knows, he may have even burned a portrait of the Führer that had once hung, as a safeguard, in his office, or destroyed one that my grandmother had saved in a drawer out of attachment. It was a wasted effort, since the local chiefs of the NSDAP fled the city without even a half-hearted attempt to destroy the registry of Mannheim party members, which the Americans found intact when they arrived.

But Karl didn't clear away his Nazi past completely. In Opa's papers, my father found a very strange heraldic drawing: a knight's helmet on a background of black and gold plants partly shielding an imaginary creature—a cross between a goat and a deer with red horns and hooves, whose neck is pierced by a red arrow. Beneath it, the name Schwarz is written in complex calligraphy, with the date 1612 and this text: "The origins of this bourgeois family whose lines flourish in Swabia and Franconia are to be found in Rothenberg." Under National Socialism, genealogy was very much in vogue and even achieved quasi-official status in the service of the regime, which needed to lend its muddy theories of race a credibility that no serious science could provide. This drawing would have had only decorative value, since joining the Nazi party required a document that was more complicated to establish: a certificate of Aryanism, requiring an extensive number of detailed justifications proving the Aryan origins of the applicant and his or her spouse, at least as far back as 1800. It perplexes me that Karl Schwarz also had this nonrequired crest done in watercolor and ink. By all accounts, my grandfather was not a hardline National Socialist—he was too smitten with liberty. "He might have hung it in the offices of his company, so that whenever a Nazi client or official passed through, they would ask fewer questions and leave him alone," my father said. In the thirties, rumors circulated in Germany about business owners suspected of hiding their Jewish origins, which contributed to an atmosphere of paranoia and accusation so intense that some people even published announcements in the newspapers denying any link to Judaism. Opa destroyed his certificate of Aryanism, but strangely, he spared his watercolor, and kept it until his death. According to my father, "he liked the drawing because it gave the illusion of a glorious ancestry. And my father sometimes had dreams of grandeur." In some ways, Karl Schwarz was a man of his time.

✴   ✴   ✴

As they faced the scope of the task they'd given themselves, the Americans quickly decided to integrate the German justice system into the process of denazification. After the questionnaires were examined, the people suspected of being implicated were sent to one of a few hundred German arbitration chambers in the American zone. In Mannheim, they sifted through 202,070 forms, 169,747 of which were considered "not implicated." Of the 8,823 Mannheim citizens judged at the German hearings, 18 were classified as major offenders, 257 as offenders, 1,263 as lesser offenders, 7,163 as *Mitläufer*, and 122 were exonerated. I doubt my grandfather had a hearing. Either way, since the Americans struggled to find "clean" German judges due to the high degree of complicity with National Socialism among legal professionals, and had to resign themselves to recruiting among the old guard, Karl Schwarz wouldn't have had much to fear. Even less so once the occupiers could no longer afford to appear uncompromising while German personnel were urgently needed to deal with the numerous problems confronting their own society: malnutrition, a housing crisis, the lack of coal for heat. . . . Furthermore, American attention soon turned from former Nazis to focus on a new enemy—the Soviet Union and the Communist bloc. A rigorous start was followed by bungled measures, as the Americans attempted to wrap up the denazification process as quickly as possible in order to accelerate the reconstruction of western Germany, which was on the edge of Communist enemy territory.

Unlike the Americans, the British were much less interested in denazification based on sanctions in their northwestern zone, which included Hamburg, Lower Saxony, North Rhine–Westphalia, Schleswig-Holstein, and the western sector of Berlin. Above all, they aimed for reeducation through newly created media outlets in the region. Sometimes democratization was imposed with an iron fist, as in the case of a British commander in the small town of

Steinfurt, who forced the inhabitants to watch a film made during the liberation about concentration-camp victims. The relationship between the local population and their occupiers was much more distant than in the American zone, and the British were often regarded as a kind of colonial invader, particularly when they commandeered apartments in towns that were already suffering from an acute lack of housing after the bombardments. In truth, the British didn't always have a choice about requisitioning, since they were very much weakened economically by the war and had difficulties financing the costs of the occupation. For the most part, they lived in parallel worlds. The British reserved a certain number of train cars, trolleys, businesses, and cinemas for themselves, with signs posted that read "Keep Out" or "No Germans." They also reproduced their model of clubs, and though they occasionally allowed some Germans entry, this mingling was rare. The British quickly abandoned the idea of decontaminating German society and merely focused on banning former Nazis from applying for the most senior civil service positions and catching the biggest fish. They were so indulgent toward wartime complicity that some Nazis under American occupation hurried to reach their zone.

More than anything, the British were eager to rebuild the economic power of Germany, in which they had their own vested interests. And so they proved to be accommodating if the accused were part of the Reich's economic elite, as was the case with Günther Quandt. He was not a hardline National Socialist, but an opportunist who waited until Adolf Hitler came to power in January 1933 to finance and then join his party. A familial tie reinforced this financial proximity, since the industrialist's second wife, Magda Ritschel, whom he had divorced, had gone on to marry Joseph Goebbels, the future minister of propaganda, in December 1931, with the Führer himself as best man. Despite the fact that he was in conflict with Goebbels over the custody of his son, Quandt's loyalty to Hitler paid off, as he amassed a colossal fortune and became one of the Nazis' largest military suppliers. During the massive labor shortage caused by the mobilization of men to the front, Quandt exploited some 50,000 forced laborers—prisoners of war and detainees in concentration camps, who were "loaned" by the Reich at low cost. In 1946, the Americans arrested Quandt, but he escaped the Nuremberg Trials thanks to the British, who "overlooked" the documents concerning his case and didn't send them to the Americans, then continued the farce by officially classifying him as a *Mitläufer*. In January 1948, the Americans, for their part, refrained from investigating further and liberated him. Soon after, the British army rushed to do business with this weapons specialist.

Quandt was a rare specimen. He made equipment that the whole world wanted, in particular, the battery for the "magic weapon" the Nazis developed during the war—the V2, the first operational ballistic missile and the precursor of intercontinental missiles and space flight. After the war, the Quandt family, which is now a major shareholder in BMW and other high-profile companies, was steeped in denial about the suspect origins of their fortune until a 2007 television documentary called *The Silence of the Quandts* forced them to acknowledge their past.

As for the French, whose zone was the smallest—it included only a little strip of land at the French border and the northwest of Berlin—they also quickly realized the advantages of being lenient toward industrialists who, in return for this generosity, offered promising business opportunities. In general, the French acquired a reputation as the occupying force least interested in denazification. They preferred to accuse the Germans as a whole, without differentiating individuals by their degree of culpability or hoping to reeducate them. The feeble number of judicial procedures they undertook was in part due to the fact that France itself, having closely cooperated with the Third Reich, had a postwar administration rife with

former Vichy collaborators who feared that accusations against the
Nazis would return to haunt them. Among the Allies, General de
Gaulle, who governed France after the war, was most in favor of policies that would weaken Germany, hoping for it to be permanently
divided and to pay maximum reparations. This stance was apparent
in the occupiers' vindictive attitude toward the local population, who
feared the French agenda. Though the French were only invited to
the victors' table at the last minute because of their collaboration
with the Reich, they acted like a true occupying force—confiscating
apartments to house their own teachers, engineers, and officials,
exploiting German labor, and requisitioning food in abundance,
while many Germans were living in basements, hungry and cold,
with no fuel to warm themselves. There was even a series of rapes.

In the Soviet zone, which spread across the five easternmost
Länder—Thuringia, Saxony-Anhalt, Saxony, Brandenburg, and
Mecklenburg-Vorpommern, as well as eastern Berlin—the denazification measures were applied not only to the Nazis, but also
to "undesirables" whom the Soviets wished to get rid of. These
so-called Class Enemies included the Junkers, who were the largest
landowners, as well as members of the economic elite, social democrats, and other detractors of the new Communist regime, which
the occupying authorities quickly tried to put in place following the
Moscow model. The Soviets also left the *Mitläufer* in peace, perhaps because they recognized the opportunity to recycle them into
good Communists. However, the more heavily implicated Nazis
had more to fear in this zone than in the others, since they could
not claim, with the Soviets, to have become Nazi party members
to oppose Bolshevism, an argument that carried a certain weight
in the West. As a result, many Germans preferred to flee the East,
especially because of its infamous prison conditions. Thousands of
presumed Nazis and "undesirables" languished in former concen-

tration camps, where at least 12,000 perished. Thousands of others were deported to the Soviet Union, where many of them also died.

In March 1948, the Soviets had already chased more than 520,000 former members of the NSDAP from civil service, particularly from the administration and the judiciary, where they quickly replaced them with "loyal" Communists. In less than a year, these new judges and prosecutors had been "trained," and by 1950 they took on a series of expedited trials called the *Waldheimer Prozesse*, backed by the authority of the newborn German Democratic Republic (GDR). In two months, approximately 3,400 people accused of committing Nazi crimes were tried, without witnesses and without legal assistance, before these inexperienced judges and prosecutors. Their judgments were determined in advance to obtain the maximum penalty, without distinguishing among *Mitläufer*, true offenders, or enemies of communism. These phony trials were above all designed to legitimize, after the fact, the internment of thousands of people in special camps. More than half of the accused were given sentences of up to fifteen to twenty-five years in prison; twenty-four of them were executed. Then the GDR decided that the era of denazification was over and threw itself into a long denial of its historical responsibilities in regards to the crimes of the Third Reich, designating the Western Federal Republic of Germany (FRG) as the sole heir to that somber past.

Germans did not support denazification of the population as a whole, which was perceived as an unbearable humiliation, a *Siegerjustiz*—a conqueror's justice designed to take revenge. But they were largely in agreement with the idea of prosecuting the authorities of the regime.

In November 1945, at the behest of the Americans, a trial opened in Nuremberg against twenty-four high officials from the Third Reich, before an international military tribunal under the authority of the four Allied powers. Treating "the war and the atrocities committed in its name not as politics by other means, but as a crime for which high-ranking politicians and military officers could be held responsible as they could for any other crime" was unprecedented, argues the lawyer Thomas Darnstädt in his 2015 book, *Nuremberg: Bringing Crimes Against Humanity to Justice in 1945*. The major points were developed in advance in Washington under the direction of Justice Robert H. Jackson. The Soviets, who were afraid of being accused of crimes themselves for the abuses of the Red Army and the nonaggression pact they signed with Hitler in 1939, asked that the international criminal jurisdiction accorded at Nuremberg only apply to Allied powers. Judge Jackson refused: "We are not prepared to lay down a rule of criminal conduct against others which we would not be willing to have invoked against us." The British, who had their own intensive bombardments of German civilian populations in mind, negotiated a compromise: the rules of criminal conduct would be applied to everyone, but the Nuremberg trials would only be responsible for Nazi crimes. More than two thousand people were mobilized to prepare for the trial, sifting through at least part of the miles of archives left by the ultra-bureaucratic regime.

A year after the Nuremberg trial opened, the verdict came down: twelve of the accused were condemned to death by hanging, including Hermann Göring, the Reich's second in command; Joachim von Ribbentrop, the minister of foreign affairs; Ernst Kaltenbrunner, the last head of the powerful Reich Main Security Office (RHSA); Wilhelm Keitel, the head of the armed forces high command; Julius Streicher, the founder of the anti-Semitic newspaper *Der Stürmer*; and Alfred Rosenberg, ideologue of the Nazi Party and minister of occupied territories in the East. Three were condemned to life in prison, including Rudolf Hess, Hitler's former deputy. Two others—Albert Speer, architect and minister of armament, and Baldur von Schirach, head of the Hitlerjugend

(Hitler Youth)—received a twenty-year sentence. Four organizations—the NSDAP, the Gestapo, the SS, and the SD (Security Services)—were classified as "criminal organizations." The judges decided against a petition by the prosecution to include the German General Staff and the Supreme High Command of the Wehrmacht (OKW) on that list.

The trials demonstrated a resolve, on the part of the Allies, and especially of the Americans, not to let Nazi crimes go unpunished. They defined a new category of wrongdoing: crimes against humanity. But in the short term, these measures didn't have the desired results. Justice Jackson stressed the prosecution of "crimes against the peace of the world" and "conspiracy." This approach reinforced a myth that would take a long time to dismantle: that the Nazi crimes were the result of a secret plan developed by a small group of commanders surrounding Hitler that gave orders to people who were for the most part ignorant that they were participating in a criminal enterprise. Another problem jurists emphasized during the Nuremberg trials was the idea of a tribunal where the victors judged the defeated, imposing silence on the Allied war crimes: the Vichy collaboration; the massive American and British bombardments against German civilians; the atrocities committed by the Red Army in the Reich's eastern territories; the atomic bombs dropped by the United States on Japan. But one of the greatest failures of the trials was to neglect the genocide of the Jews, as this offense did not yet exist. According to Thomas Darnstädt, "even in the face of this incomparable Nazi crime, there was still a taboo in international law against interfering in the 'internal affairs' of a sovereign state," or so the crimes against German Jews were considered. Only crimes against foreign Jews were taken into account, and just after the war, many aspects of the Reich were still poorly understood. Experts had not yet analyzed the proceedings of the 1942 Wannsee Conference, where the Nazi commanders developed their plans for the Holocaust, which by then had already begun.

Between 1946 and 1949, in keeping with the aims of Nuremberg, the Americans organized twelve more trials in their zone in three years, held under their sole authority—bringing more than 185 doctors, generals, economic leaders, jurists, high-ranking bureaucrats, and commanders of the Einsatzgruppen into court. Twenty-four were condemned to death, thirteen death sentences were carried out, and most of the rest received long prison sentences. At the same time, American public indignation in response to the images of concentration camps that had begun to circulate in the press led the United States to create a military tribunal on the grounds of the Dachau camp, to try the personnel of the six camps situated in the American zone. Approximately 1,600 of the accused were condemned, and 268 of the 426 death sentences were carried out.

In the three Allied zones in the West, approximately 10,000 Nazis in total were condemned by German and Allied tribunals. Of those, 806 were condemned to death, and a third of them were executed. These figures reveal a certain effectiveness, considering the amount of time they had. However, many people who deserved imprisonment for their crimes during the Reich succeeded in slipping through the wide loopholes in the net cast by the Allies. To escape, you had only to pass as a *Mitläufer* by falsifying a few papers and paying one of the *Persilschein*, those false witnesses to "innocence" or "cleanliness," who were named after Persil washing powder. These witnesses were rarely verified by the occupiers, partly because they were overwhelmed by the scale of the task, and also because their motivation quickly began to flag in the context of the Cold War.

One of the largest discredits to the Allied cause was their own conduct in profiting from their position of strength by stealing German technological knowledge. From the beginning of the twentieth century, the spectacular achievements of German scientists were envied the world over. Between 1900 and 1939, thirty-four were awarded a Nobel Prize (fifteen in Chemistry, eleven in

Physics, and eight in Physiology or Medicine), a quarter of them to Jewish Germans. During the same period, fourteen French scientists got the prestigious prize, twenty-two British, and seventeen Americans. The Reich's defeat was the chance for these countries to help themselves to the kind of technological expertise they lacked, expertise that was especially important in the context of the Cold War. Through an American operation called Paperclip, scientists were discreetly taken out of Germany en masse and installed in positions at American companies and universities, so that those who had collaborated with the Nazi regime (such as Wernher von Braun, the father of the V2 ballistic missile, member of the NSDAP and the SS) wouldn't fall into the hands of international justice. It was partly thanks to the breakthroughs of these experts in chemical weapons, space exploration, ballistic missiles, and jets that the United States benefited from a technical advantage during the Cold War. Numerous innovations from other sectors were also stolen, including electron microscopes, cosmetics formulas, recording devices, insecticides, and a machine for distributing paper napkins. The United Kingdom also partook of the feast. The historian John Gimble estimates that the Americans and the British made off with German intellectual property worth $10 billion at the time, the equivalent of $100 billion today. The French were much less involved in this siphoning off of German expertise. Unlike the other Allies, they didn't think it was possible to take German technologies out of their context and apply them at home. Nonetheless, the French military and aeronautics sectors brought several hundred scientists to France, particularly those who had worked on the V2 rocket. Newly transplanted German engineers participated in the development of the first fighter jet engines, the first Airbuses, the first French rockets, submarines, torpedoes, radar, and tank engines, allowing France to make important advances in its military capabilities. As for the Soviets, they put thousands of German experts—including Wernher von

Braun's assistant—on trains to the Soviet Union with their families, enlisting them without ever asking their permission. These German scientists opened the way, at least indirectly, for the USSR to launch *Sputnik*, the first man-made satellite, in 1957.

Despite these kinds of conflicts of interest, the Allies at least had the integrity to sanction, sometimes strictly, a number of war criminals and Nazi officials, giving Germans the foundations of a vague understanding of the harm a regime like the Third Reich could enact. Thanks to these efforts, my aunt Ingrid, who was born in 1936, told me that she had known in early adolescence that "the Nazis had committed crimes," because "it was mentioned in school, and even in the media," where she had seen photos of concentration camps. I was astonished, since my father, who was born in 1943, had always described a total amnesia after the war. Then I realized that Ingrid had gone to school at the moment when the Americans in Mannheim had begun trying to "reeducate" the people, but by the time my father was educated, the parenthesis of denazification had already closed.

In 1949, the Western occupiers authorized the fusion of their three zones to found a new Federal Republic of Germany and allowed Germany to benefit from the Marshall Plan, a program that offered loans to most states in Western Europe to help with their reconstruction after the war. My father often says, "Germany was lucky to have been treated with such leniency after the crimes it committed." Without the Cold War, Germany's fortunes might have been very different.

At the end of the 1940s, the Allies withdrew from the vast project of denazification. They lacked hindsight and didn't understand all the complexities of the Nazi regime, but above all, outside forces could not do this work for the Germans. It was up to them to change their mentality and take charge of their own democratic fate. There was reason to be pessimistic.

II

Germany, "Year Zero"

After the war, my father's family never talked about politics, and in general, discussions were rare at the dinner table—children were not allowed to speak unless they were spoken to, and breaking this rule meant a beating from Karl, who had an authoritarian idea of fatherhood. In the apocalyptic atmosphere of postwar Germany, the priority was not revisiting the past but pulling together a new life. The Schwarz family occupied a three-room flat on the second floor of an apartment building, which was built in 1902 by my grandmother's father, a carpenter who bequeathed it to her—the sole survivor of his brood of nine children—in 1935. Though it had been severely damaged by the Allied bombardments, this building on Chamissostrasse was miraculously spared the worst, while the buildings on the other side of the street were reduced to barren ruins. This urban disfigurement still made a few people happy: "It was an extraordinary landscape for childhood adventures—we could run, jump, climb, hide, and discover piles of treasures," my father remembers.

❋ ❋ ❋

During the war, Mannheim and the neighboring town of Ludwigshafen, at the confluence of the Rhine and the Neckar rivers,
were targeted by more raids—304 in total—than any other city
in the region because of the infrastructure of their ports and their
roles as industrial centers. But in fact, the British were also inten-
tionally aiming for the densest residential areas, as they did in
many of their aerial attacks. To them, Mannheim seemed particularly suited for experiments with a type of offensive called
"carpet bombing," whose goal was to level an urban center to
the point where it resembled a carpet. The city seemed ideal for
these experiments because of the square blocks at its heart, which
allowed the British Royal Air Force (RAF) to precisely determine
the impact of explosions thanks to aerial photography. Luckily for
my grandparents, their building was located just outside the city
center. But some bombs were so powerful that the blasts could
harm residences for miles around.

My grandfather scrupulously documented such damage to his
property as it happened in order to get reimbursed by the German
authorities. My father and I peeled apart those files, which Opa
carefully kept in his cellar for his whole life, as if he feared that
years after the war, someone would come to challenge the losses
he had sustained, to demand that he return his compensation.
After each raid, the authorities would come to survey the damage
and assess the level of reimbursement, which was often paid out
much later: "Through air pressure following the bombardments
during the aerial attack on the night of August 5 and 6, 1941, the
building sustained damage to the roof and windows. Walls and
ceilings were torn. The damage was recorded by a housing official
and an architect. The sum of 4,841.83 Reichsmarks will be allocated. Furthermore, compensation totaling 340.67 Reichsmarks
was allocated." This letter from the Mayor's Office is dated May
15, 1943—not only more than a year and a half after the events in
question, but also in the middle of the Third Reich's unraveling.

I find it quite awe-inducing that despite the chaotic context, the German bureaucracy continued to function with such precision.

The most devastating attack in Mannheim happened on the night of September 5–6, 1943. In a few hours, a fleet of 605 Royal Air Force planes dropped 150 mines, 2,000 bombs, 350,000 fire-bombs, and 5,000 bombs of white phosphorus. The inhabitants took refuge in some fifty-two gigantic bunkers hollowed out of basements. It was thanks to this infrastructure that the number of civilian victims of the bombardments in Mannheim was limited to approximately 1,800 dead, which is not many, considering the intensity of the assaults. When the inhabitants emerged like zombies from their underground hiding places, the city center was nothing more than dust, ruins, and flames. My grandfather's entire petroleum products business, which was located near the port, was reduced to ashes. The apartment building had also been hit, but the bunker built in the basement to serve as a refuge for the tenants had survived. And that space is still there—the large steel beams on the ceiling and the huge armored door, hermetically sealed, and so heavy that, as a child, I couldn't open it by myself when I went looking for preserves in the cellar. It was my aunt Ingrid who told me, much later on, that at the start of the war members of the NSDAP had sent men to transform their basement into a private bunker. Having one was a privilege compared to those who had to make a run for one of the public shelters scattered throughout the city.

By the time the September raid occurred, my grandmother, like many other women and children fleeing the increased bombings in the city, had already left Mannheim with six-year-old Ingrid and my newborn father. "He was a sickly child," my aunt says, "he caught bronchitis and couldn't stop coughing. The doctor said, 'With all this dust from the ruins, you'll have to flee the city!'" Their first stop was in the Odenwald, a pretty region of hills just behind Mannheim. "We lived with two elderly sisters, and they couldn't stand the baby's cries anymore. So they said to my mother: 'Lydia, you have to go elsewhere, it's too much for us.'" Their journey took them to Franconia, in Bavaria, to the home of Karl Schwarz's parents. "They were poor peasants who already had three children to feed. We lived on top of one another, and since there weren't enough plates to go around, we plunged our spoons directly into a pot in the center of the table. I thought that was funny." Oma, who was much less amused, couldn't stand imposing in such a way and went to the mayor of the village, threatening to "create some mischief" if he didn't find her a place to stay as soon as possible. "I went with her and she said something horrible to him like: 'I'll hang myself, or throw myself in the river with my children,'" my aunt remembers. A farmer offered her a room, in exchange for which my grandmother had to work long hours in the fields, no matter the weather, and milk the cows each day. I found photos from this exile, which lasted for two years. Ingrid with her two blond pigtails, agile as a gazelle in the green hillsides, and my father, his hair shimmering with golden highlights, worn like a helmet over his chubby face, stomping in front of a pen of geese, bursting into laughter. Sometimes Opa appears in these photos, but he rarely came to see them during that time.

When the war broke out in 1939, Karl Schwarz was thirty-six, but he didn't get conscripted, perhaps because of his age or because the burst of victories in Poland, Scandinavia, the Benelux countries, and finally in France in June 1940 had made replenishing the troops unnecessary. The unleashing of Operation Barbarossa on June 22, 1941, changed the terms, launching more than 3.3 million Axis soldiers against the Soviet Union on a front that stretched from the Baltic Sea to the Carpathian Mountains—a scope that was unprecedented in military history. The faster the Reich entrenched itself in this soldier-devouring war, the worse my grandfather's chances looked of escaping the calvary of the Eastern Front. Karl, a bon vivant who had no intention of playing the little Nazi

Lydia and Karl Schwarz in 1943, with their daughter, Ingrid, and son, Volker (my father), in Oberschefflenz. Lydia had gone to the German countryside with the children to escape the bombings in Mannheim.

soldier on the glacial Russian steppes, had to skillfully maneuver to avoid this fate, since his Nazi Party membership was no longer sufficient protection. He had to convince the higher-ups of the absolute necessity of his presence in Mannheim for the functioning of his business, since his clients, deprived of their petroleum products, would be at risk of ceasing their essential activities for the Reich . . . Considering the very modest size of his company, and the pressing need for men on the front, Karl Schwarz must have displayed an uncommon talent for persuasion to successfully gain his exemption from required military service in the Wehrmacht. This was probably the moment when he had the idea of adding the Wehrmacht to his list of clientele, likely negotiating an advantageous price for them. In this way, he became useful to the economy of the Reich. I must at least recognize a certain talent that got him out of serving as cannon fodder for a band of suicidal, megalomaniacal Nazi criminals. It was only recently, in going through the endless filing cabinets stacked in the basement, that the context of Opa's exemption emerged in another light. In a letter dated March 4, 1946, Max Schmidt, his partner in the Mineralölgesellschaft Schwarz & Co., accuses my grandfather of informing the Nazi authorities that he wasn't a member of the NSDAP, with the sole intention of forcing him to be drafted into the army in Karl's place in 1943. "You told me that my not belong-ing to the party obliged you to send me to my military duties: this is not the product of my imagination, but the reality, which, like other declarations, you now refuse to acknowledge. What's more, you always twisted things to your advantage, while treating me like a necessary evil who could bring in money and contracts." And he adds, "I did not become a soldier voluntarily. Enlisting me in the Wehrmacht gave you the chance to take control of the com-pany. . . . the partner who stays at work has no right to profit on the back of the one who is drafted." While he pled his own cause with the authorities, my grandfather must have realized that if, by arguing that the company needed a director, there was a chance to escape the Wehrmacht, it was either for himself or his business partner, but certainly not for both of them. And it was perhaps at that moment that he let slip, just in passing, that Max Schmidt, well, he didn't have his party card.

From spring 1943 on, with his wife and children in the country-side, Karl lived alone. The evenings must have become a bit sad on Chamissostrasse in the half-empty building whose inhabitants were either exiled from the city or at the front, braving death and cold, with the exception of three or four souls who continued to live together amid the ghostly architecture of apartments riddled with cracked, cardboard-covered windows and gaping holes in the ceiling, floor, and walls. To distract himself, my grandfather would go down a perpendicular street, the Lange Rötterstrasse, to a cabaret that was called Eulenspiegel, named for the joker and wit of folktales.

Many cabarets, variety shows, and theaters in the Reich were allowed to pursue their work up until September 1, 1944, when the minister of propaganda, Joseph Goebbels, suddenly ordered them to close under the auspices of *Totaler Krieg*, total war. Until that date, artists were exempt from the armed services, since their role seemed essential in turning public attention away from the horrors Hitler was in the process of enacting. The establishment doesn't exist anymore, but in my grandfather's papers, I found a sheet of letterhead printed at the top in pretty, red calligraphy: *Eulenspiegel—Parodistischer Kabarett*, parody cabaret. At the bottom of the page, in small type, were excerpts from positive newspaper reviews. From the town of Saarbrucken: "Rarely is the art offered to us in such excellent form, with a repertoire of popular songs and classics, and a sharp, high-spirited wit." From Mannheim: "The Eulenspiegel rapidly gained public support through its displays of originality, intelligence, and—what a rare treat—quality."

The letter, dated February 2, 1948, reads: "We hereby confirm that Mr. Karl Schwarz belongs to our troop," and the paper is signed by the director of the cabaret, Theo Gaufeld. Whatever the purpose of this document, which by all accounts must have provided my grandfather an alibi to protect him from any irregularities after the war, it reveals that Karl must have habitually frequented this establishment. In truth, he'd cozied up to a woman, Mrs. Gaufeld, who was an artist and the director's wife. He grew close enough to the couple that after his factory was destroyed in September 1943, he moved his office and his stock of oil barrels just next door to their apartment, into a brick factory on the outskirts of Mannheim, where he lived until the end of the war. And since it's impossible that Mr. Gaufeld didn't know about the intimate relationship linking his wife to their new friend, it's likely that they began a kind of ménage à trois, which would last until my grandfather's death. When Oma understood that the Gaufelds, who had so kindly taken care of her husband while she was away, were more than just friends, she was overcome with sorrow, and never really got over it. Luckily, she made this painful discovery much later, not right after the surrender of May 8, 1945, when she returned to Mannheim with her children. Another trauma awaited her: the city of her birth had vanished.

Mannheim was one of the most devastated cities in southwestern Germany. Seventy percent of the center of Mannheim and 50 percent of the rest of the city had been destroyed. There had been the destructive September 1943 attack, followed by many others. Then, on March 2, 1945, with the war nearly over, Royal Air Force bombers had returned once more, unleashing a storm of fire that polished off what remained of the historic city. At the end of March, Mannheim laid down its weapons when the Americans arrived, unknowingly escaping the worst, since if they had encountered German resistance, the Americans had a secret plan that proposed dropping several nuclear bombs on German cities, with Mannheim and Ludwigshafen included among the proposed targets. If Oma arrived by train, she would have seen the great baroque castle next to the station perforated from every side, with only one room in five hundred still intact. To reach Chamissostrasse, she would have traversed the wide commercial arteries, once illuminated by department stores displaying an opulence that drew people from all over the region to do their shopping. Karstadt, No. 1 Otto Spuler, and recently Aryanized old Jewish establishments such as Kaufhaus Kander, Gebrüder Rothschild, and Hermann Schmoller & Co. had, for the most part, collapsed like houses of cards under the bombs. There was no trace left of the cafés that set out their pretty terraces in the summer to serve cream pastries and coffee to ladies, besides a few letters torn from their signs and broken dishes with café insignia, buried under the mountains of debris piled on either side of the roads. Whole streets had been wiped off the map, transformed into vast vacant lots, dotted here and there with the broken facades of apartment buildings, anchored like theater sets in the void. I imagine Oma, a very faithful Protestant, searching for the familiar outline of a church and finding nothing in its place but the skeleton of a nave, the fragments of a stained-glass window, and a cross balancing over an empty, soundless bell.

How many Germans like my grandparents had seen their home-towns, the cement of their lives and identities, so destroyed? Hamburg had been transformed into a hellscape of flames, which cost 40,000 people their lives and demolished half of the apartments; Dresden, a baroque masterpiece, became a ghost town after a burst of bombs killed approximately 25,000 inhabitants. Hanover, Nuremberg, Mainz, and Frankfurt were 70 percent gone, while the whole Ruhr industrial valley—Cologne, Düsseldorf, Essen, Dortmund—had crumbled under attacks. Some communities were more than 96 percent destroyed, such as Düren, Wesel, and Pader-born. In total, almost one in five German families lost their homes. Between 300,000 and 400,000 civilians were killed, at least as many were disabled for life, and millions of others were traumatized.

On February 14, 1942, the British Air Ministry had issued the Area Bombing Directive to the commander-in-chief of the Royal Air Force's Bomber Command, Arthur Harris, which directed him "to focus attacks on the morale of the enemy civil population and in particular the industrial workers." The order added: "You are accordingly authorized to employ your forces without restric-tion." The next day, the commander-in-chief received an additional clarification: "ref the new bombing directive: I suppose it is clear the aiming points will be the built-up areas, and not, for instance, the dockyards or aircraft factories where these are mentioned in Appendix A. This must be made quite clear if it is not already

understood." Arthur Harris earned the nickname Bomber Harris.
Before starting this book, I hadn't heard of him. While I studied
in London, I must have passed his statue outside the church of
St. Clement Danes dozens of times without paying any special
attention to it. But ever since history's memory has become an
obsession of mine, everywhere I go, I track it through all its diverse
manifestations, generally devoting myself to this work alone, since
not everyone is as enthusiastic about spending a day with the
dead. And so I was able to use a quick visit to London to visit the
statue of Arthur Harris, erected by the Bomber Harris Trust in
1992 and unveiled by the late Queen Mother as a monument to
the glory of the RAF despite fierce criticism coming from some
voices in both Great Britain and Germany. This time I read the
inscription: "In memory of a great commander and of the brave
crews of Bomber Command, more than 55,000 of whom lost their
lives in the cause of freedom. The nation owes them all an immense
debt." The bombing of civilians was intended to undermine the
morale of the German people and their support of Hitler's war,
but historians now agree that these attacks did little to shorten
the conflict. These raids—which began as retaliation for the devastating German assaults on Coventry, and also on London and
Rotterdam—took the form of a murderous vengeance. In the last
months of the war, although the defeat of the Reich was assured,
the British and Americans bombed Germany almost daily.

Beyond the human toll, these ravages cost Germany huge
swaths of its cultural and historic identity. It's enough to look at
photos of Mannheim, Berlin, and Cologne before the war—and see
another country become visible. Yet even if the Allies committed
crimes whose gravity they still struggle to recognize, the Reich
must still take primary responsibility for this spiral of violence,
since if it had never unleashed the war in Europe, Germany would
never have been disfigured by what followed. And above all, it
was not the bombs that made people suffer most, but rather the

murderous fanaticism of the Führer that cost 5 million German soldiers their lives on the battlefields.

My grandparents were not directly affected by the slaughter on the battlefields. But how many of their friends and family mourned loved ones lost in this vain war that Hitler was determined to prolong? Karl's sister, Hilde, was married to an officer in the Wehrmacht who was caught by the spark of National Socialism and died on the Eastern Front, like the other 3.5 million soldiers who paid with their lives for their Führer's fanatical refusal to beat a retreat from the Soviets, who had an obvious tactical advantage. After the failure of his plan, which predicted conquering the USSR in a few weeks during the summer of 1941, Hitler pushed his men to march on through the glacial winter up to the gates of Moscow, without any equipment to protect them from the cold. Without gloves or coats, in temperatures approaching minus 58 degrees, they were ordered to attack and to maintain their positions no matter the price. "We didn't know where the front was. We stayed on our knees, or collapsed in the snow. The skin of our knees stuck to the ice," wrote one Wehrmacht soldier. Unable to dig trenches to protect themselves in the icy, rigid ground, the German soldiers were squashed like flies, picked off by Russian bullets or overcome by cold and hunger. My aunt Ingrid's boyfriend, who was hostile to Hitler, lost toes from frostbite at the gates of Moscow. A year later, despite warnings from his generals about the catastrophic state of the troops, the Führer once again forced them to attack, against Stalingrad this time, in an offensive without any hope of victory, which amounted to condemning his men—the 220,000 soldiers of the Sixth Army—to certain death. They were surrounded. Clothed in thin coats and without provisions, many died of cold and hunger. Only 6,000 ever came back home.

✿   ✿   ✿

In North Africa, another theater of operations, the death toll was low by comparison, with several tens of thousands of deaths on the German side, because General Erwin Rommel, nicknamed the "Desert Fox," who led the German Afrika Korps against the British in North Africa and the Middle East, had the courage to disobey Hitler. During the battle of El Alamein, despite the evident logistical impossibility of pushing back the enemy, the Führer had sent one of his infamous *Durchhaltebefehl*, his orders to hold the line: "You have no choice but to show your troops either the way of victory or the way of death." At the start, Rommel, who was otherwise very loyal to his commander, obeyed, but then he ordered all his mobile units to withdraw to the west. After the Allied landing in Normandy on June 6, 1944, which confirmed the inescapable defeat of the Reich, Rommel exhorted the Führer to put an end to the war, but this only served to provoke the rage of a tyrant blinded by his outsized ambitions. Though Erwin Rommel's audacity and triumphs had thrilled Germany and terrified the enemy, a little while later he was suspected by Hitler of having participated in a failed coup of officers against the Nazi regime and received the order to kill himself, which he carried out. Despite a growing number of generals who tried to reason with him, Hitler remained stony until the end, strengthened by a coterie of persistent supporters among the high command. A few months before they surrendered, in their suicidal folly, the Nazis in charge could find no better course than widening the circle of sacrificial victims by recruiting thirteen- and fourteen-year-olds. They formed a *Volkssturm*, a "tempest of people," charged with defending, practically without weapons, towns that would certainly fall to the enemy. These children were deliberately slaughtered to preserve the image of Germans who fought to the death, an image that flattered the Führer's vanity.

The Germans who lived through the last months of the war remember it as an apocalypse. Germany was collapsing, burning,

exploding, tearing itself apart, agonizing in a hell worthy of Dante.
In the confined atmosphere of his bunker under the Chancellor's
Palace in Berlin, where he had taken refuge with his entourage,
Adolf Hitler paced like a lion in his cage as his gloom deepened into
destructive madness, preferring shipwreck to surrender, to teach
his own people a lesson, since they'd proven themselves "unworthy"
of the National Socialist revolution. On April 30, after killing his
dog, he shot himself in the head, while his companion Eva Braun
poisoned herself with cyanide. On May 1, it was Joseph Goebbels,
Hitler's notorious minister of propaganda, who took cyanide along
with his wife, after feeding it to their six children, little angels and
model "Aryans" whom they had co-opted to make their propaganda
films more moving to the German people. Once the arrival of the
Red Army seemed inevitable, suicide spread like an epidemic.
Clergymen, especially in Berlin, worried about the surge of faithful
who came to confess that they always carried a capsule of cyanide
with them. The number of Berliners who died at their own hands
in the last weeks of the war probably exceeds 10,000. In Demmin,
a little town in eastern Pomerania that fell to the Red Army on
April 30, 1945, between 700 and 2,000 people committed suicide,
including many women who killed their children first. Other towns
suffered the same fate. My aunt remembers her mother's despair.
"The Americans were already in the country and my mother said
to me, 'We will not lose the war! The Führer will win! If we lose
the war, I'll kill myself!' That made an impression on me."

If Oma didn't act on her words, it was perhaps because compared
to others, her own fate wasn't so terrible. After crossing the center
of Mannheim in ruins, her heart must have lifted when she saw the
family apartment building, and a chance for her to reconnect with
her childhood, still standing. The walls, a bit of roofing, and part
of the stairs had been torn out, and all the windows had shattered.

Little by little, the residents returned from exile and moved back into their apartments, but they had to share them with those who had lost everything. In Mannheim, out of 86,700 apartments, only 14,600 were spared by the bombs. Faced with a grave housing crisis, eight people had to live in an apartment the size of those in the Chamissostrasse building, which were all identical at 300 square feet. Opa escaped the rule by pretending that his brother Willy lived with his whole family under their roof. Nonetheless, my aunt remembers that they regularly hosted relatives in need and that she slept in the living room, behind a big sheet that had been transformed into a curtain. On the ground floor, an old bachelor who lived alone found himself with an entire family of refugees. "We called the refugees the *Rucksackdeutsche* [Germans with rucksacks on their backs]; we guessed that they had been through a nightmare," she says.

The German civilians who sacrificed the most were probably the 12 million to 14 million people expelled from the German territories in the northeast, from Czechoslovakia, and, to a lesser degree, from southeastern Europe, whose lands were torn from them after they'd lived on them for generations. Those from the northeastern territories fled under particularly terrible conditions before the advancing Red Army, whose violence had been stoked by the villages the Wehrmacht had burned during their retreat from Russia, and by the deaths of millions of Soviet prisoners of war at the hands of the Germans. More than 1.4 million German women were raped, and hundreds of men were sent to the gulag and condemned to forced labor. In Czechoslovakia, the situation was less bloody, but the forced departure of 3 million Germans was also a painful memory. Under the Austro-Hungarian Empire, the German Sudetenland, which designated the region of Bohemia and Moravia in the northwest of the country, had prospered and developed an important glass and crystal industry. The situation there had deteriorated after the dismantling of the empire and the proclamation, in 1918, of an independent Czechoslovakian state, which discriminated against the German minority. Invoking his "blood brothers," Hitler annexed the Sudetenland in October 1938, cheered on by an immense majority of local people, who wasted no time in discriminating against and expelling the Czechs in the region. After the defeat of the Reich, vengeance switched sides and it was the Czechs' turn to expel nearly all the Germans, treating them like lepers, throwing them into the streets, where thousands died of exhaustion, sickness, or at the hands of roving assassins. Edvard Beneš, the president of Czechoslovakia, decreed that all German possessions should be "seized," i.e., stolen. In 2002, the Czech president Václav Havel officially condemned the expulsions. The welcome for these refugees was not warm in West Germany, where there were already so many local homeless. Empathy is rare when everyone is suffering.

On Chamissostrasse, my grandparents couldn't count on their tenants to get by, as they had financial problems of their own, and the damage insurance from the September 1943 raid still had not been paid out. My grandfather spent whole days making the rounds of the authorities. By chance, before the huge bombing, he had created a list of all their possessions, which I found in the basement in Mannheim. As I read this list enumerating each piece of clothing, each furnishing, each accessory my grandparents owned, I was thrust back into the decor Oma lived with when I was very young, which I had only vaguely remembered. After her death—when I was six—my father had completely transformed the apartment. With a bit of a lump in my throat, I clearly saw my grandmother's bedroom, filled with dark, heavy furniture, an idyllic painting of the German countryside, a bed that was much too big for the size of the room, and above it, an imposing cross which Lydia prayed to every evening. The apartment consisted of a living room, a big kitchen where Oma spent days making large sheet cakes for the Sunday *Kaffee und Kuchen*, coffee and cake, and a *Herrenzimmer*, the men's living room, where, in the armchairs facing the Art Deco cabinet and matching desk, men were permitted to smoke a pipe or a cigar if the finances allowed. I found another list dated the day after the devastating bombing of September 1943. Opa's tally of losses—including "a canary and its cage," a "doorknob," "empty bottles," and "empty fruit cases"—gives an idea of the stretched financial situation my grandparents were in at the time.

Quickly, Karl Schwarz found a much more effective solution than state reimbursements to improve conditions for his family. The Allies had of course taken control of his business, but they didn't know he still had a stock of barrels of oil and gasoline in a brick factory on the outskirts of town. In such scarce times, these reserves were worth gold on the black market, and my grandfather brought home treasures: cartons of eggs that he stored in the courtyard shed, apples by the hundreds kept chilled in the cellar, whole hams which hung in the bathroom, and even—a forgotten luxury in these hungry days—fireworks and *sekt*, sparkling wine for the New Year. He was the only one on their street to have a car, and "there was always plenty of space to park it," my father jokes. In the neighborhood, Karl Schwarz's family seemed particularly well provided for, while other kids arrived at school with empty stomachs, wearing shoes with holes. "People were a bit jealous of us," says my aunt, who has always given my grandfather credit for "knowing so well how to make good for his family."

Everyone did what he could in this rock-bottom version of Germany. One of my father's great distractions as a child was to rush to the window as soon as he heard the big jeeps honking their horns at the door of the building—American soldiers coming to pick up friends for an evening out. "The woman downstairs had two daughters, and one of our neighbors was actually married but didn't know if her husband would return, so she had to live," he remembers. Many German prisoners of war couldn't return home until several years, even a decade, after the end of the fighting, leaving their spouses in a state of destitution and uncertainty. Two million never came back from the Soviet Union, forced to work in horrifying conditions as payback after the Reich killed or abandoned 3.3 million of its 5.7 million Soviet prisoners of war.

For a German woman at the time, it was better to have a husband declared dead than one declared missing, for in the first case, she could have immediate access to a pension, while in the second case, she would most likely have to survive for several years without any benefits, waiting until his death had been confirmed. "The young women of Mannheim resigned themselves to going out with the Americans, who took them to their barracks, where they could dance, see movies, get a meal, and enjoy themselves a little with the young men, who were alluring in their uniforms," my father says. Sometimes these meetings gave way to pretty love stories, like that of one of the girls from downstairs who married an American and whose daughter, Cynthia, became my father's childhood friend before her parents moved to the United States in 1949. For others, like the neighbor whose husband was a prisoner of war, these dates were a form of prostitution. Everyone in the apartment building knew, but it wasn't looked down upon, since the cigarettes the Americans handed out sometimes allowed an entire family to survive. "Officially, the Americans had forbidden their soldiers to fraternize with German girls, but that only lasted a few months. And if my father allowed them in his apartment building, it was probably in exchange for a few things and some cigarettes." Since the collapse of the Reichsmark, cigarettes had become the fiat currency of the black market, and it was impossible not to trade on it, since ration tickets allowed for only 800 to 1,500 calories per day for an adult in 1946, depending on supplies. Many went hungry, and some died—of cold as well, since coal was also rationed and the winter of 1946–47 was harsh. Opa has a picture in his photo album of the frozen Rhine, where Mannheimers strolled on the ice as if it were the Neva in St. Petersburg.

Other new visitors made their appearance at the apartment building: the "uncles." Since war widows had to remain single to get their pensions, they didn't have any interest in remarrying. The custom was to pass off a new companion as an uncle, since the law forbade nonmarried couples from living together. The owner of each building was charged with enforcing this law or else paying a fine, but Karl Schwarz turned a blind eye, since he was no saint in matters of legality. He was generous by nature and shared his windfall from the black market freely with family and friends around a large Sunday table. "The discussions revolved around pensions that they worried they wouldn't get because they had been bureaucrats or soldiers for the Reich, products that were impossible to find, and the neighborhood gossip . . . those were the preoccupations of the moment, not who did what under National Socialism," my father explains.

Sometimes, Mannheimers would pity those who had an even worse fate, like the Berliners, whose future seemed as grim as streets of rubble, haunted by wandering refugees looking for rats to eat, women who prostituted themselves for soldiers, and children eyeing the passage of trucks to gather any scraps of coal that might bounce off. Made in 1947 in Berlin, Roberto Rossellini's film *Germany, Year Zero* is one of the most arresting eyewitness accounts of this world encircled by the void. Navigating through the phantasmagorical relics of the capital, the Italian director tells the story of a twelve-year-old boy, Edmund, who helps his miserable family by picking up odd jobs. To save his sick father, he calls on his old schoolmaster for help, and the man encourages him, following the eugenic Nazi ideology, to get rid of the feeble link in the family who threatens the survival of the group. After poisoning his father, Edmund commits suicide by throwing himself from the top of a ruin.

III

The Ghost of the Löbmanns

My grandparents thought the past was buried forever beneath the wreckage of the Third Reich, but it reared its head one morning in January 1946, when Karl Schwarz found an envelope in the mailbox with a return address that immediately implied bad tidings—Dr. Rebstein-Metzger, Lawyer, Mannheim. In the letter, the lawyer made clear that his client, a certain Julius Löbmann living in Chicago, was suing Mineralölgesellschaft Schwarz & Co. for approximately 11,000 Reichsmarks by virtue of a law instated in the American zone to give reparations to Jews who had been dispossessed under National Socialism.

Neither my father nor his sister—who usually likes telling family stories—told me the story of this letter and what it unleashed. I knew that Opa had belonged to the NSDAP, and I also had a vague idea that at the start, the *Mineralölgesellschaft* had once belonged to Jews. My father must have told me that detail when I began to study the Third Reich in class, but I was still too young to take an interest in the ramifications of this secret. It was only much later, after a remark by Aunt Ingrid, that I decided to dig around in Opa's filing cabinets in the basement of the Mannheim building, which had stayed in the family after the death of my grandparents.

Among the papers, which had yellowed with age but whose typed characters were still readable, I discovered a contract stipulating that Karl Schwarz had purchased a small oil company from two Jewish brothers, Julius and Siegmund Löbmann, as well as from their brother-in-law Wilhelm Wertheimer, who was also Jewish, and whose sisters Mathilde and Irma they had married. The Siegmund Löbmann & Co. business was located by the Mannheim harbor near the river Neckar. But it is mainly the date that matters: August 1938, a year of relentless descent into hell for the German Jews, as they experienced a sharp acceleration of persecution and discrimination and were forced to abandon their assets for a very low price.

I started to search for the Löbmann family and found few traces of them. I hoped to identify Julius's descendants in Chicago, where he was living when he claimed reparations from my grandfather, and I trembled when a thread of Internet searches led me to a "Loebmann" family living in Chicago. But my next discovery, of a long list of Loebmanns in the Chicago White Pages, put an end to my hopes. It was like looking for a needle in a haystack. I tried looking on the Wertheimer side. This was how I stumbled upon an article mentioning a certain Lotte Kramer, née Wertheimer, one of the last living people who had witnessed the *Kindertransport*, a British rescue operation that gave more than 10,000 Jewish children safe passage from Germany and Central Europe to Great Britain between 1938 and 1940. I found her in a retirement home in Peterborough, a little town an hour north of London. On the phone, she confirmed that she was the daughter of Sophie Wertheimer, the sister of Mathilde and Irma, and immediately agreed to meet me.

Lotte Kramer is ninety-five. She's a small, frail woman, with delicate movements, polite as only the British can be. She had arranged two armchairs facing each other, close enough for us to hear each other, and she told me her life story, and what she knew of the Löbmanns' lives. "My mother, Sophie, and her two sisters were very close," she said, taking a black-and-white photo of three young women down from the wall. The youngest, Mathilde, has a handsome face, determined and open, with a big bow in her hair and another at her neck. Next to her, Irma, the oldest, wears a crocheted collar that brightens her tired features. The third one, Sophie, is seated with a medallion around her neck and has an uncertain gaze, filled with vague hope.

The Wertheimer sisters in Mannheim in the 1930s: from left to right,
Mathilde and Irma (the wives of Julius and Siegmund Löbmann),
and, seated, Sophie (the mother of Lotte Kramer).

Lotte was born in 1923 in Mainz, a large city in Rhineland-Palatinate, where she grew up. She often traveled the sixty miles separating Mainz from Mannheim to visit her much-loved cousin Lore, the daughter of Siegmund and Irma Löbmann. She

remembered their long walks in the gardens at the foot of the Was-
serturm, their strolls in lively streets, and the unmissable *Kaffee
und Kuchen* her aunt Irma, "a splendid cook," would make. "We
sometimes went on vacation to the countryside all together, to
a village where the Löbmann family originated, where they still
had family living on a farm. We were very close." The Wertheimer
sisters had three brothers: Siegfried, who moved to America in
the twenties; Paul, who fled to France when the Nazis came; and
Wilhelm, who invested in Löbmann & Co. at the beginning of
the thirties to help his brothers-in-law save the company, since it
had been hard hit by the economic crisis of 1929. Thanks to this
intervention, business was back on track, before lapsing again
due to growing discrimination against Jewish companies under
National Socialism.

Lotte was nine years old when Hitler came to power. In January 1933, the German president, General Field Marshal Paul von
Hindenburg, finally gave way before the growing electoral success
of the NSDAP, which became the country's first political party with
more than one third of the votes in 1932. He named the head of
the party, Adolf Hitler, chancellor. The latter hurried to dissolve
the Reichstag, held new legislative elections, and carried out an
aggressive political campaign marked by dubious negotiations,
threats, and political pressure, all with the goal of enlarging his
parliamentary base into an outright majority. In March 1933, he
had to content himself with 43.9 percent of votes. In Mannheim,
a city where the Social Democratic Party (SPD) and the Communist Party (KPD) were traditionally strongly represented, the
number of NSDAP members was no more than a hundred at the
end of the 1920s. But with the 1929 economic crisis, the number
of unemployed people tripled, and in 1932, the Nazi Party became
the largest political force in the city, with 29.3 percent of votes.
Shortly after they came to power in 1933, the local Nazi authorities crushed the SPD and the KPD, forbade newspapers, and

forced the mayor of Mannheim to watch the flag of the republic
burn before shutting him up in a hospital. Quickly, a new wave of
anti-Semitism began spreading in Mannheim, which was home to
the largest Jewish community in Baden, with approximately 6,400
members. The change was felt across the whole region. "Suddenly,
anti-Semitic propaganda was everywhere, in the street, in the
newspapers, on the radio," Lotte remembers. "One day, with my
class, we went to see a propaganda film for children, the story of a
boy who converts to Nazism. It made a big impression on us—we
all wanted to be like him." Each day when she returned home
from school in Mainz, she passed the Center for Hitler Youth. "I
was jealous, I dreamed of taking part in it—they looked so happy
in their uniforms." Most of all, it was their normalcy she envied as
a little Jewish girl, carrying on her child's shoulders the weight of
the exclusion, humiliation, and shame inflicted on her community.

In an excellent book titled *Arisierung und Wiedergutmachung in
Mannheim* (Aryanization and Reparations in Mannheim), the historian Christiane Fritsche explains how, without any national law to
justify it, anti-Semitic measures were undertaken on the local level
in many areas. The Mannheim Chamber of Commerce set the tone
when, at the end of March 1933, it got rid of its Jewish members,
including its acting president and a third of its personnel. At the
same time, as in other places in Germany, numerous Mannheim
institutions and associations of industrialists, business owners,
lawyers, and doctors excluded Jews at an alarming rate at their
own initiative and without any outside pressure, depriving them of
essential professional networks, sabotaging their reputations and
their clientele, and precipitating their financial ruin. The regime
itself ruled on the fate of civil servants on April 7, 1933, when it
allowed the dismissal of all "non-Aryan" functionaries, including
university professors and scientists.

Another way of stigmatizing and isolating Jews was to call for a boycott of Jewish agencies, companies, and businesses, not at the national level, but locally. Nazi organizations and representatives of the NSDAP, who were very impatient to act, banded together to start a daylong boycott of Jewish stores planned for April 1, 1933, and announced beforehand through newspapers and flyers. Across the country, uniformed members of the SS and the SA planted themselves in front of businesses, department stores, banks, doctors' offices, and legal practices to prevent customers from entering, and scrawled anti-Semitic messages on the windows, haranguing the crowd or brandishing placards that read: "Germans! Defend yourselves! Do not buy from Jews!" Many businesses closed their doors and lowered their metal grates, either because they had been warned or because they were observing Shabbat as they usually did. Other businesses were sacked and pillaged, and their Jewish owners were beaten up. Even if the majority of the population hadn't actively participated, this day proved that such acts would not encounter resistance from other citizens. Christiane Fritsche explains that a few months later, the minister of economics made it clear to the Chamber of Commerce and Industry that "differentiating between Aryan and non-Aryan companies was not possible," as "the boycott of non-Aryan businesses would considerably hinder economic reconstruction." Since the Jews played an important role in the German economy, a certain number of Nazi leaders in Berlin feared that these actions would interfere with economic recovery and the lowering of the unemployment rate, which were the government's priorities. According to Fritsche, that is one reason why, in the first years, no law was instated that discriminated against Jewish economic activity. But on the local level, this policy was not respected.

One of the most effective instruments in Mannheim was the local Nazi newspaper *Hakenkreuzbanner*, which advocated daily for the boycott of 1,600 local Jewish businesses, publishing their names and addresses, and sometimes the names of the clients who still frequented them, accusing them of disloyalty to the Führer. The newspaper also threatened to publish the names of *"Juden-liebchen,"* women who had allegedly been involved with Jews. These intimidation campaigns paid off in a medium-size city like Mannheim, which had some 280,000 inhabitants. Public humiliation had more impact there than in a big, anonymous city like Berlin. Another method of harassment, Fritsche observes, was to spread false rumors about the dirty kitchen of a Jewish restaurant or the sexual behavior of a Jewish businessman. Sometimes it even went as far as a *Schmutzprozesse*, a dirty trial intended to discredit someone on the basis of false accusations of crooked business, sexual predation, or the concealment of stolen goods. Even if he was acquitted, the accused would see his reputation destroyed, and his company would usually go down with him. Jewish entrepreneurs were also often denied public contracts and forbidden from exhibiting in trade shows. Other local rules prohibited Jews from decorating their windows with "Christian" motifs before Christmas, meaning no angels, Christmas trees, or mangers, labeling them as non-Aryan and significantly reducing their sales, which were crucial during the holidays. The four big Jewish department stores in Mannheim were the main targets. The city even forbade its employees from buying anything there and imposed penalties. By 1936, hammered at every turn by these slander campaigns, three of the four had already been sold to "Aryans" due to financial difficulties.

"I think the Löbmanns hung on, since I don't remember noticing any big changes to their way of living when I visited them. That's to say, they lived modestly, and they were pretty religious, more religious than we were," Lotte Kramer says. The Löbmanns' business wasn't retail, and they were probably less affected than others by this witch hunt. Their clients were not as visible as those who entered a tailor's shop or a bakery, and they were probably harder to intimidate with threats of slander. But some of them must have gone elsewhere, as I discovered by looking among Opa's papers at a statement of the total annual turnover at Siegmund Löbmann & Co. after 1933, revealing that the company had also suffered from the disloyalty of certain clients, whether it was motivated by fear or anti-Semitism.

At the beginning, the enthusiasm for National Socialism in German society had more to do with a renewed confidence in the strength of their Fatherland than with the Nazi leaders' anti-Semitic obsession, and their loud claims that only when Germany was purified of its "non-Aryan" elements would it be reborn from the ashes, granting its people the power of racial harmony, a power unequaled in human history. This frenzied idea arose from a complete myth, since like all humans the Germans had already mixed countless times with other peoples over the course of the millennium that preceded the arrival on earth of Adolf Hitler and Joseph Goebbels, who had none of the so-called morphological Aryan characteristics. Many citizens were too preoccupied to bother with chasing out Jews simply because they were Jewish. But when this harassment began presenting opportunities for personal gain, the passion for the racial cause intensified at all levels of society. Even in educated circles, there were few university professors, researchers, lawyers, and judges who would oppose the exclusion of Jewish colleagues when their empty posts became a windfall for those who remained. The case of the philosopher Martin Heidegger, who was rector of the University of Fribourg in 1933–34 and a member of the Nazi Party until the end of the war, illustrates the reigning climate at the time in universities, where the majority of professors wished for quotas to be instated to limit the "overrepresentation" of Jews in the university, and in cultural and intellectual circles in general. In 1929, in a letter to Victor Schwoerer, vice-president of the German Association for the Support and Advancement of Scientific Research, he confided: ". . . we're talking about nothing short of focusing on an urgent choice we have to make. Either we restore our German intellectual life with true, down-to-earth vigor and educators, or we succumb to the increasing Jewish takeover in every sense." Other academics were simply jealous of the success of their Jewish colleagues.

Removing the competition and getting off scot-free was also the main reason for a sudden interest in anti-Semitism in the economic sector. Profiting from colleagues in difficulty was so tempting that in Mannheim, some went so far as to put it in their windows: "Shop here at a German store." Jewish business owners in distress started to take out their medals from the First World War, pinning them to their jackets, while others tried to get through by offering discounted prices and installment plans, even for products that were already cheap. Christiane Fritsche writes, "Within weeks of the seizure of power, without changing any of the corresponding laws, a change of awareness took place for many Germans at breathtaking speed: being Jewish or Aryan suddenly mattered for business." It was surely in this context that Karl Schwarz had that heraldic crest drawn and hung in his office, to attest to his Aryan roots.

This discrimination was just as cruel in the social world: Jews were forbidden to go to cinemas, dances, movie theaters, public pools, and athletics centers, and barred from all sorts of associations. There's a photo of men and women in bathing suits, visibly distraught, running down the docks along the Rhine in Mannheim, trying to escape members of the Nazi SA paramilitary group who arrived in the midst of the swimmers to beat up Jews. This scene preceded a radical step in the process of their exclusion from the community: the racial laws from Nuremberg in the summer of

1935 that reduced Jews to second-class citizens, depriving them of the rights and status associated with German citizenship.

For her entire adolescence, Lotte watched the position of Jews become rapidly more precarious. "In my class, five of us were Jews, and even if we didn't have great political awareness, we understood that our situation was not good, we talked about it amongst ourselves. Our mothers had changed, they were worried, we had to come home right after school, keep a low profile, don't talk to anyone." One day her parents told her that she was no longer allowed to go to the German school and would be transferred to a Jewish establishment. "The teacher was very kind, he apologized to the parents and even proposed to hold make-up classes in the evening if we needed them." Despite these persecutions, in 1936, only 1,425 of the 6,400 Jews in Mannheim had left the city, while on the national level, out of a community of more than 500,000 Jews, about 150,000 had decided to flee. The latter had probably been threatened the most—because they were engaged in politics, or had lost their jobs as civil servants, or were facing bankruptcy in business. Paradoxically, they would eventually be grateful to have been targeted first, as it allowed them to get out in time.

For better or worse, the Löbmanns had succeeded in continuing their business, and, as with most German Jews, leaving was not an option. Especially because it was tantamount to leaving their fortune to the Reich. As was often the case under the Third Reich, politics were a disarming contradiction in how to treat the Jews. On the one hand, the Nazis wanted to make their lives so unbearable that they would have no choice but to leave, and on the other hand, they created insurmountable obstacles to their departure. The tax on currency transferred out of Germany kept going up, passing 20 percent in 1934 before reaching a prohibitive rate of 96 percent in 1939. They also had to add the *Reichs-*

fluchtsteuer, a newly established tax for fleeing the Reich. Above 50,000 Reichsmarks, emigrants had to give the regime 25 percent of their savings and their revenue. Not to mention the administrative labyrinth they would have had to go through to obtain the prohibitive amount of paperwork necessary to legally emigrate from the Reich. But deep down, the main reason Jews resisted leaving was because they did not want to leave Germany, and certainly not for Palestine, a semi-desert with an arid climate and a culture that was vastly different from their own. And they loved Germany. How could the Löbmanns and others continue to be so attached to a country that treated them this way? Why weren't they more alarmed, considering that from today's perspective, all the warning lights were flashing red? In fact, for a family of entrepreneurs like the Löbmanns, the signs were murkier, and the initial absence of national laws against Jewish businesses allowed them to entertain the illusion that despite everything, it was possible for Jews to subsist economically under the Third Reich. Even more so because a parallel economic universe had formed, made up of Jewish stakeholders and clients, that softened the effects of the local boycott.

All this was combined with a dose of self-imposed blindness. Lotte Kramer, whose father "kept repeating that he didn't want to leave," explains that their desire to stay was so great that it took only a small sign of solidarity from the heart of German society for them to feel reassured. "At school, I had a friend who wasn't Jewish. When Jews had to leave the school, her mother said to mine, 'I want our daughters remain friends.' My mother had to convince her that it was too dangerous. But these reactions restored trust." People shared positive stories, like that of a couple who fibbed to the police when their neighbors were threatened, or a little anonymous package of medicine found on the doorstep of a Jewish family whose children were sick. "My parents had very good non-Jewish friends, Greta and Bertold, and when the situation worsened, they came over in secret, late at night, to find out if everything was OK and to bring us things that we hadn't been able to buy for ourselves. They took a lot of risks." The tragedy was that while they thought they were helping, these good souls unknowingly encouraged the community to think that there was still time to escape the trap—a trap that was deadlier than anyone yet suspected. I've wondered what sign of solidarity could have kept the Löbmanns' hopes alive, and I think it was the faithfulness of their many clients. I found a list, several pages long, that Opa recovered when he bought the company. This long inventory of names reveals another Germany, one that hadn't renounced its loyalties.

Lotte Kramer gave me another explanation for their illusions. "We experienced a certain normalcy, since life continued within the Jewish community. Perhaps in the country, in the villages, people felt the isolation more quickly, but in the big cities like Mainz and Mannheim, you could forget what was forbidden because we did everything internally. There was a Jewish school, a Jewish sporting club, there were dance classes, parties, concerts, and lots of friends . . . there was also the synagogue, which played an important role in strengthening the community, and the Löbmanns often went to synagogue." These little indications Lotte Kramer revealed were like missing puzzle pieces in my understanding of why the vast majority of German Jews believed, up until the last minute, that they could lead a respectable existence in their country while hoping the Germans would come to their senses and stop repudiating the Jews who had devoted their many talents to science, philosophy, literature, the arts, and the economy, Jewish gifts that had made it possible for Germany to shine brightly. In the end, they accommodated the degrading measures, preferring humiliation to exodus.

From 1936 on, the regime, which until then hadn't favored removing Jews from the economic sector, began to change course. Once unemployment was greatly decreased, the priority became Aryanizing Jewish assets. In 1938, Berlin strengthened measures to force Jews who hadn't yet sold their businesses to transfer them to "Aryans." For Siegmund Löbmann & Co., the first blow was the drastic reduction of quotas concerning the amount of raw materials Jews were allowed to have, which was fatal to a petroleum products business. Jews were then forced to write down all their assets in detail in a register: real estate, businesses, life insurance, securities, cash, jewelry, art, and complete household effects. Soon after, an ordinance demanded that all Jewish-owned businesses be visibly labeled as such. At the same time, political persecution of the community increased with police raids, arbitrary imprisonment, and the destruction of religious sites. The Löbmanns must have given up all hope when they finally decided to sell their business to finance their departure. But they weren't the only ones to become pessimistic in 1938; thousands of other Jews put their businesses on the market at the same time, creating a crushing surplus. In these conditions, it wasn't difficult to tell whether the seller or the buyer had the upper hand.

The thought of getting a good deal in this buyers' market was probably part of what motivated Karl Schwarz to leave the Nitag petroleum company, though he had a good managerial position, a comfortable salary, and enough respect in 1935 to have been selected as a representative to the Deutsche Arbeitsfront, the Nazi labor organization that forcibly replaced all independent trade unions. He actually acquired his NSDAP party membership in that same year, perhaps because his new responsibilities made belonging preferable, and certainly because he was seduced by the advantages of such an affiliation. But it's unlikely that he did it out of ideological conviction. For Opa was a hedonist, a pleasure seeker who had little interest in the sadomasochistic displays of power in which the National Socialists excelled. Nazism demanded a blind discipline that had nothing in common with his independent spirit and the freedoms it craved. He liked to ski alone in the mountains overhanging Fribourg and to camp near lakes where he could exercise his passion for *Freikörperkultur*—the culture of free bodies, i.e., nudism, a movement that started in Germany at the end of the nineteenth century. He was an individualist, in contrast with the cult of community that reigned among the Nazis. Being at the Nitag company, obeying a boss who imposed the rules, sticking to the routine of salary and the humiliating wait for a promotion every year, must have weighed on him. He must have started to dream of independence, to think that with his talent for getting by, his ease in communicating, he should go into business for himself, especially since he'd learned in his youth how to make petroleum and kerosene in a laboratory. He kept the certificate from that apprenticeship, which attests: "During this time, we were always satisfied with the initiative, leadership, diligence, and behavior of Mr. Schwarz."

Perhaps my grandfather wouldn't have dared to strike out on his own, if his colleague Max Schmidt hadn't one day indicated his own scorn for this docile life. I imagine them meditating over their exit plan over an after-work beer during the *Feierabend*, or happy hour. And in fact, the plan involved plenty of scheming, since Karl and Max were not only planning to start a competing business together, but also to steal seven of their Nitag colleagues and their clients with them. The circumstances that afforded the opportunity to acquire Jewish businesses at low prices must have intensified this conspiratorial atmosphere, since they were about to profit from the distress of the Jews. The two founders likely consulted the register of Jewish businesses that still needed to be Aryanized, which included about a third of the 1,600 that had once been in Mannheim. The others were either already sold or had been liquidated after going bankrupt. What was their state of mind when they met the Löbmanns? Did they feel embarrassed? Guilty? Arrogant because they knew they had the upper hand? I don't know but I can offer a clue: unlike other buyers, Karl and Max feebly negotiated the already discounted sale of the Jewish company, since they payed 10,353 Reichsmarks, which was 1,100 less than the seller's price. Knowing that the price was curtailed by the Nazi authorities who had to validate the transaction, they might have felt a spark of empathy that prevented them from milking the situation any further.

There were certainly many crueler profiteers than my grand-father—like the pitiless vultures who squeezed as much as they could out of Jews who faced growing difficulties finding a buyer and a pressing need for money to finance their flight. Nonetheless, in this instance Karl Schwarz conveniently followed a practice endorsed by the Nazis: to pay only for the material value of a Jew-ish business and not spend a cent on its immaterial value, which could often be what was most precious about it—the years spent building a reputation, a clientele, a service, a product, a brand, the development of formulas or patents.

After the sale, Julius Löbmann accepted a 400 Reichsmark monthly payment to accompany Opa on business trips and intro-duce him to the clientele of Löbmann & Co. over several months, delivering precisely the type of resource that Karl Schwarz and Max Schmidt had not paid for. To my mind, the understanding between Karl and Julius must not have been contentious for those trips to be possible, especially because it was forbidden for Jews to go on business trips. Inns and restaurants that for years had welcomed these guests posted "No Jews Allowed" signs in their windows. Everywhere, the situation of the Jews was visibly unrav-eling. Professional limitations accumulated. They automatically received a second first name on their identity papers to distinguish them more easily: Sara for women and Israël for men. Then a big J was stamped on their passports. During their travels, Opa must have been the one to lie about Julius—to the police on the roads, to the innkeepers, to the proprietors of restaurants. This shared risk-taking must have brought them together. But it came to an end after the pogroms of November 1938.

Julius and Opa were on a trip together in the Black Forest, an idyllic setting with hills and pine forests. When they came back to Mannheim on November 10, anti-Semitic hate had crossed a new threshold of cruelty. A pogrom of devastating violence had been unleashed throughout the Reich by members of the NSDAP, the SA paramilitary force, and the Hitler Youth, actions that Hitler had "clearly endorsed," writes the historian Dietmar Süss in his book *One People, One Reich, One Führer: German Society Under the Third Reich*. According to his calculations, "as a direct or indirect consequence of these pogroms, 1,300–1,500 people died, 1,406 synagogues were destroyed, tens of thousands of businesses were looted, and 30,756 Jewish men were arrested and sent to concentration camps." Lotte Kramer remembers this "Crystal Night," so named by the Nazis after the millions of pieces of broken glass. "We got a call from an uncle who lived across from the synagogue, where our school was also located. He said to my mother, 'Don't send your children to school! The building is burning!' My father got a message that he should disappear for the day, and he hid in the woods. With my mother, we climbed to the attic, where we peered from the little window at people looting stores; luckily, they didn't come to our house. My father came back at nightfall, and I slept in my parents' bed that night. For the first time, I was truly afraid."

In Mannheim, the violence began at dawn on November 10. Three synagogues were destroyed, one of which was even pulverized with explosives, and dozens of Jewish men were arrested and later sent to the concentration camp at Dachau. As was often the case, one main motivation behind this criminal impulse was greed—most of the stores were looted, and many apartments were too. The

National Socialist gangsters launched plundering raids, barging into rich and poor homes alike, stripping away what they could carry and destroying the rest—china, furniture, artworks. Many citizens in Mannheim were shocked by this barbarism, as Opa might well have been too, coming back from his travels to find this desolate spectacle in front of his van—carpets of glass shards strewn over the ground, books in flames, furniture thrown from windows in pieces on the sidewalk—with Julius at his side, crazed with worry after learning that some of his family members had been arrested. That day, they put an end to their illegal cooperation, which had become too dangerous. Soon after, Julius's family members were released, and it became urgent to arrange their departure for the United States. They had contacts in Chicago and in New York, where Irma and Mathilde Wertheimer's brother Siegfried lived. He wouldn't stop singing America's praises in his letters to his sisters. The Löbmanns started to send furniture to Chicago thanks to the money from the sale of the company. A gesture that was either optimistic or naïve, since obtaining a visa for the United States was already very difficult before 1938, and later it became an impossibility.

In July 1938, faced with the intensification of the Jewish refugee crisis, the American president, Franklin D. Roosevelt, had called an international conference in hopes that the participants would agree to welcome more Jews. After Italy and the USSR declined the invitation, representatives from thirty-two states and twenty-four aid organizations got together for nine days in Évian-les-Bains, on the banks of Lake Geneva. In the majestic salons of the Royal Hotel, an oasis for tiaraed heads and renowned artists that was nicknamed "the most beautiful hotel in the world" at its opening in 1909, the international delegates took turns at the podium expressing their profound compassion for the fate of Europe's Jews. But not a single one offered their hospitality, with the exception of the Dominican Republic, which asked for subsidies in exchange.

The United States, represented by a simple businessman named Myron C. Taylor, refused to raise its fixed quota of 27,370 visas per year for Germany and Austria. Once one of the most influential countries on the planet had set the tone, the rest speedily followed suit. Despite the huge colonial empires Britain and France possessed, none of those options were considered, whether it was Palestine, Algeria, or Madagascar. France claimed it had reached "an extreme saturation point regarding refugees." The Australian delegate explained that his country, one of the largest in the world, didn't have "racial problems" and "didn't want to import them." The Swiss representative, Heinrich Rothmund, the chief of immigration police, let it be known that his homeland was only a transit country. This notorious anti-Semite had never bothered to conceal his hostility toward the Jews, whom he considered a "foreign element" threatening the Swiss with "Jewification." I imagine these representatives of the "international community," with troubled faces, falsely distressed, taking refreshments between two genteel speeches in the shadow of the elegant pergola of this hotel where Marcel Proust, the son of an Alsatian Jew and a hardline Dreyfus supporter, had written passages of his masterpiece *In Search of Lost Time*. The future Israeli minister Golda Meir, who had been invited to Évian as a "Jewish observer from Palestine," later wrote: "Sitting in that wonderful hall listening to the representatives of thirty-two countries standing up one after another and explaining how terribly glad they would be to receive a larger number of refugees and how terribly sorry they were that they unfortunately could not—it was a shattering experience."

What figures were they talking about? It was about dividing, among thirty-two countries directly or indirectly in possession of large territories, some 360,000 Jewish members of the German population, and about 185,000 Austrian Jews as well. The immigration of these mainly urban populations, who had demonstrated their predisposition to intellectual, entrepreneurial, and artistic occupations, would have benefited anyone who welcomed them. Especially countries like Argentina that were constantly looking for candidates to inhabit their immense, underpopulated territories. But before the Évian conference was even over, the Argentine foreign ministry sent a directive that ordered, under the cloak of secrecy, all the Argentine consulates to refuse visas to any people "who are believed to have left or are leaving their country of origin because they are considered undesirables or have been expelled from the country, regardless of the reason for their expulsion." In other words, Jews. It is hard not to take this unjustified rejection as the symptom of an international epidemic of anti-Semitism that went far beyond the borders of the Third Reich. China, which was absent from the Évian conference, was one of the few countries to accept European refugees, even without visas. Lacking the option to set up a life elsewhere, almost 20,000 Jews went to Shanghai, where they struggled with the language barrier, the cultural differences, and difficult economic conditions. Even at that distance, they were caught by the Nazis. At the end of 1941, under pressure from their German ally, the Japanese, who were by then occupying part of China, imprisoned European Jews in a ghetto where 2,000 of them perished. Even after the torments of *Kristallnacht*, the international community didn't budge. Only Great Britain made a gesture, agreeing to welcome 10,000 Jewish children into families, the *Kindertransport* that helped Lotte Kramer. But at the same time, it closed Palestine, one of the main gateways out of Europe for the Jews, since it was under a British mandate. Afraid that refugees would heighten the already sharp tensions between the local Arab and Jewish communities, it set the immigration quota for Jews at 75,000 for the whole period between 1938 and 1944, while almost 10 million Jews were still living on the European continent.

After November 1938, and the consecutive abolition of the few remaining rights the Jews possessed, a breath of panic blew through the Jewish community in Germany, and hundreds of thousands who up until that moment had resisted, suddenly understood that they needed to leave as quickly as possible. They rushed en masse to the consulates of countries across the globe, but these, which had become more and more reluctant over the previous years to give visas to German Jews, tightened up even more in the face of this whirlwind of despair. The diplomats had received orders. "My father went to the American embassy and waited for a very long time," Lotte Krämer says. "He came back to the house with a number, but he was so far down on the waiting list . . . we knew we didn't have a chance. My parents also tried Panama and Ecuador, from there they might have made it to the U.S., but they didn't get anywhere." Despite the fact that many applicants from Europe already had family in America as well as experiences suggesting their ease of assimilation, the United States remained utterly unmoved by their fate, and stuck to its meager quotas.

One of the most dramatic episodes was the spring 1939 voyage of the *Saint Louis*, a transatlantic ocean liner from Hamburg headed to Havana with 937 passengers on board, nearly all German Jews who were trying to get to Cuba before traveling on to try to enter the United States. But Cuba, which had actually given the visas in Germany, had changed its immigration rules in the meantime, in the context of a political scandal in which certain provocateurs riled up public opinion against Jews and organized an anti-Semitic demonstration before the boat's arrival. Only twenty-nine passengers were allowed to disembark, and the *Saint Louis* was chased from Cuban waters. It found itself near Miami, so close to the coast that the passengers could see the lights. The captain, Gustav Schröder, and various Jewish organizations tried to convince President Franklin D. Roosevelt to grant them asylum. In vain. The White House decided not to let them in, egged on by an American population whose unemployment rates, due to the economic crisis, had made them allergic to immigration, and especially to Jews entering the

United States, whose competition they feared more than they pitied their situation in Germany. Then it was Canada's turn to be asked, but there once again, the highest immigration officer, Frederick Blair, blocked their passage. When they returned to Europe in June 1939, Captain Schröder refused to deliver his passengers to Germany and let them off in Belgium. A quarter of them later died in the Holocaust.

The Löbmann family never got their visas. It's possible that, having sent their furniture to the United States, they reflexively clung to that nearly impossible option so as not to lose their material possessions. But even obtaining a visa wouldn't have been any guarantee of safe arrival, since to get to other countries by sea, they would have had to cross one, if not two, intermediate countries—France, Portugal, Belgium, the Netherlands, Switzerland, where many shady intermediaries demanded that their palms be greased in amounts that increased at the same rate as Jewish distress. Travel agencies, consulates, drivers, smugglers, innkeepers, corrupt functionaries . . . so many got rich off of anti-Semitism! But the Löbmanns didn't have much money at their disposition, since the sum they'd gotten from the sale of their company had been, following the new rules, kept in an account controlled by the Reich, from which they could take out only small amounts at a time. However, leaving Germany was not totally impossible yet. After the pogroms in November 1938, 40,000 Jews were able to emigrate. Lotte Kramer was among them. Her teacher in Mainz had heard of transports for children organized by Great Britain and told her parents to find her a place. "My mother spoke to her sister Irma, who managed to place her children, Lore and Hans, in the convoy. I didn't want to be separated from my parents, but I was with my cousins and it was a bit of an adventure." In 1939, almost 80,000 Jews succeeded in fleeing, and 1,000 of these were from Mannheim. Some of them settled in India or Kenya, destinations that had not been their first choice.

The Löbmann family may have hesitated to let go of the American plan, to hightail it out of there to an unknown destination with the basic necessities. This aversion to improvisation was their downfall. The longer the Löbmanns waited, the more their fortune diminished, and with it, their chances of leaving. The organized looting of Jews redoubled in force. To punish them for *Kristallnacht*, where they had been the victims, the regime demanded atonement in the form of a new tax—a Jewish property tax that amounted to extorting 25 percent of the wealth of those who possessed more than 5,000 Reichsmarks, which included the Löbmanns. Then, in February 1939, they were ordered to give up all their silver, gold, and platinum, as well as any pearls or precious stones, for ten or twenty times less than what they were actually worth. The Jews stuck in Germany were caught in a dramatically deteriorating situation. Hitler had decided to definitively exclude them from economic life and from the working world. Those who had lost all their means were forced into constructing roads or collecting garbage, while those businesses that hadn't yet been Aryanized were sold for next to nothing. Some lawyers were cynical enough to go find owners who had been imprisoned in Dachau to make them sign the bill of sale. Land was seized from synagogues, Jewish organizations, and Jewish cemeteries. In Mannheim, even the Protestant church participated in this sinister carving up of land.

Very early on the morning of October 22, 1940, government forces burst into the homes of the Löbmanns and also the home of Wilhelm Wertheimer, Irma and Mathilde's brother. They ordered them to prepare to leave immediately and to pack their suitcases as fast as they could: each adult could have a maximum of 100 pounds of baggage and 100 Reichsmarks, and was advised to bring a few days' worth of water and food. Their accounts, their titles, and their properties were seized. Several hours later, they were on the platform at the Mannheim train station, with 2,000 other Jews from the city, about to board trains without knowing their destination. About half the community had fled in the previous years. Eight Jews killed themselves the morning of the raid. Several hundred had succeeded in going into hiding; those who were married to Aryans were spared. On October 23, a convoy consisting of nine trains started out, transporting 6,500 Jews, among them 4,500 other Jews from southwestern Germany.

After traveling across the Rhine at Kehl, the train arrived at night at the demarcation line separating France into a zone occupied by the Reich to the north, and a southern "free zone" administered by a French government of limited autonomy based in Vichy. The Reich had received word that an internment camp located in Gurs, in the southwest of France, was mostly empty. It had originally been set up by the French government at the end of the Spanish Civil War to control those who fled Francisco Franco's regime. Vichy protested the transport, arguing that such a measure had never been part of the plan. But faced with the fait accompli, in the end Vichy yielded. After two painful days of travel at the mercy of the brutal SS, the passengers, including many elderly, arrived at the Gurs camp, located in the free zone where in theory the Germans didn't have jurisdiction.

Administered by Vichy, this diverse internment camp would, for the duration of the war, hold detainees, Jewish and otherwise, of all nationalities besides the French, whether they were deported by the Nazi regime from European countries under their control or rounded up by the Vichy regime in the free zone. There were no executions and no torture at Gurs, but hundreds of detainees died from unsanitary conditions, of hunger and cold in barracks without windows, facilities, or running water, where rain leaked in and the beds consisted of sacks filled with straw thrown on the mud floor. Irma, Siegmund's wife, fell gravely ill and was sent to a hospital in Aix-en-Provence. Siegmund managed to be transferred to the internment camp at Milles, near Aix, to be closer to her. Escaping from the Gurs camp was pretty easy: the nonelectrified fences were only six feet high, and there weren't any watchtowers. But few tried to escape, since the real challenge came after, when an anxious game of hide-and-seek would begin with the police. It was probably because such an exploit was impossible with children, elderly parents, or a frail wife that most detainees in Gurs chose family over freedom.

Several religious and humanitarian organizations had been authorized to enter Gurs to bring food and medical care, and to ease the daily life of the interned. One of them, the international Jewish organization HICEM, helped Jews to pull together the necessary paperwork for an application to emigrate. Those who succeeded were transferred to Marseille, a large French port on the Mediterranean, in hopes of embarking overseas. This was how, in March and April 1941, Julius, Mathilde, their son Fritz, Wilhelm, his wife Hedwig, and their son Otto, left for Marseille. Thanks to the precious help of the team that manages the memorial at Milles, one of the leading institutions in France for teaching this legacy to the younger generation, I was able to reconstruct the rest of the family's course. The men were put in the Milles camp, placed under the authority of Vichy, where numerous German artists and intellectuals were interned, among them Golo Mann and Lion Feuchtwanger. The women and children were sent to Marseille hotels that had been transformed into housing. Hedwig and Otto, who was nine at the time, were placed in the Hôtel Bompard, while Mathilde and Fritz, who was twelve, were at the Hotel Terminus les Ports. They suffered from malnutrition there, and from poor hygiene, vermin, lack of clothing, and cold. The rooms contained up to eight beds, electricity was limited, and showers were rare. Some hoteliers had no scruples about pocketing the compensation from the Vichy administration and spending only a little bit on the detainees. But compared to the camp at Gurs, their living conditions had certainly improved. International charitable associations held classes for the children and sewing courses for the women, but above all, most women could circulate freely about the city, going to the beach, and pursuing the administrative steps required to emigrate. According to archives at the Milles camp, Hedwig tried to get American visas for her family. Mathilde probably did as well.

But they arrived too late. Up until July 1, 1941, this goal might still have been achievable, thanks to the help of the American vice-consul in Marseille, Hiram Bingham IV, who procured visas and false papers for Jews. And thanks to the complicity of Varian Fry, who co-founded an unofficial, private rescue network with the support of Eleanor Roosevelt. He had succeeded in rescuing more than 2,000 French and German refugees, primarily artists, university professors, and scientists, including Claude Lévi-Strauss, Max Ernst, André Breton, Hannah Arendt, and Marc Chagall. In response, and also under pressure from Vichy, in 1941, the State Department in Washington revoked the Marseille consulate's power to grant visas, confiscated Varian Fry's passport, and suddenly transferred Hiram Bingham to Portugal.

Hedwig Wertheimer and Mathilde Löbmann's attempts to emigrate fell apart in the summer of 1942, when they were transferred with their sons to the camp at Milles and reunited with their husbands, Julius and Wilhelm. The atmosphere was heavy. Deportations to the main French transit camp at Drancy had begun, officially to send detainees to work camps in Eastern Europe. When they saw adults and children packed like animals on freight trains without water, some wondered why they would also send unskilled kids to work. Rumor had it that Vichy no longer hesitated to turn over Jews to the Germans, and some even spoke of massacres. Hedwig and Mathilde must have sensed the danger. Like other mothers, they decided to trust their sons to L'Oeuvre de Secours aux Enfants (OSE), a Jewish organization. Witnesses described heart-wrenching separations, screams of children torn from their mothers, who fought to keep a certain expression of calm so as not to worry their children. Otto was placed at the Château de Montintin, south of Limoges, where about 100 German Jewish children were hidden under the protection of a doctor. Fritz was sent to a similar group intending to save children from deportation. In Spring 1943, Otto and Fritz were transferred, probably because their hiding place had become too risky. They must have wept with joy when they were reunited in one of the last refuges in France, situated in the Italian-occupied zone. In Izieu, a little village perched above a branch of the Rhône, Sabine Zlatin, a Polish Jew and resistance member, had established a colony with her husband to protect children from deportation. For the first time, Fritz and Otto could reconnect with their childhood light-heartedness. At the Izieu memorial, photos show these children in a big meadow, their hair blown by the wind, or in a group in front of the house, the older ones carrying the little ones in their arms, or in bathing suits on the dock of a lake. These photos could be those of any happy childhood, and they are always smiling in them, without a hint of foreshadowing. The Italian-occupied zone had always been the safest for the Jews, since, unlike the French, the Italians refused whenever possible to hand over the Jews in their territory. But in July 1943, the situation in Italy was upended by the Allied landing in Sicily and the ensuing bombing of Rome, which destabilized Mussolini. In September, the British landed in Calabria, and in the chaos Italy surrendered, and the Wehrmacht invaded northern and central Italy, as well as the Italian zone in France. In April 1944, Sabine Zlatin sensed danger approaching and left to find another refuge for her charges. It was precisely during her absence, on the morning of April 6, when the children were preparing to eat their breakfast the first day of Easter vacation, that two trucks of Wehrmacht soldiers and a car full of Gestapo agents arrived to brutally load up the forty-four children, Sabine Zlatin's husband, and six teachers, sending them to the Drancy camp. The order was given by the head of the Gestapo in Lyon, Klaus Barbie, a man who became famous for his mad obsession with tracking Jews and resistance members, whom he would subject, with an unconcealed pleasure, to a variety of tortures he prided himself on inventing.

On April 15, 1944, Fritz Löbmann and Otto Wertheimer, aged twelve and fifteen, were deported from Drancy to Auschwitz on board a convoy with thirty other children from Izieu. The day they arrived, they were gassed.

Two years earlier, Hedwig, Mathilde, and Wilhelm had been transferred to the Drancy camp near Paris. On August 17, 1942, they set out again, onboard convoy number 20. Destination: Auschwitz. On September 2, it was Siegmund's turn to reach Drancy, and from there he was deported five days later on convoy number 29. Destination: Auschwitz. His solitude must have increased his distress even more. His wife, Irma, was listed among the deported from the Milles camp, but she must have been saved in extremis, perhaps by the doctors who demanded her emergency internment at the Aix-en-Provence hospital.

Julius Löbmann was also on the list, but he wasn't deported. He'd successfully managed to flee during one of his daily shifts in the village of Saint-Cyr-sur-Mer, where he worked with a group of forced laborers. He must have decided quickly when he understood that his family would not escape deportation. Only he could leave—the others were caught in the trap of the camp perimeter. I imagine him saying goodbye to his wife, his son, his brother, and his brother-in-law, and not sleeping a wink the night before his escape. Then the day of it, watching for the best moment to slip away, disappearing in the forest of pines near Saint-Cyr-sur-Mer or jumping from the truck as it returned. The chances of getting out, for a Jew on the run, left to his own devices without money, without contacts, and knowing nothing about France, were slim under a regime that collaborated with Germany and had established its own anti-Jewish measures under the passive eye of the population. At least, if fate didn't decide to be generous and put in his path one of those brave French humanists who hid Jews in their attics or cellars during the war, bringing them what they needed to survive. Even this scenario could end badly, if the guardian angel was denounced and arrested by the Gestapo or the French police, and those under his protection were captured or abandoned in their hiding places without help. Without such an arrangement, the only recourse was to be ingenious and audacious, which Julius was, according to Lotte Kramer. So as not to risk betraying his origins, he pretended to be deaf and mute and applied to be an elevator boy in a grand hotel on the Côte d'Azur, probably between Nice and Menton, in the Italian-occupied zone. I don't know if his boss guessed whom he was hiring, but he was good enough to overlook the lack of papers offered by this funny lad with blond hair and light eyes like a German. After the German invasion of the Italian zone in October 1943, Julius must have watched Wehrmacht and SS officers descend on the hotel. How many times a day did he undergo the ordeal of taking these men to their floors, of brushing those uniforms in that small elevator, of feeling his hands tremble as he pressed the buttons, his heart pounding in fear that a look, a reflex would escape him, a *Bitte schön* or *Danke* or *Guten Morgen*—one word and he would be lost. In summer 1944, he was delivered from this tension after the Allied troops disembarked in Normandy, then in Provence, and chased out the occupiers. He might have gone to Drancy, and learned that his family had been sent to Auschwitz. I don't know if, at the time, Julius knew what Auschwitz meant.

In summer 1941, the British knew that SS commandos, whose radio signals they had decrypted, were committing massacres in Eastern Europe. After that, the Allies received more indications thanks to sources in the German army, in the Polish resistance, or among Jewish activists. In spring 1942, *The Daily Telegraph* was alarmed: "More than 700,000 Polish Jews have been killed in one of the largest massacres in world history." More and more, the media began to relay this information, and even the gas chambers were mentioned. On December 17, 1942, the Allies publicly and unanimously condemned these "bestial methods of extermination." In truth, the American, British, and Soviet governments had already been informed that at least 2 million Jews had been killed and that 5 million others were in danger. The BBC replayed the declaration, which notably confirmed: "No one ever heard from the deported again. Those who could work were exploited in camps until they died of exhaustion. The sick and the infirm died of cold or hunger or were ruthlessly killed." Since this information was being censored in France by Vichy, Julius must have harbored some feeble hope, particularly for his little son, Fritz, who was still so young—the Nazis couldn't possibly kill children. Once free, who could Julius go to for help? All his family, all his friends had disappeared, and liberated France completely neglected the Jews. There was nothing left for him but to join his relatives in America, in Chicago, where his family had planned to flee before being picked up during the raid in Mannheim.

While he crossed the Atlantic aboard a boat, leaving a burned, bloodied Europe behind, a profound sense of sadness must have come over Julius at the idea of being alone on this journey, a journey his loved ones had once thought of, with bitterness, as a last resort. He'd never imagined it would become an impossible dream—to be all together on the boat, saved from the wreck of their country and continent. As his eyes fixed on the horizon where this much-desired American land would soon appear, Julius must have sensed that he would never share this new world with his son, Fritz, his wife, Mathilde, or his brother, Siegmund.

IV

Karl Schwarz's Denial

Chicago was a first choice for Europe's Jews, since, after New York and Warsaw, it sheltered the third-largest Jewish community in the world, with a Jewish population of 275,000. The most influential and best assimilated were from Germany. As the first to arrive after 1840, they had created a vast network of educational, social, and religious institutions that gave the community a solid, thriving framework. At the turn of the twentieth century, Jews from Eastern Europe and Russia fled violent pogroms in their countries and flowed in as well, and in the thirties they were joined by the victims of Nazi persecution. Non-Jewish celebrities were also exiled in the city, including Ludwig Mies Van der Rohe, one of the founders of modern architecture, who left Germany not so much out of political resistance but because the regime, an enemy of modern art, didn't appreciate his work. His minimalist architecture of "almost nothing" left an imprint on Chicago: skyscrapers of steel and glass, and the imperial Crown Hall on the campus of the Illinois Institute of Technology, an imposing, open rectangle of dark gray metal and windows, placed in a verdant garden.

It is likely, in this context, that Julius Löbmann quickly met other exiles—perhaps even friends or former citizens of Mannheim who had known his family, his business, and with whom he shared memories of a German existence that had vanished forever. After all, of the 3,500 Jews from Mannheim who had succeeded in leaving the country, almost half had gone to the United States. This was how Julius met Erna Fuchs. Like him, she was from the Baden region, and her family had left in 1937 to settle in Chicago. He didn't wait long to marry her, since according to documents from the archives in Karlsruhe, Erna had already taken the name Löbmann in 1949 and lived at the same address as he did. Quickly remarrying a Jew from his own country who understood what he had been through must have spared Julius a great deal of loneliness. Though the Jewish community in Chicago was welcoming, many could not imagine what those from Europe had endured under Nazism.

As for American society, the chilling coldness it had displayed in the past didn't inspire much trust. In 1938, while the Jews of Europe clearly faced a grim fate, polls had shown that more than 80 percent of Americans were still against raising immigration quotas. One year later, other polls revealed that more than 60 percent of Americans were against a bill introduced by Senator Robert Wagner and Representative Edith Rogers, which would have welcomed 20,000 German Jewish children in addition to the fixed quota. The bill was blocked by anti-Semitic lobbyists before it was even submitted to Congress for a vote. Did Julius make the connection between the American lack of solidarity and the fate of his family, caught in the trap because they couldn't get visas? In spite of this dark history, many Jewish immigrants were grateful to the United States for letting them in and giving them a real chance to integrate and succeed in society, which few other countries offered. The heavy German accent of Heinz Kissinger, a Bavarian Jewish refugee who came to New York in 1938, didn't stop him from becoming a legendary American secretary of state. How many Jewish letters contained this admission of patriotism:

"We've already become real Americans!" Many who had left for other countries couldn't say as much. Even in Israel, assimilation was difficult for Jews who refused to learn Hebrew, and they experienced a profound nostalgia for their homelands.

When the end of the war was announced, Julius Löbmann must have held out hope, pouring energy into phone calls, knocking on doors in Chicago to find out if anyone had news of his son, his wife, or the others. Then he must have seen images of the death camps in the American media, showing the living dead, emaciated, next to mountains of corpses. His hope, of finding his loved ones alive, must have suddenly been cut short. What traces remained of those who had vanished? A few photos, objects, clothing, furniture the family had sent to Chicago from Mannheim before they were deported. Unless these items had never arrived, since after the invasion of the Netherlands, the Nazis had helped themselves to a number of containers full of goods from German Jews that were waiting in the port of Rotterdam to be sent to their owners overseas. This theft was the last straw for refugees, many of whom had emigrated with only basic necessities after being robbed by the Reich. For them, exile was accompanied by a steep financial and social decline from which they never recovered, frustrated by the language barrier and the challenge of getting their diplomas recognized in a foreign country. This decline was particularly hard on those who'd had successful careers in Germany, and who found themselves, at the age of more than forty or fifty, plummeting to the bottom rung of the social ladder. A woman from Mannheim who was the head of several large department stores and reigned over a thousand employees became a cleaning lady in New York. Upstanding businessmen who were models of success in their native land suddenly became relegated to the rank of assistant. Lawyers and doctors found themselves reduced to exhausting manual labor and had no choice but to take it on, even if they were old or sick, since there were no social services in the United States, adding financial instability to humiliation and deprivation. Some preferred to kill themselves.

Julius Löbmann must have benefited from the aid of friends or Jewish organizations, since he didn't seem to have lived in poverty, if you believe the address listed on the letters he sent to my grandfather. I discovered that at the start of 1947, he lived in a tidy cooperative of little brick buildings in Wicker Park, a neighborhood that housed many Polish immigrants. Two years later, I found him with his new wife, Erna, in Kenwood, a pretty residential neighborhood of Georgian and Art Deco houses on the edge of Lake Michigan, which once served as a refuge for Chicago's elite. The couple lived in a house that was unpretentious, but agreeable, on a wide, quiet street, bordered with trees and elegant houses, not far from synagogues and Jewish schools.

This was Julius's situation when he claimed reparations from the two owners of the *Mineralölgesellschaft*, Karl Schwarz and Max Schmidt, in January 1948, through his lawyer Rebstein-Metzger. Shortly before, a law had been instituted in the American-occupied zone in Germany which ruled that all the assets that had been stolen or "forcibly sold" under the Nazi regime had to be returned to their owners or heirs. The *Rückerstattungsgesetz*, or restitution law, gave a legal framework to allow victims of Nazism to legally contest all property transfers that took place after the Nuremberg Laws of September 15, 1935. The American zone had the earliest and most unequivocal way of dealing with this question. Pan Am even had an advertising campaign in the United States on this theme: "Going to Germany for your restitution claims? Daily flights by PAA to principal German cities." They offered discounted tickets, but these were still out of reach for Julius and most other refugees, while those who could have afforded them didn't really want to revisit the countries that had attempted to annihilate them. The British waited two years before instituting, in turn, a law similar to the one created by the Americans. In the French zone, on the other hand, the law was more flexible, since it included a clause for "faithful buyers" and fixed the start of the period of presumed abusive acquisition on June 14, 1938, the date of the text that forced Jews to list their businesses and shops in a public register, so as to facilitate their Aryanization. Before that date, the French required the plaintiff to provide proof that the transaction had been illegal.

In Mannheim, it was the American version that prevailed. Karl had undoubtedly heard about the *Rückerstattungsgesetz* because he was directly concerned. Starting in the postwar period, the American authorities had held his company in trust after having identified, thanks to intact records, the thousands of Jewish businesses and lands that had been Aryanized in Mannheim, and the *Mineralölge-sellschaft* figured among these. All the same, Opa must have thought that he was one of those who had paid a "faithful price" and would soon be released from the suspicion of having taken advantage of Jews. Many buyers were thinking along the same lines, because the Nazi regime had devised the perfect way of making people become complicit while still keeping their consciences clear: making their crimes legal. In Karl's mind, it was therefore totally legal to consult the public register of Jewish businesses for sale and to pay the market price of the moment, and this was all within the framework of a contract validated by the authorities. Especially since he seemed to be convinced that the transaction took place in "a most amicable manner," as he repeated in many letters to Julius Löbmann's lawyers, which he copied and kept in the cellar in Mannheim.

My grandfather assured Mr. Rebstein-Metzger that he didn't take up the business capital of the Löbmann business, but had simply purchased the material goods and created his own business on that foundation. He considered himself particularly generous in paying at least the going price for objects without any value. "In the appraisal of furnishings, each item was evaluated down to the smallest (a ball of string, wrapping paper, stamps, pencil sharpening machine, etc.)," he stressed. According to him, he had also spent a sum of 5,000 Reichsmarks for packing materials and empty fuel drums scattered among the Löbmann clients that he'd never been able to recover. In his view, it was apparent that "it was not an actual Aryanization," and so he could not imagine "on what grounds Mr. Löbmann would like to make restitution claims." The lawyer replied: "The sales and transfer contract clearly shows that it was a purchase of the business as a whole and not only the sale of equipment. You even stipulated the right to keep the company name Siegmund Löbmann & Co. with or without any further addition. The only correct thing is that you merely paid for the material goods, as was common for this type of sale at that time. I also cannot discern that you at least paid for these items adequately." My grandfather could find nothing better to do than aggravate the issue by writing again to Mr. Rebstein-Metzger that "the equipment consisted of 'very old pieces,' which had a lower market value at the time, and apart from that, it would have been difficult to find a buyer because they were so ugly."

After several fruitless exchanges with the lawyer, Opa took the initiative of writing directly to Julius Löbmann: "My wife and I sincerely rejoiced in the fact that you at least made it out of this ordeal alive. We deeply regret the fate of your brother and brother-in-law. Did the families also perish? Even if, like most Germans, we did not wish for your fellow-believers' atrocious fate, from now on we all must suffer for it. Our dispute, which I did not anticipate, is just one example, since I certainly never put you in a difficult situation and all our agreements were made in the most amicable way . . . Our financial conditions are dismal. I think you may have completely mistaken ideas of the scope of our business." He signed off with: "How is your family? I hope they are doing well. My wife has already had to undergo two operations for intestinal ulcers this year, and has to have a further operation in September. There's always something."

Others had certainly abused the situation more than my grandfather, who negotiated a discount that was only 10 percent off the initial price. Nonetheless, five years after the war, he didn't seem to understand that the Third Reich was by nature an illegal regime, and that, by consequence, all transactions that occurred during its time should be seen in this light. He must sincerely have been shocked when he learned that the Jews the Nazis said had been deported to the east for their labor had actually been killed in squalid camps. But he failed to comprehend the scale, to the point of comparing his pain with Julius Löbmann's: "From now on we all must suffer for it." And this dissonant remark: "There's always something."

When they were asked to give Jews back what they were owed, many "Aryanizers" reacted like Karl Schwarz—asserting their own misfortunes and their difficulties in keeping themselves afloat. This state of mind was enabled by the fact that it was shared by the vast majority of Germans, and therefore rarely encountered any critique. The lack of guilty feelings, the intentional, supportive blindness allowed people to reject, en masse, all responsibility for Nazi crimes. Instead of showing empathy for the victims of Nazism, they endlessly pitied their own fates. The German Jewish political theorist Hannah Arendt, in exile in the United States, made a trip to Germany from August 1949 to March 1950 and was appalled by this population's "lack of emotion, callousness, cheap sentimentality." She wrote: "It is hard to tell whether they somehow purposely refuse to mourn or if they have a true inability to show emotions." Several years later, in 1967, the psychoanalysts Alexander and Margarete Mitscherlich delivered their response to this question in a shocking book, *Die Unfähigkeit zu trauern* (The Inability to Mourn). According to them, "denial and suppression of feelings" was the consequence of trauma, not from the crimes committed by the Reich, but from the loss of the idealized authority figure Adolf Hitler represented: "Hitler represented an idea of omnipotence, his death and his devaluation by the victor also meant the loss of a narcissistic object and thus an ego or self-frustration and devaluation." With this failure, the Germans who had clung to the Führer and National Socialism found themselves "naturally exempt from their personal responsibility." Such denial opened the door to a staggering misrepresentation of the past.

This attitude would become even more deeply entrenched as the 1949–63 government of the first chancellor of the Federal Republic of Germany (FRG), Konrad Adenauer, gave it a moral justification and a legal framework. "The denazification has caused much misfortune and much mischief," Adenauer declared during one of his first speeches to the nation, on September 20, 1949. "The wars and the turmoil of the postwar period have sorely tested so many and created such temptations that one must understand some misdemeanors and offenses." Where it seemed "defensible," the chancellor said, the federal government was determined "to let bygones be bygones." These words were hailed beyond his own supporters, since denazification was largely unpopular, even with the Social Democrats.

The birth of the FRG was expected to draw a *"Schlussstrich,"* to put an end to the practice supposedly imposed by the Allies, of dividing Germans into two classes, "politically clean" and "politically unclean." The wish to (re)unite the people for the task of reconstruction was understandable, but in truth, the goal was to vindicate the whole of the German people, with a few minor exceptions. In this spirit, the first measure the Bundestag hurried to enact was an amnesty law that would benefit the tens of thousands of Nazis condemned to a maximum penalty of six months by the tribunals. These included persons guilty of bodily harm leading to death. The law was also in favor of those who had gone underground to escape the tribunals.

This was only a prelude. In 1951, a new law called the 131er-Gesetz allowed the reintegration of more than 300,000 bureaucrats and career soldiers that the Allies, especially the Americans, had terminated for their alleged proximity to the regime, including thousands who had been involved in crimes. Even former members of the Gestapo benefited. On March 31, 1955, the beneficiaries of this law represented approximately 77 percent of the Ministry of Defense, 68 percent of the Ministry of Finance, 58 percent of the Governmental Press Office, and 40 percent of the Ministry of the Interior. *The Frankfurter Rundschau*, one of the few newspapers to criticize this policy, revealed that at the Ministry of Foreign Affairs, two thirds of the managerial positions were occupied by former members of the NSDAP. Adenauer hurried to deliver a response in agreement with the spirit of his times: "We cannot establish a foreign ministry without having people—at least for now—in leading positions who understand our history. . . . I now believe we should stop ferreting out Nazis." The most susceptible areas were in education and justice, where a very high percentage had belonged to the party. From then on, professors who had taught the virtues of Nazism had to teach those of democracy, and former judicial employees of the Reich had to defend the rule of law. The judges and the prosecutors, hardly motivated to condemn what they had fostered, let investigations against Nazi criminals drag on and closed cases. Besides, they were well placed to exempt themselves, which explains why practically none of them were tried despite being heavily implicated under the Third Reich.

*   *   *

Since a "fresh start" mentality was so popular, Bonn presented
a new amnesty law, which would finally end denazification. This
new step was carried out by the liberal FDP party, which held the
Ministry of Justice in Adenauer's government and was very popular
among former Nazis because it defended their cause. The party
had garnered 11.9 percent of the votes in 1949 with the slogan:
"Stop denazification, stop taking away rights, stop disenfranchise-
ment! No more second-class citizens! Vote FDP if you want civic
equality." Under the influence of the FDP the law introduced
the attenuating circumstance of *Befehlsnotstand* (obeying orders
given in a state of emergency), which de facto freed the accused
from any liability (or stripping of his responsibilities), as in the
Reich's very hierarchical system, everybody was obeying orders,
even war criminals and high officials. In its wake, the number of
legal proceedings dropped to next to none. The myth that it was
impossible, under Hitler, to disobey an order without risking your
life gained official status.

In his five-year exchange with Julius Löbmann and his lawyers,
Karl Schwarz never departed from his tearful tone. From the first
letters, he proposed a deal to Julius: "I am the last person to take
a handout or make his living at another's expense. I can also imagine that you need every penny you earn. Without acknowledging
the legitimacy of your claim, I propose to pay you 4,000 DM in
monthly installments of at least 200. In our current circumstances,
200 DM is tantamount to taking the bread from our mouths. This is
the best offer imaginable without endangering our own existence."

Under the varnish of denial, my grandfather let slip an admission that the price he had paid, however legal, might not have
been "suitable": "If we had let a Nazi expert verify the sale," he
wrote to the lawyer, "the price wouldn't have exceeded half the
sum we paid." If Karl didn't get the deal verified, it might have
been out of sympathy for the Jews. But this statement also reveals
that he had been aware that the "estimates" by the Nazi party were

My grandfather, Karl Schwarz, in front of his oil company,
Mineralölgesellschaft Schwarz & Co., Mannheim, 1965.

ridiculously low, and that the Löbmanns were forced to name a
realistic price if they didn't want to risk delaying the official vali-
dation of the contract and, by extension, the payment they needed
to finance their exile.

Julius Löbmann didn't respond. After four months, my grandfather raised his offer to 5,000 Marks. These repeated gestures
were, in my opinion, the result of Karl's guilty conscience mixed
with the fear of having to go before the tribunals, which were quite
strict about reparations to Jews.

Konrad Adenauer, a former opponent of Nazism who had been
chased out of the mayor's office in Cologne in 1933 after having

refused to officially welcome Adolf Hitler and unfold the NSDAP flags, clearly understood his country's duty to "repair" the crimes committed under the Third Reich. In September 1951, he declared: "The Federal Government and the vast majority of the German people are aware of the immeasurable suffering that was brought upon the Jews in Germany and in the occupied territories under National Socialism (. . .) unspeakable crimes have been perpetrated in the name of the German people, which commits us to moral and material reparation." The Germans might have been comfortably settled into amnesia, but other countries hadn't forgotten. The world watched with distrust as the Federal Republic of Germany took its first steps as a democracy, and Adenauer knew it. His goal was to anchor his country in the Western camp, with the hope of gradually recovering complete sovereignty and the respect of the international community. To this end, he had to increase gestures of goodwill, which would essentially translate into the dispensing of "reparations." The first step was the restitution of the astronomical quantity of goods and money stolen from Jews by individuals, businesses, and especially the state—an enormous bureaucratic, financial, and legal challenge. There was no precedent in history to fall back on. Millions of claims piled up on desks, and these requests had to be treated on a case-by-case basis. In 1957, 98 percent of cases had been processed. But the victims sometimes had to wait long years before receiving the last slice of their restitution, and those who had once been wealthy never recovered the equivalent of their lost prosperity. The next step was more delicate. It meant compensating people for "nonmaterial" damages: the death of a loved one, imprisonment, abuse, torture . . . the proceedings were long and painful for the victims, since it wasn't easy to demonstrate the cause-and-effect relationship between poor health and persecution under the Nazis. Despite the weaknesses and injustices of this system, it allowed the country to bandage certain wounds, and mainly to rescue Jews from their precarious position, while during this time East Germany and Austria stood out for their continued show of indifference.

The FRG also had huge reparations to pay to foreign countries. It sent a total of 971 million DM to countries in Western Europe between 1959 and 1964. But the most symbolic reparations agreement was the one between Konrad Adenauer and the Israeli foreign minister, Moshé Sharett, signed during an icy ceremony in 1952. In the guise of "compensation" for the genocide of the Jews, the FRG undertook the payment of 3 billion Marks in equipment and services to Israel over the following twelve years, and 450 million Marks to the Jewish Claims Conference, an organization representing the interests of Holocaust survivors outside Israel. In Jerusalem, heated debate and violent protests preceded this signing, which was denounced as Germany's attempt to buy back its conscience with "blood money." But financial need eventually convinced this brand-new country to accept the offer. In March 1953, the agreement was approved by a slim majority in the Bundestag, the German parliament, thanks to support from the Social Democrats, while most representatives of the parties in power voted against it, revealing their incapacity to face the reality of the Holocaust. Adenauer had resisted internal pressure because he knew that this gesture was essential to making his country "respectable" in the eyes of the international community. But this act was motivated by political calculation and carried out by a man who was isolated at the top. It didn't originate in the remorse of the German population. Many were even opposed to giving aid to German Jews, who were perceived as being "on the side of the victors." Rumors circulated that Jews were profiting from the situation by claiming assets that they had never possessed, and a virulent anti-Semitism resurfaced. The Germans were far from being cured.

❋   ❋   ❋

Strictly speaking, I didn't find anti-Semitic statements in Opa's letters, but faced with Julius Löbmann's stubbornness, his tone, which at the start was relatively amicable, suddenly changed. In response to Karl's gushing messages in letters that were several pages long, the plaintiff eventually sent him a very brief, cold message informing him that the process had begun and that he didn't plan to intervene on behalf of Karl Schwarz, who would have to "wait to see what came of it." Despite a certain goodwill on my grandfather's part, his endless laments, his denial, and his little paternalistic remarks must have left Julius unmoved in his decision to claim the maximum: 11,241 Reichsmarks for the intangible value of the company. Undoubtedly outraged by this demand, and succumbing to the panic of having to pay a sum he couldn't pull together promptly, Opa tried to reverse the roles in presenting himself as the victim: "Mr. Löbmann still seems to have inflation figures in mind, because his demand is extremely excessive, especially since in our case any claim for reimbursement is unfair . . . Even before Hitler's time, the Löbmann company wouldn't have found anyone stupid enough to pay 10,000 Reichsmarks. Unfortunately, we realized too late that we had been cheated. In all fairness, we should get several thousand Reichsmarks back." As proof of his words, he sent the lawyers the growth record of the Löbmann company's profits, revealing, according to Karl, the mediocrity of its intangible value, which he'd been accused of not paying for:

1929: 7,884.84 Reichsmarks
1930: 4,762.45 RM
1932: 11,581.81 RM
1933: 9,198.63 RM
1935: 7,811 RM
1937: 11,864 RM
1938: 6,961.79 RM

Didn't Karl Schwarz understand that these figures were insep-
arable from the context and that they only served to confirm the
injustices the Löbmanns had suffered? The first two years were
marked by the global economic crisis, then, when the business had
barely begun to recover, the Nazis came to power in 1933, causing
a new slump, due to the calls for boycotts among other things.
The revival of profits after 1935 corresponded to a lull after Jewish status was determined by the Nuremberg Laws in 1935. And
as for the drop in 1938, it was due to the increasingly precarious
state of the Jewish population, and then the sale of the business.

Julius Löbmann's new lawyer, Dr. Janda, was accustomed to
the Aryanizers and the way they twisted the truth, and he set my
grandfather straight: "The sale of the assets of Siegmund Löbmann
& Co. took place under the compulsion exercised by the then Nazi
legislation against Jews. If you now claim that you were grossly
deceived by the owners of Siegmund Löbmann & Co., this is a
bold statement, to say the least. The purchase price was reviewed
and approved by the NSDAP, and it is not to be assumed that
this party was given to disadvantaging Aryans in favor of Jews." I
was quite astonished by the firmness of this lawyer, a rare pearl
at a time when most legal professionals remained attached to the
Reich they had served. Clearly, Karl Schwarz missed the point
that this rhetoric, without ever precisely saying so, was inspired by
stereotypes about the tendency for Jews to be deceptive, greedy
swindlers, and that these clichés were scandalously inappropriate,
not to mention hurtful to his case. In his position as a victim of
the war, Karl Schwarz had surreptitiously slipped into posing as
a victim of the Jews.

In a German society that had been saturated with propaganda from
the National Socialists, it was these types of slippages that Konrad
Adenauer absolutely had to control if his country was going to be

reintegrated into the international community. The chancellor was glad to forgive his people for past crimes, on the condition that they clearly broke with National Socialism and adhered to democratic principles. But these ideals were far from being unanimously held. Abuses of language multiplied among politicians, as if the Allied retreat from political affairs after 1949 had removed their inhibitions. Some made no secret of their allegiance to the Third Reich, such as the Socialist Party of the Reich (SRP), which saw itself as the successor to the NSDAP and began to collect worrying regional support. They weren't content with denying particular Nazi crimes and disputed whether crimes had been committed at all. Outside Germany, people began to worry about this "renazification." And Adenauer was eager to ask for the SRP to be barred from the constitutional council, which agreed in October 1952. But the danger also came from within the very interior of the government, since in the heart of the coalition partner FDP, a group of neo-Nazis secretly resolved to take the reins of the party and topple the democracy. The British secret service uncovered the conspiracy and launched a spectacular wave of arrests in 1953. Despite the unrest that such an intervention on interior German affairs by outside forces could generate, Konrad Adenauer went along with it. He had established a very clear limit and the new Germany would not tolerate it being crossed. Open adherence to National Socialist ideas and anti-Semitism was taboo from then on.

However, a sizable mismatch remained. While declaring democratic values, Adenauer's government gave impunity to those who had incarnated their opposite: Hans Globke, co-author and commentator of the Nuremberg Race Laws, was named as state secretary of the Federal Chancellery; Theodor Oberländer, an early convert to Nazism, who had been in charge of Germanization measures in Poland, was named federal minister for displaced persons, refugees, and war victims. On the other hand, those who had actively resisted the Nazis or even attempted to assassinate Hitler had no chance at a career in politics, or of being acknowledged, during the Adenauer period. This very courageous minority of Communists, social democrats, unionists, religious groups, military, and others who had made tremendous sacrifices were treated like traitors by the Germans, who marginalized them in the political scene.

Instead of mobilizing for these heroes, the Germans led a fierce campaign to liberate German war criminals imprisoned abroad and in Allied prisons in Germany, under the pretext of defending "soldiers' honor." Among them were the worst types: the *Gauleiters*, commanders of the death squads, personnel from the camps, doctors in the euthanasia program. Under general pressure, the Allies gave in. Of the 3,400 war criminals still interned in 1951, there were only 30 left abroad by May 1958, and practically none in the Allied prisons of West Germany.

Even prominent Nazis were liberated, such as Ernst von Weizsäcker, the high commissioner of the Ministry of Foreign Affairs, who was one of the people responsible for the deportation of French Jews to Auschwitz. Or the entire management of one of the German companies most implicated in the Shoah: the chemical giant IG Farben, whose Zyklon B was used to gas millions of people. Among other German companies such as Siemens, IG Farben had built an external facility near Auschwitz, called the Buna camp, to take advantage of nearby manual labor. Between 1942 and 1945, tens of thousands of Auschwitz detainees worked like slaves at Buna, among them the Italian chemist and writer Primo Levi. The life expectancy there was a few months, in accord with the Reich's concept of Jewish "extermination through work." After the war, the IG Farben company was dismantled. Among the lucky ones pardoned was Friedrich Flick, condemned to seven years in prison at Nuremberg. A generous supporter of the NSDAP, he built his arms empire in corrupt coal mining in occupied territories, by buying successful Jewish businesses for a

pittance, and by exploiting more than 60,000 forced laborers, tens
of thousands of whom died. Until his death in 1972, Friedrich Flick
refused to pay a dime of reparations to the people he had forced
to work, and it was only under pressure from public opinion that
his heirs eventually gave in and began to pay several millions to
victims of slave labor.

This wave of pardons also benefited Alfried Krupp von Bohlen
und Halbach, the son of Gustav von Bohlen und Halbach and
Bertha Krupp, and the heir of an arms empire. Gustav Krupp first
refused to support the NSDAP. But after Adolf Hitler's rise to
power in 1933, he gave in and even created a fund for donations to
the German economy, which brought in 700 million Reichsmarks
to the NSDAP before the end of the war. One part of the Krupp
family was opposed to this support, which Gustav had prominently
displayed by hanging a swastika flag from the pediment of his house
in Essen. The family conflict and the moral decline of the Krupps
inspired the splendid Luchino Visconti film *The Damned* (1969).
The patriarch's son, Alfried, who took the reins of the empire in
1943, was not part of the resistance. On the contrary, he preceded
his father by supporting the SS as a "benefactor" beginning as early
as 1931. Beyond delivering indispensable materials to Hitler for
the war effort, the Krupp company exploited more than 100,000
forced laborers, including 520 women "rented" from Buchenwald
who were forced to forge steel in suffocating temperatures and
handle toxic substances without protective gear. Once pardoned in
the early 1950s, Flick and Krupp regained most of their fortunes
and their empires.

In this context in which the bloodiest criminals and the worst
crooks and slavers in the Reich emerged practically unscathed, my
grandfather's fate must have seemed very unjust. After all, hadn't
Konrad Adenauer absolved all the *Mitläufer* when he declared:
"The vast majority of the German people abhorred the crimes
committed against the Jews and did not participate in them."

Karl Schwarz had not been among those who slit Jewish throats and marched over corpses to do business. Richard Greiling had settled in Switzerland, but in 1935 he returned from exile with the sole intention of doing business on the backs of the Jews. He bought five companies for next to nothing, including three in Mannheim. One of these, a huge corset-manufacturing company, occupied most of a block of houses close to my grandparents' building. Greiling renamed the company Felina and for a time had some of his corsets made in the Łódź ghetto in Poland. After the war, the past caught up with him, but he dragged out the restitution process so much that the Jewish family, who were exiled to Canada, ended up contenting themselves with relatively low reparations. The Felina company, whose logo was visible in my childhood from Oma's living room balcony, still has its offices there.

On the other hand, there were the "goodwill buyers," a rare species: people who bought businesses as a favor to friends or Jewish bosses, so that the assets would remain in good hands. There were also people who were simply more honest than others who went behind the Nazi authorities' backs and arranged to pay, under the table, the intangible value of the company. Karl Schwarz couldn't boast of having been one of them, even if he seemed to truly believe it. "Due to the high purchase price, we helped to facilitate their timely emigration." "Removal," the lawyer corrected. Later my grandfather wrote to Julius Löbmann: "I now have to atone for the things that went horribly wrong for you, even if this is a great injustice, as I cannot be made responsible for these dreadful things." I'll never know if Opa was pretending or if he truly had trouble understanding the connection between the crimes of the Third Reich and his participation in pillaging the Jews. I think he found himself in a sort of fog somewhere between the two. The fact is, like many of his countrymen, he had genuinely profited from the Aryanization of Jewish assets, and no one had forced his hand. As Christiane Fritsche emphasizes in her book, Aryanization had not been an order, or a measure imposed from on high, but "a sociopolitical process involving numerous actors and profiteers": the state and the buyers, but also middlemen, real estate agents, brokers, banks, notaries, lawyers, and auction houses. This Nazi crime probably implicated the widest circles of German society. While the people were mainly guilty of apathy toward the deportations of Jews, they excelled in ruthlessly pillaging them, both in taking the initiative and in their ability to put aside scruples. By demonstrating their aptitude for crime, they encouraged the regime in its inhumane enterprise, paving the way for murder.

Seeing that his opponent stuck firmly to his position and avoided corresponding with him except through the intervention of lawyers, my grandfather raised his offer once more, to 8,000 Marks, which represented about a quarter of the value of the building on Chamissostrasse. He wrote him one last letter: "There seem to be misconceptions about our situation. If I hadn't worked day and night, and every Sunday to sell something, often at an unprofitable price, we would have closed down. Apparently, you want your revenge. But I certainly did not put you through anything that could morally justify your move. I have no words for your manners. At any rate, they will bring you no blessings . . . I have already heard about many restitution cases, but few have gone about it as rigorously as you have." He closed his letter with an appeal: "If you still have any sense of justice at all, you will review your claim and make a lesser demand so that at least I can also keep on existing." These contradictory emotions, which Karl Schwarz seemed incapable of mastering, perhaps touched Julius Löbmann, who accepted the offer and put an end to his pursuits.

My aunt Ingrid has a pretty good memory of this painful iron fist, since she was between twelve and seventeen at the time. "It was terrible, my father was extremely anxious. Besides Julius

Löbmann, there was also my father's former partner who wanted out of the business, and my father had to pay his part. There were also many repairs to pay for on the apartment building and a solidarity tax for those who had particularly suffered from the war. My father was drowning in debts." My grandmother was also very upset, my father remembers. "She was a rather brave woman, she went to see the judges and said, 'We don't have this money. Do you want to ruin a family with children?'" For all these expenses, my grandfather had to take out a mortgage on the apartment building, and for years to come he would lament what he considered an injustice, as if the Jews, and not Hitler's disastrous politics, were the origin of his troubles.

V

Oma, or the Discreet Charm of Nazism

My grandmother Lydia wasn't an expert in politics, but she regularly watched the news on a television set Karl exhibited on their living room sideboard like a trophy. In the fifties, they were the only ones in the building to allow themselves such a luxury, and the neighbors often rang the doorbell, asking if they could watch. "We couldn't say no to these neighbors. They were a bit like family, especially since we spent part of the war together in the bomb shelter in the basement—that's bonding!" my father jokes. "We pushed the furniture into the corners and brought chairs from here and there, making straight rows in front of the screen like at the movies." Sometimes a friend would come to see Lydia, and together they would discuss some news story they interpreted as a sign of German society's inevitable decay. My father remembers that in those moments his mother would let slip a mild regret—"That would never have happened under the Führer!"—a sentiment that became harder to tolerate the more my father came to understand the level of crimes this same Führer had committed.

My father had already inherited a scar from this nationalist sickness, in the form of a first name that left no doubt about the spirit in which his birth had been celebrated: Volker, composed of two words *Volk*, from the old High German for "people," and *Kämpfer*, for "fighter." Together they meant *Volkskämpfer*, "fighter for the people." My father escaped the worst, since the belligerent enthusiasm of the time had caused a renaissance of old baby names that were much more explicit than his. The mother of one friend had been hard hit by this wave, with a name that signified a battle-hardened femininity: Helmtraud, meaning "faithful to the helmet." She had been born one year before my father, in 1942, a year of widespread euphoria, when the Reich, buoyed by its staggering victories in Europe, had launched an offensive in North Africa, and then against the enormous Soviet Union, and stolen victory after victory with disconcerting ease, reinforcing the myth of the invincible German warrior, whose symbol was the helmet. When my father was born in April 1943, the German conviction that they were the race chosen to rule the world had already diminished after brutal defeats in the East where many German households lost a son, a husband, a brother, or many loved ones at once. This development encouraged parents to exercise a certain caution in the choice of Hitleresque first names, which disappeared as quickly as they had come.

More than Opa, Oma developed a certain emotional attachment to the Third Reich. This tie wasn't ideological in nature—like many Germans, Adolf Hitler had allowed her to dream. Born in 1901, Lydia was twelve when she lost her mother, who died after giving birth to her ninth child. She had already witnessed the deaths of six brothers and sisters, one after another, as was common in that era, when a little infection, a simple cold, could turn out to be fatal. The youngest would soon be carried off in turn, and Oma found herself alone with an older brother, a gentle dreamer with fragile health, whom she loved dearly. Shortly after her mother died, her father moved in with a woman who favored her own children, and she forced Lydia to do the housework.

For her thirteenth birthday, on August 1, 1914, Lydia's gift was the German declaration of war against Russia. The gears were turning: they would drag Europe into a world war that no one had wanted and which, in its ferocity, would surpass everything humanity had previously known. Far from spoiling Oma's birthday, the event must have brightened it, since in Germany—and in a number of other countries—the declaration was celebrated with euphoria, at least by part of the population. The photos from that time show men in the middle of the street throwing their hats in the air, their faces radiant with joy, or soldiers, arm-in-arm on train platforms, with playful looks in their eyes and flowers in their rifles, as if they were off on a lark with their friends. This sense of elation was short-lived, however, and the burdens and sacrifices of the war would bring a brutal end to Lydia's innocence, thrusting her into the heavy responsibilities of adulthood. With 13 million men at the front, the women and teenagers of Germany had no choice but to work very hard in factories and fields to make up for the lack of labor. During that time, the eldest sibling often had to look after all the children in the household, or even all the kids in the apartment building, who had to be watched, bathed, cared for, and fed. During the war, a total of 400,000–700,000 civilians, many of whom were children, died of cold, sickness, and most of all hunger. In this miserable atmosphere, letters arrived regularly from the front, sending a wave of emotion down the street. The news was often bad. Families lost not only a husband, a son, a father they had loved, but also the perspective that things would once again return to normal once the man returned.

Lydia was lucky enough to be spared such a fate. Her father was too old to be drafted, but she had the profound grief of losing her much-loved older brother, who died of tuberculosis during the war, and whom she mourned all her life. From then on, she was the last child, alone with her father, a hard worker who rarely took a day

off, busy preserving the excellent reputation of his carpentry business, whose woodwork—stairs, plinths, carved wooden doors—
decorated the most beautiful mansions in Mannheim. With her
sense of devotion, she would have very much liked to become a
nurse, a career that would have fitted her like a glove. But her
father flat-out refused, based on the then-widespread idea that in
an honorable family, the women didn't work. In place of a career,
he sent her to spend a year with the nuns in the Black Forest, to
instruct her in domestic duties, a necessary asset for a fifteen-
year-old young lady about to reach marriageable age. In the middle of the war, with daily life punctuated by death and despair,
Lydia ended up welcoming this time away as a blessing, and she
would later speak of it with emotion to her daughter Ingrid. The

My grandmother, Lydia Koch, Mannheim, circa 1916.

fact that this year of sewing, washing, ironing, and cooking with the sisters was one of the best years of her adolescence gives an indication of the types of entertainment prevalent in the lives of young middle-class women at the time.

My aunt remembers that her mother carefully kept a scrapbook of poetry that her classmates from the Black Forest had inscribed with little notes of friendship. Did she perhaps flip through it from time to time to feel, in the moments where she touched rock bottom, the happy memory of whispered nighttime chats in the dormitory, wild bouts of girlish laughter, and the sharing of simple dreams—the only youth she'd been allowed to have?

Lydia was seventeen when the armistice was signed, on November 11, 1918. But in truth, the war was still haunting Germany, a country on the brink of social, economic, and political collapse. In the cities, no one could escape the monstrous spectacle of hundreds of thousands of wounded with deformed faces, bodies torn apart, pierced, mutilated by the new weapons of large-scale destruction that this world war revealed in all their ignoble efficiency. These men who were incapable of working, and sometimes abandoned by a social system that was deficient or bankrupt, were reduced to begging in the street, and it wasn't rare for the workers who tended the streetlamps to find these veterans' stiff bodies on the sidewalk at dawn.

Two million soldiers died at the front, and four million were wounded. For the widows and survivors, the wartime struggle continued, aggravated by a deceptive peace built on shame, defeat, and humiliation, trampling under the Allied heel a country already on the edge of a financial precipice. To answer the unreasonable demands for reparations set out in the peace Treaty of Versailles— payment of an enormous sum, military and other supplies, the loss of patents for inventions, commercial sanctions, the dismantling of certain factories—the Bank of Germany printed an unlimited number of bills. Germany was thrust into the fatal whirlwind of inflation and hyperinflation, and every day, thousands of people who had lost their possessions overnight were put out on the street. Unemployment, hunger, and illnesses raged, and many babies died in infancy.

An atmosphere of civil war floated in the air. Popular revolts targeting the monarchist regime multiplied, stirred by German Marxists from the Spartacus League and inspired by the Bolshevik revolution in Russia. Kaiser Wilhelm II first ordered the army to march on the insurgents but ended up abdicating. The Weimar Republic was proclaimed. Shortly after, the Spartacus League called for a general strike in Berlin and the downfall of the government. The uprising was violently suppressed by the army with the help of the *Freikorps* of veterans. The figureheads of the moment, Rosa Luxemburg and Karl Liebknecht, were savagely assassinated, unleashing bloody fights in the street between the radical left and the *Freikorps*. The latter would soon support a new movement, young men in brown uniforms calling for National Socialism behind a leader by the name of Adolf Hitler. In 1923, they launched a failed coup. After that, the atmosphere calmed down a bit as inflation was curbed, and the economy slowly began to recover.

It was during these years of respite, the "Golden Twenties," that Lydia met Karl. The country was vibrating with new artistic and intellectual excitement. The Bauhaus revolutionized architecture and artistic reflection in a resolutely modern sense, marked by the idea of industrial progress and the emergence of mass culture; German cinema triumphed with masterpieces of expressionism by Fritz Lang and Friedrich Wilhelm Murnau. An ardent desire for lightheartedness had taken over the Germans, who were eager to forget the torments of the past in the opulent sequins and feathers of dancing girls, the dark humor of political cabarets, and the unfettered atmosphere of *Tanzcafés*, where the orchestra played jazz and imported liquor was served. In his ambivalent paintings, the artist Otto Dix immortalized this hedonistic euphoria.

One day, Oma ventured into one of these temples of dance to try out a few steps of the Charleston, and Karl's eye was drawn to this honest young woman, whose simplicity ran counter to the manners of her peers, who had been liberated by the war and their inclusion in the workforce. He must have liked that she was different from him, a man about town and a lover of sensual pleasures. Lydia was nonetheless a woman of character, with an independent spirit, and in no hurry to marry. The sudden death of Karl's father, who left three younger brothers and sisters in his care, accelerated their union. In 1926, Lydia and Karl were married. I have a faded black-and-white photo as the only souvenir of the day. In it, Lydia looks tender and misty, her face obscured by a white veil and her neck straightened by the high collar of her dress, while Karl seems serious, looking directly out from beneath his slim glasses. How young they are!

Out of love, Lydia took care of her spouse's brother and two sisters, the youngest of whom was eight years old, with a maternal affection. She agreed that they would all live together in a three-room flat. In return, Karl had a certain talent for amusing his wife thanks to a rather respectable salary. I found several photos where you can read the happiness and insouciance of their first years, at a tipsy table with friends and an accordionist, during a trip to the countryside in Karl's big car, or on a boating excursion. Her husband's way of life was a bonus for serious Lydia, who smiled a lot in those days. In photos from a carnival, she poses in a sailor's costume, with a cigarette in her hand, or in a Spanish dress, with some wild accessory in her hair.

Lydia in 1929, newly married and dressed as a sailor at a local carnival.

Shortly after, when Germany had just barely begun to recover
a taste for the good life, the nightmare returned, this time in the
form of a devastating global economic crisis, unleashed by a crash
in the United States. American investors who had an urgent need
for capital withdrew their investments from Germany all at once,
leading to the collapse of German banks, massive waves of layoffs,
and a drastic lowering of salaries. Between 1929 and 1932, the
number of unemployed workers grew from 1.4 million to more
than 6 million. When Adolf Hitler was named chancellor in 1933, I
don't think Oma was particularly enthusiastic. She and her spouse
hadn't voted for Hitler in the presidential elections of 1932, but
for Paul von Hindenburg, a World War I military hero who gained
widespread support. But in federal elections the following July and

November, the NSDAP emerged in the lead, clearing the way for its leader to become chancellor. Thanks to Karl's stable position as a manager in the Nitag petroleum company, my grandparents didn't desperately need to believe in the miracle of a man chosen by Providence who would save them from their economic misery. Nonetheless, Oma had a charitable spirit and could only hope for the end of this disaster that tossed children into the street and drove men to suicide because they could no longer provide for the needs of their families.

And thanks to the strong interventionism of the National Socialist state, which undertook big public works such as the construction of highways, developed considerable industry for the military, and introduced great numbers of Treasury bonds, the German economy righted itself after several years. The price was record levels of national debt. But people preferred not to look too closely, since they were reassured by the possibility of finding work. The number of unemployed people went from 5.6 million in 1932 to 2.7 million in 1934, and by 1939 it was practically zero. The endless lines disappeared in front of businesses where Germans had waited, armed with ration tickets, for the right to a scrap of bread, a cabbage, or a few potatoes, and the shop windows were full once again. However, the standard of living remained well below that of the French and the Americans, and the German people still had to economize. Despite these privations, the Reich was lucky to have risen on the heels of such a collapse, making the living conditions it offered seem miraculous. Especially after the summer of 1935, when the government could proudly announce that unemployment had dropped to 1 million. Hitler was promoted to the status of "Savior" of all Germans, without divisions in class or wealth.

In truth, despite its promises and its references to socialism, the National Socialist Reich did not treat all men equally, even among so-called Aryans. Hitler was respectful of social class, and when the bourgeoisie understood that he wasn't going to revolutionize the established social order, they unhesitatingly supported him. Where access to higher levels of schooling was concerned, the regime didn't do anything to counteract the lack of social mobility through education, and in business, it privileged employers over employees: tariff regulations, contractual freedoms, and the right to strike were abrogated, while union power was destroyed, its assets confiscated, and its leaders imprisoned, all under the pretext of one of Hitler's most important objectives, the "destruction of Marxism" in Germany. Besides, a new elite had risen: the Party bosses and bureaucrats of the Reich, who abused their power and gave themselves all kinds of privileges.

Yet the labor class didn't rebel. Most likely, after the nightmare of the economic crisis, they, too, hoped for material comfort and social harmony. It was even easier to give up the battle against the bourgeoisie, since Hitler had presented, on a silver platter, other forces responsible for society's ills: democracy and Jews. German social democrats and Communists in exile watched in amazement as more and more laborers joined the new regime. Besides employment and the end of economic precarity, the Reich offered the labor and middle classes the novel concept of social mobility through work, which followed from the party's Darwinist view of the world and its adage "may the best man win" (on the condition that they were Nazi and Aryan). In fact, this selective meritocracy that valued productivity and performance more than certain kinds of social origin gave a whole group of young people unparalleled career chances in the civil service, the many Nazi organizations, and especially the army, where the need for personnel was too significant to reserve positions of responsibility for those families belonging to the traditional military caste.

But above all, the Reich spread a feeling of social equality by generating a sense of belonging to the same *Volksgemeinschaft*,

or "people's community"—the utopia of a social body, united and
equal, in communion with the Führer. This was the meaning
behind the "Sunday stews" where NSDAP officials would share a
table with the poor, eating the same cheap, hot meal that all restaurants were required to serve. According to the historian Norbert
Frei, "One of the most notable successes of National Socialist
social policy was how they spread a feeling of social equality." The
Volksgemeinschaft was the basis of the Nazi ideology that infiltrated all of society thanks to a mass of organizations acting at all
levels—professional, social, educational, festive, sporting, tourist—
to replace the old structures. The Germans quickly adapted to
these changes, particularly because they brought a streak of joy
and good humor to the calendar, increasing the number of holidays, parades, and celebrations. At the Nitag company, Opa was
responsible, as a delegate of the German Labor Front, for organizing excursions and parties for everyone. His mission was to sell
the idea of a joyful, harmonious company that brought together
managers and workers, to make them forget the suppression of
unions and grave breaches of the right to work.

It was the end of grimness and desolation. People ate, worked,
and amused themselves once again. An air of jovial optimism
floated in the street, at work, and in the cafés, and even the faces
of ordinary citizens were bathed with renewed confidence. Smiles
and laughter had come back, and prettily dressed women strolled
down the aisles of the suddenly resuscitated department stores,
buying fabric for a new dress or paying for some little treat—a hat,
an evening bag for a trip to the theater or to a concert. The quality
of cultural programming had greatly declined under the National
Socialist censor, but to compensate, a large variety of entertainments were offered by the state at prices that were accessible to the
majority, which contributed to fostering a sense of social equality.
After the model of Fascist Italy's Opera Nazionale Dopolavoro
(National Recreational Club), which Hitler greatly admired, the

Nazis created the Kraft durch Freude (KdF), or Strength through Joy, which offered courses in gymnastics, dance, sports, excursions, nature hikes, theatrical and musical evenings, checkers tournaments, and even contests for the most beautiful village.

The objective was not at all social—it was ideological. It sought to reinforce allegiance to the *Volksgemeinschaft* and through it, allegiance to the Führer and the state, supremely powerful protectors, guarantors of the physical and psychological health of those citizens with Aryan blood. In exchange, the people had to let themselves be completely guided by an unwavering loyalty to Adolf Hitler, even in private life and thought. They also had to serve National Socialism through hard work, and if necessary, war.

The Reich also provided vacations, which German workers enjoyed thanks to a centralized tourism organization and an increase in the length of paid leaves. I visited a symbol of the rise of mass tourism in the Baltic Sea on Rügen Island, a high-end vacation spot where the nineteenth-century German bourgeoisie built handsome white wooden villas decorated with corbel arches and sculpted balconies. In a pine forest bordering a luminous beach, I walked for a whole hour along a deserted six-story building dotted with gaping holes. This Prora property stretches for three miles, surrounded by barbed wire to prevent people from going inside. It seems Hitler himself had the idea for this titanic project—a leisure center equipped with a multitude of rooms and modern comforts, large enough to house up to 20,000 vacationers, who would have the free time to stretch out by two wave pools and divert their spirits in a gigantic performance hall. This dream remained unfinished, as did the construction, which was interrupted by the war. In vacations and leisure activities, the KdF particularly emphasized health and fitness. For Hitler was fanatical about physical hygiene, eating a vegetarian diet, forbidding anyone to smoke in his presence, and abstaining from alcohol. His companion Eva Braun was passionate about gymnastics, as the Russian film director Alexander Sokurov displayed with delicious irony in his masterpiece *Moloch*. This obsession was consistent with the eugenics and racism of Nazi ideology, which aspired to create a "new man" of purely "Aryan" blood, handsome and sound of body. It was a Nazi's duty to take care of his body and a mother's duty to feed her children accordingly. Purging the *Volksgemeinschaft* of the supposedly "impure" blood of Jews wasn't enough. The Nazis favored the strongest, those in the best health, over the old, the sick, and the weak, with the idea that the former would be more useful in wartime. In 1937, Hitler congratulated himself on his "German racial politics" in a speech at Nuremberg: "How beautiful are our girls and our boys, how bright is their gaze, how healthy and fresh are their attitudes, how splendid are the bodies of the hundreds of thousands, the millions that are trained and cared for by our organizations. . . . It is the rebirth of a nation through the deliberate breeding of a new human being."

Oma wasn't very athletic. When she was young, she accompanied her spouse when he went skiing in the Black Forest, and I found photos of them, astonishingly at ease on their wooden skis, alone in the middle of a vast, unspoiled expanse. Love had given her wings. Later she put on a little weight, and Karl stopped asking her to go with him on his solitary escapades in the mountains or his naked camping trips by the lakes. Perhaps she was also tired of these extravagances and hoped for other diversions. The KdF had more than one arrow in its quiver, and in addition to athletic vacations with Spartan tendencies, it offered the exact opposite: the voluptuousness of a cruise. This was how Lydia, who had never traveled in her life, set out one day with 1,500 other passengers for five days on a large white ship, brand new and equipped with modern cabins and hot running water, headed for the sumptuous fjords of Norway, one of the Nordic countries whose "purity of race" Hitler admired. This passenger ship, built in 1937, had been christened with the name of the former NSDAP chief in Switzerland, Wilhelm Gustloff, a fanatical anti-Semite who was assassinated at Davos by a Jewish student. On board, there were several restaurants, a hairdresser, stores, an indoor pool, a gymnasium, and a theater. "My mother often talked about that voyage," Ingrid says. "She enjoyed herself as she rarely had before—she danced, she drank—she said there was a fantastic atmosphere on board." The Reich had six cruise ships at its disposal and offered destinations that people could have only dreamed of, such as Madeira, an archipelago southwest of Portugal where the cream of British society typically spent winters. Their jaws must have dropped when they saw a horde of middle-class Germans disembarking. Up until the war, more than 700,000 Germans benefited from this luxury that was otherwise unimaginable for the European middle class. Even so, 99 percent of workers didn't have this privilege because even the subsidized prices of cruises remained prohibitive.

This daring mixture of glamour and socialism had a very positive influence on the popularity of the regime, especially with women, who spoke of their wonderment to friends and family long after they returned from their trips, as a Nazi Party observer noted with satisfaction. Already, the Führer benefited from the particular affection of female citizens, moved by both a protective instinct for this grown boy with no family, and a fascination for this man with a supposedly magnetic charisma and voice. Besides that, Hitler had been careful to keep quiet about his relationship with Eva Braun, whom he refused to marry so he could preserve the illusion of a Führer married to Germany, and therefore to all German women. He also knew how to nourish his adoring fans by raising the status of Mother's Day to a national holiday, which was a way of signaling the importance of the mother and housewife in the project of National Socialism, as both a breeder of good little Aryans and an essential support for man's mission. Twelve million women were members of Nazi organizations, and at the end of the war, many bemoaned the Führer's defeat, and some even killed themselves. Oma also admired him, and if she didn't belong to organizations, it was perhaps out of respect for her father, Heinrich Koch, a die-hard social democrat who had been so moved the day he personally met Friedrich Ebert, the legendary president of the SPD. But since she was involved with charities and had many female friends, it's likely that she participated in Nazi initiatives to help the poor.

Even without a social life, it was hard to avoid Nazi ideology, since it had penetrated the most intimate nooks and crannies of private life. It forbade sexual relationships with Jews and encouraged men and women to procreate, outside of marriage if necessary. "I wonder if my mother was influenced by this spirit when she had me," my father confides. "She was forty-two, which, at the time, was quite old to decide to have a child, especially in the middle of the war." The ideology was also imposed on children's education. A book by the Austro-German doctor Johanna Haarer made a big splash and sold 160,000 copies between 1934 and 1938. It was called *The German Mother and Her First Child* and had three key words: *breeding*, *obedience*, and *cleanliness*. "My mother didn't subscribe to that ideal, on the contrary, she spoiled me a little too much," Volker explains. "As for my father, he was more inspired by the old model of education, patriarchal and harsh." To correct any cases of parental incompetence in raising little Nazis, the regime enrolled young people aged ten to eighteen in Hitler-approved organizations. At the Association of German Girls (BDM), "Aryan" girls learned "to care for the warmth of the hearth of the house" as "guardians of the purity of the blood and the people" and to "raise heroes from the sons of the people." The masculine equivalent, the Hitler Youth, exercised its brainwashing capabilities on 98 percent

of boys from that age group, indoctrinating them into the racial
and social Darwinist ideology, and requiring physical and mental
training intended to prepare them for combat. The HY even participated in violent actions, like the boycott of Jewish stores and
Kristallnacht. Some completely brainwashed kids even began to
spy on their professors at school, their parents, and their neighbors.
Despite the radical, obligatory quality of these institutions, they
were popular, perhaps because they also treated children equally,
no matter their wealth or social status.

Not all women venerated Hitler. Unlike Oma, those who had
entered the workforce and tasted the early stages of emancipation
during the twenties experienced the Nazi regime as a stinging
rebuke. The Führer declared war on "women's liberation," which
according to him was a phrase "invented by Jewish intellectuals."
During a speech at the Nuremberg rally in 1934, he said, "It is
not right for women to enter the man's world. We find it natural
for these two worlds to be separated." With the irony of history,
that rally actually owed its international importance to a woman:
Leni Riefenstahl. Hitler was blown away by her talent and had
given her carte blanche to make propaganda films like the dizzying *Triumph of the Will*. The rhythm of montage and the takes,
breathtaking in their newness and power, would make a strong
impact in German theaters and abroad. It perfectly renders the
giddy atmosphere of these party rallies, where mystical displays of
power subjugated the viewers and the participants, uniting them in
a halo of warlike camaraderie—illuminated by raids with torches,
unbreakable military discipline, and an aesthetic marked by flags,
raised salutes, imposing architecture, and shouted appeals for radical action. Opa, who didn't have the soul of a warrior or a fanatic,
gave way to curiosity and went to Nuremberg to see this pompous
spectacle, which was said to amaze even those least sympathetic
to National Socialism. That was just the idea—to hypnotize, to
turn attention away from persecutions, arrests, and the brutality

that subjected one part of the population, while the other was drinking sparkling wine on a cruise or marveling at the grandeur of the Reich at Nuremberg. The targets were Jews, Communists, socialists, unionists, journalists, intellectuals, and men of power who were judged too ambitious. The Reich also targeted homosexuals, the weak, the sick, and the marginalized, who, from 1934 onward, were subject to forced sterilization presented as a "Law for the Prevention of Diseased Offspring." There was no place for them in a eugenic state.

What did my grandparents know of this violence? They lived in a city where information circulated rapidly. In the thirties, people knew about the concentration camps and poor treatment of the detainees, the assassination of political competitors and opponents was an open secret, and the persecution of Jews took place in broad daylight. The raids by the SS and SA, shouting, stomping their boots, and sowing terror, probably irritated many Germans who would have preferred this crackdown to take place out of sight of their homes. But they resolved their moral qualms by deciding that Adolf Hitler, the man who had their loyalty, was either far removed from these raids or was doing something legitimate. What this demi-God did and said had the value of truth, of law. Sigmund Freud said as much in *Group Psychology and the Analysis of the Ego*: "Conscience has no application to anything that is done for the sake of the object; in the blindness of love, remorselessness is carried to the pitch of crime." The cult of the Führer grew to even more outsized proportions as the unemployment rate dropped and he accumulated diplomatic victories. The reintroduction of obligatory military service, the remilitarization of the Rhineland in violation of the Treaty of Versailles in 1936, the annexation of Austria and the Sudetenland in 1938 gave Hitler the status of a prophet who had brought glory to the Reich and won vengeance for the "Shame of Versailles." For his fiftieth birthday, on April 20, 1939, he received an avalanche of love letters and gifts worth 3 million Reichsmarks, which he donated to charity.

Even the majority of the aristocratic elite, who were reserved at first, quickly gave in. In 2004, I interviewed Baron Philipp von Boeselager, who was born in 1917. "You can't imagine the excitement that reigned in those days. At the beginning, we scorned Hitler in my circle for his proletarian origins and rejected the party for its vulgarity, but that changed once Hitler gave nobles their role in the army. We had watched our older brothers humiliate themselves after 1918, kept from the army and forced to lick the boots of the Allies, and this man saved them from idleness and shame." During the war, Philipp von Boeselager joined Hitler's army, but bit by bit, he began to realize the criminal aspect of the Reich, and he participated with his brother in a 1944 conspiracy against Hitler led by his officers. The conspiracy was uncovered, but they escaped the wave of executions because their names were not divulged.

More generally, the conservative, educated elite was seduced by the Führer's antisocialist, antidemocratic tone, and his rejection of the rational thinking that had characterized the Weimar Republic. The exultant belief in an irrational force that would forge a powerful, respected new Germany brought down their guard, one by one. At the start, the SS was mainly attractive to the lower and middle classes as a means for social climbing, but from the mid-thirties on, the level of education among its members grew. The French historian Christian Ingrao followed the careers of eighty senior administrators at governing bodies responsible for suppression in the Third Reich: roughly 60 percent had studied at a university, and 30 percent had their doctorates. Senior army officers drawn from conservative families with thoroughly Christian values would organize massacres of prisoners of war and the destruction of entire villages; brilliant lawyers would deliver meticulous reports intended to legitimize the crimes of the Reich in glacial language; experts in ancient languages and civilizations would lend their knowledge to determining whether or not certain isolated peoples in the East had "Jewish blood" and if they had a right to life or death; doctors would transform themselves into sadistic executioners. Careerism and conformism alone aren't enough to explain these dark metamorphoses and what they say about the mystery of evil.

Allegiance to the Führer was often a convenient alibi. In the eyes of my grandmother, it was completely possible to adore Hitler without considering yourself a Nazi, which permitted her to feel unconcerned with the crimes of the Reich. After all, the German Evangelical Church, which was a strong guiding force for Oma's conscience, had given the Führer its blessing, hoping that the hated democracy would be followed by a Christian-authoritarian regime. On holidays, some churches unabashedly flew the Nazi flag from their steeples, letting its blood-red fabric flutter around the Christian cross. Oma didn't belong to the most Nazified wing of the Protestant Church, the Deutsche Christen (DC), but she also didn't join the Confessing Church, which opposed the Reich with rare courage. The Catholic Church was more circumspect about the new regime. Some priests opposed the new order but were quickly arrested, and resistance to the Führer weakened after the Vatican, gleaming with apathy, failed to support the dissenters. In the end, Protestant and Catholic churches gave the Reich the names of Christian citizens who had Jewish origins.

Of course, criticizing Nazism was a perilous exercise, and opposing it could be deadly. The party had no shortage of informers: hostile neighbors, envious colleagues, or jealous husbands hurt by their wives—people who exploited the political situation to settle a score. Besides, social and political pressure for Germans to participate in the *Volksgemeinschaft* was high. Any reluctance was poorly received, and could lead to continued harassment from Nazi Party accomplices—the end of government aid, rejection from a university, the loss of a job, or even exclusion from society. Although terror played a role, the Third Reich's key to success came from the adherence of the people, won over by the government's impressive seduction campaign. It was hard to escape the ever-present propaganda. "My parents had a radio. I was too small to understand, but I remember that it was always the same tone, the same rhythm—propaganda eventually entered everyone's minds by force, including my mother's," my aunt Ingrid remembers. Once the majority of newspapers had been forbidden in Mannheim, there was only one anti-Semitic rag left, the *Haken-kreuzbanner*. There were also films and placards to promote the Reich, showing nothing but harmony, pleasure at jobs well done, pretty family scenes, a bucolic return to nature, and even love, as in one photo showing a young couple with their arms around each other on a beach, caressed by a large Nazi flag. After the suffering they had endured since World War I, who didn't like to be mesmerized by this totalitarian utopia starring the Germans as a superior race? "It was wonderful to be a chosen people," Alexander and Margarete Mitscherlich write in *The Inability to Mourn*. I don't think that Oma and Opa were susceptible to these ways of flattering their egos or these dreams of absolute power. But Karl's little sister Hilde was engaged to a man who burned with passion for the domineering mission of National Socialism. He sent her letters from the Eastern Front, pouring out his hatred for "*Unter-menschen*," the subhuman, inferiors to the supposed "Aryans."

When the war broke out in 1939, Oma was thirty-eight and Ingrid was two and a half. Germans who had admired the Führer because he had so far avoided war were worried, and this made a stark contrast with the hawkish enthusiasm that had swayed so many in 1914. They now knew what kind of carnage modern, technological warfare could produce, and they trembled at the idea of losing their hard-won comforts. With clear victories for the Reich, the atmosphere quickly shifted, and the Führer's popularity reached its height. In addition to his numerous talents, he had become the best commander-in-chief in German history. As so often happens, material pleasures added to belligerent pride. People rejoiced at receiving products seized from occupied countries—the butter from Denmark, the woolen goods, the oil, the wine from France— right up until the Führer had the misguided idea of launching an attack on Russia in June 1941. The Germans were dismayed, and as they had suspected, the tide began to turn and the war came closer to their own hearths, arriving from the sky in the form of devastating aerial raids. The population was caught in a trap of spiraling, hellish suffering, of death and destruction. The Allies succeeded in traumatizing the Germans, and yet they missed their principal goal: to make them rise up against Hitler. The population said: "Allied warfare is inhumane, not our leader!" Even when defeat was assured, the bureaucrats, the NSDAP, the SS, and the judges continued to apply the *Führerprinzip*, obstinately and passionately attacking all those "harmful elements," the weak, the saboteurs, the defeatists, the deserters. And all the while, in the east, the machine exterminating Jews continued to run at an insane rate, guided by men who killed mechanically. "The fascination with Hitler and his demands was not only sadism, but also masochism, the pleasure of submission," Margarete and Alexander Mitscherlich wrote.

The indoctrination was endless. Even more deeply rooted, in my view, than it was for the Bolsheviks, since the majority of Germans had succumbed through seduction rather than through fear. The shock of the Führer's death, when he killed himself on April 30, 1945, and the routing of the Reich, came at the height of this bewitchment, and partly explains the pathological amnesia Germans plunged into after the war.

Some never came out of it, like Emma, whom I interviewed in 2005. This woman came from a modest family of peasants in the Sudetenland who were chased out of Czechoslovakia in 1945 and resettled in Bavaria. I met with Emma in a retirement home. She was seventy-eight at the time, stuck in a wheelchair, and perhaps because of her medication, she struggled to keep her eyes open and to articulate. Nonetheless, she told me how, one night in July 1945, her family had been brutally torn from their house by the Czech police and forced to leave all their possessions. They found themselves walking several hundred miles in the midst of a cortege of refugees, while the villagers jeered at them and hit them as they passed. Sixty years later, nothing seemed to have altered her feelings—not time, not the revelation that the Reich had committed crimes far worse than the expulsion of the Germans by the Czechs. I asked her, "But, in 1938, were you happy that Hitler annexed your lands?" She confessed, "Yes, we all hailed him as a savior, and if I could do it again, I would." I asked her why. Emma thought for a moment, then said: "Before, we only had potatoes to eat, and after the annexation, we had meat in our soup." I was struck by this answer, and what her unsettling honesty revealed about how simple the motive for political loyalty can be. "Meat in our soup."

VI

The *Mitläufer*'s Son

Very early on, my father developed an interest in the crimes of the Third Reich, mixed with the frustration of not being able to share it with anyone. In his family, no one discussed the war or National Socialism. Jews had come up only briefly, in the early fifties, when Karl had to pay reparations to Julius Löbmann, and the memory of the domestic tension around that episode was still raw enough that Volker preferred to avoid asking questions about such a thorny issue. Especially because Karl Schwarz was an irascible father, and it was better not to provoke him without first having considered the consequences, which alternated between withholding small things and actual smacking. As he neared the end of adolescence and started to fear his father less, Volker dipped his toe into the water a few times; now and then, he would drop the name Löbmann. But even when he wasn't trying to tackle family history, just the history of Germany in general, each attempt was met with such an avalanche of cries that he finally gave up: "He got angry! In the oil warehouse where I was helping him, he would sometimes grab the water hose and chase me or throw utensils at my face."

❖   ❖   ❖

I can imagine these intergenerational confrontations between my grandfather, a corpulent and authoritarian man, finding his arguments lacking when faced with his defiant, slender, intelligent son. "As long as you sit at my table, you obey me!" However, Volker wasn't really interested in pointing an accusing finger at his father, since after all, he hadn't been in the SS, or in the Wehrmacht, or in the state bureaucracy; he had never held a weapon or a pen that had caused another's death. Most of all, my father would have liked to learn from his parents *how it had happened*, what they had known and not known, what they regretted doing and not doing. Since he wasn't able to talk to his father, he tried to make some headway with his mother, for whom he felt a great affection. She protested: "We didn't vote for Hitler in 1932, we chose Marshal Hindenburg!" All the same, their vote in March 1933 remains a mystery. "My mother said, in her Mannheim accent, 'the Jews, they shouldn't have killed them,' but this has a double meaning," as Volker points out. "Because at the time, many people thought the defeat could be explained as the revenge of the Jews, who, according to anti-Semitic stereotypes, had vast global networks, and as a result, it would have been better to have left them alone." Oma often added, "If the Führer had known, he would have stopped it." She had heard about the horrors of the camps from a Romany woman named Annie who lived miserably in the ruins across the street from the family's apartment building. She had become friends with this woman, who had been imprisoned in a concentration camp where she had been raped repeatedly but survived, along with a child born from one of those assaults. "My mother often invited her over to the house to give her some food, a cup of coffee, some money. In return, Annie read her cards." This empathy didn't stop Lydia from daydreaming, sometimes out loud, about that unforgettable cruise to the Scandinavian fjords.

Sometimes, when guests came to celebrate birthdays at Chamissostrasse, one of them would bring up "the good times they had in France," when German soldiers lived the "chateau lifestyle" during the occupation. "They remembered drinking champagne and buying silk stockings to bring back to their wives," my father said. There was also Uncle Kurt, who liked to brag about having been an officer in the marines when he'd really spent the war on a ship in Norway, where he'd had a child with a Norwegian woman instead of fighting. The only one who had known the real war, the worst, on the Eastern Front, didn't say anything. This was Karl's younger brother, Uncle Willy, whom no one dared to ask about anything, afraid of stirring up memories so dark they made people tremble in advance. In general, apart from silly stories told during boozy birthday parties, everyone preferred to avoid talking from personal experience, especially when it had been upsetting. "No one ever brought up the bombardments at the table either," my father says, "yet they had suffered a great deal in Mannheim. They wanted to forget everything about the war." As for the general history of Germany, if people took an interest, it was for very different reasons than Volker's. "The preoccupation wasn't with knowing what crimes the Reich had committed, but with why they had lost the war. That was what traumatized people," he said. "They debated about which bad decisions Hitler had made, as if they could, retroactively, change the course of history."

One of the largest questions was about the Führer's decision, against the advice of his high command, to halt the advance of German tanks that had encircled approximately 370,000 British and French soldiers at Dunkirk on May 24, 1940. This pause had given the Allies time to put a defensive ring in place around the city and start organizing the evacuation of their troops by sea. On May 26, Hitler ordered the artillery to take up the assault again, while Hermann Göring sent the Luftwaffe to pound the enemy soldiers who were waiting on the beaches of Dunkirk for boats to rescue them. Despite the aerial attacks, most of the troops were evacuated and four years later, many of them would return as victors during the Normandy landings. After the war, Germans endlessly debated this missed opportunity. My father explains, "They said Hitler could have used this British military catastrophe to force Churchill to sign the peace treaty he'd always wished for with Great Britain, so that he could have free rein in continental Europe." To this day, the Führer's motives aren't well understood.

The Battle of Stalingrad was another obsession. The story of the Sixth Army, isolated and surrounded by the Soviets at the end of 1942, abandoned by Hitler to its fate, remained an enigma, and people liked to invent all kinds of theories to explain it. According to my aunt Ingrid, Opa used to say, "After Stalingrad, I knew we had lost the war, and I always said so!" In truth, the tide had already turned in December 1941, when the Red Army won the Battle of Moscow. But it was Stalingrad that left a mark on people's minds, peddled by Nazi propaganda as a heroic sacrifice by German soldiers. After the war, the myth perpetuated itself, fed by books like Fritz Wöss's novel *Stalingrad: Dogs, Do You Want to Live Forever?* and the film version by Frank Wisbar that came out in 1959 and was a resounding success, even winning a gold medal at the German Film Awards. The German journalist Erich Kuby wrote: "Every German man who comes out of this movie feels exculpated." I watched it, and the first thing that struck me was the arresting contrast with the representation of the Wehrmacht in French films of the same era, which depicted Nazi soldiers as devoid of all humanity, barking orders in a language that became hideous as the vehicle of "Nazi attitude." In *Stalingrad: Dogs, Do You Want to Live Forever?* I discovered them transformed—funny, honest, and brave, with the exception of one superior officer, whose cowardice served to accentuate the good qualities of the others, while Hitler appeared as a flimsy, heartless war chief. The empathy this film elicited for the Sixth Army allowed people to consign to the shadows its participation in war crimes and massacres such as the one in Babi Yar in Ukraine, where 33,000 Jews were murdered in two days. "The Wehrmacht was untouchable at the time," my father says. "Even I didn't think it was implicated." How could German people escape the brainwashing, when it was nourished by a literature of autobiographical justification and films that gave them the heroes they so painfully lacked? The favorite was Erwin Rommel, the Desert Fox, raised to the heights of legend despite his resolute commitment to the Third Reich. The fifties were the years of unconditional rehabilitation, a reaction to the denazi-fication undertaken by the Allies, who had dared to tarnish the reputations of so many "honest" Nazis.

My father, Volker Schwarz, Mannheim, 1950.

My father's younger generation couldn't count on many people to disrupt this watered-down version of the past. Even the journalists were in cahoots, since many of them had been Nazis. Such as Werner Höfer, whose activities as a close associate of the Reich's minister of armaments hadn't prevented him from becoming a familiar face on German television after the war as the host of *Der Internationalen Frühschoppen*, a weekly program that brought international journalists together around a table to discuss political themes.

That left school. But even there you couldn't count on finding anything to offset society's cowardice. "In primary school, the history courses stopped at the Weimar Republic," my father says. "Most of the teachers had taught under the Third Reich, some had been Nazis, and the old methods were still in force: a ruler across the knuckles and a kick in the behind. The Second World War was on the agenda only in high school, where a small minority of students pursued their education, but the war was evoked in a very superficial, only partial way." Some terms were taboo, to the point that they even disappeared from the dictionary! In a piece published in 2002, the Serbian German-speaking author Ivan Ivanji describes looking in his 1956 edition of the *Duden*, the standard German dictionary, for the terms *Konzentrationslager* (concentration camp) and *SS-Mann* (SS soldier). He found nothing.

In this atmosphere of amnesia, it was largely thanks to a determined fight by a prosecutor that the Germans were suddenly forced to confront the truth they were so eager to evade. Fritz Bauer had spent the war in Denmark and Sweden after being persecuted by the Nazis, who harshly put an end to his brilliant career as a judge because he was Jewish and a social democrat. After the war, he decided to return to Germany to participate in the construction of democracy. He was one of the few who immediately understood that in order to have a sound beginning, his country would have to deeply eradicate the roots of National

Socialism and honestly confront the past. He produced his first victory in 1952, against the neo-Nazi Otto Ernst Remer, who had defamed the July 20, 1944, insurgents against Hitler as treasonous. By legally establishing that the Third Reich was an "illegal state" and that, by consequence, the uprisings and attacks on the regime and its Führer were legitimate, Bauer rehabilitated the resistance fighters and challenged reigning public opinion and the many veterans who brandished their undying loyalty to Hitler as a point of pride. The prosecutor made many enemies but gained several important political allies, who allowed him, in 1956, to be named the general prosecutor of Frankfurt and the entirety of Hesse, a post that Bauer would leverage as much as possible, uncovering crimes whose scope very few people yet imagined.

In 1958, in Ulm, Fritz Bauer opened a case against ten members of a killing squad accused of killing more than 5,000 Jews in Lithuania. The accused, who had reintegrated themselves into civilian life after the war, were condemned to sentences ranging from three to fifteen years in prison as "accessories to mass murder." They escaped life sentences because the judges refused to recognize their own will to commit murder, despite overwhelming proof of personal initiative. This trial, which was the first of such a size to be heard before a German court, shocked the public, who discovered that in the east, there hadn't only been a traditional war, but also massacres that certain West German authorities visibly tried to conceal. Facing indignation, the regional ministers of justice came together to create the Central Office of the State Justice Administrations for the Investigation of National Socialist Crimes, an independent center whose mission was to investigate crimes committed outside Germany, and particularly in Eastern Europe. For a long time, the regional prosecutors refused to cooperate with the Central Office and systematically shelved all the cases it sent them. With the exception of Fritz Bauer. Isolated in the judicial apparatus, where two thirds (if not all) of his colleagues were former Nazis, and deprived of political and police support, he resisted the pressure, acts of sabotage, and other obstacles placed in his path. With the help of rare lawyers ready to defend the same cause, he took on very delicate investigations, sometimes at the limits of what the law allowed.

One day, among the many anonymous letters full of insults and threats that inundated his office, Bauer received an envelope from Argentina. The prosecutor's hands must have trembled as he read this letter from a certain Lothar Hermann, a Jew who had fled Nazism and claimed that Adolf Eichmann was hiding in Buenos Aires under a false name. This was none other than the chief architect of the genocide of the Jews of Europe, wanted by international justice for crimes against humanity. Without mentioning the letter, Bauer asked the German authorities if, by some chance, Eichmann were to be found, would they be prepared to demand his extradition? The answer was no. No one wanted a momentous trial that would dig up the Nazi past of a country that was trying to present a fresh face to the world, and certainly not for a key figure of the Holocaust who must know all the various actors, including those who had managed to reinvent themselves in the new German democracy. What an embarrassment, if, in the middle of the trial, Eichmann suddenly pointed a finger at the judges, the prosecutors, crying: "Come on! We knew each other before, don't you remember?"

But as a guardian of justice, Bauer was capable of twisting the law when it seemed unjust to him, even at the risk of being ousted and dragged before the tribunal for treason. He secretly asked Mossad, the Israeli intelligence service, to find Eichmann in Buenos Aires. In May 1960, under the noses of the Argentine authorities, agents picked up the Nazi criminal and forced him on a plane intended for a delegation from Israel, so he could be tried in Jerusalem. Faced with this news, Chancellor Konrad Adenauer pretended to be hearing Eichmann's name for the first time. In reality, there were many in Germany who trembled when his capture was announced, this man who could so easily denounce them. Perhaps no one was more afraid than the chancellor's right-hand man, Hans Globke, a co-author of the Nuremberg Laws during the National Socialist era. Germany put pressure on Israel to spare Globke in the trial and avoid embarrassing the young republic—and in the end, the accused didn't divulge a single name of a living person who hadn't already been tried. Even though the "perfectionism" with which he led his exterminating mission had weighed heavily on the destiny of the Jews, he denied all responsibility: "The mass murder is the fault of political leaders alone. My fault is my obedience, my submission. . . . But also the subordinates are victims. I am such a victim." On June 1, 1962, he was hanged, after these last words: "Long live Germany, Argentina, and Austria," and "Gentlemen, we'll meet again soon." Bauer considered the trial, which hadn't led to any others, to be something of a failure.

In fact, it marked an important advance: for the first time, hundreds of victims had testified in front of international TV cameras. In Israel, the testimonies of these witnesses changed the minds of those who hadn't experienced the Holocaust, especially the minds of people who had criticized survivors either for not having fought harder or for collaborating through the *Judenräte*. These were councils formed by order of the Nazis and composed of Jewish community leaders, who were forced to provide logistical help with the organization of ghettos, forced labor, and deportation. The trial allowed the horror the Jews had been through to burst out into the open, along with a clearer picture of why they had hoped to improve their terrible fate by collaborating.

In Germany, even if the Eichmann affair didn't have the impact Fritz Bauer had hoped for, many households followed the trial's unfolding and were shaken. My aunt remembers clips of the hearings that regularly aired on televised news. "Eichmann's face left a strong impression on me. I found that man repugnant, in what he said and in the way he said it, like a robot." My father, for his part, barely remembers. But he had already started to find answers on his own to questions people couldn't or wouldn't answer.

In 1958, at the age of fifteen, Volker read *The* SS *State*, published in 1946 by the German sociologist Eugen Kogon, which was the first analysis of the Nazi concentration camp system. The work of this former Buchenwald detainee revealed the inhumane living conditions, the crushing work, and the merciless cycle of death: "The German concentration camps were a world of their own, a state of their own—an order without right, into which the human being was thrown, who now, with all his virtues and vices—more vices than virtues—fought for bare existence and mere survival," he writes in the preface.

My father also read *Doctors of Infamy* by Alexander Mitscherlich and Fred Mielke, a chronicle of the 1946–47 trials in Nuremberg of doctors in the service of the Reich who had carried out experiments on living human beings: Jewish detainees, prisoners of war, and the mentally ill. The list of experiments was long: hypothermia, bone transplants, toxic gases, sterilization . . . These men had also participated in the euthanasia program for the "incurably ill." In general, more than a few doctors had enacted the eugenic, racial politics of the Reich step by step, completely abandoning the ethics of the medical profession. Volker even asked permission to read *Mein Kampf* from one of his schoolteachers, a young man in his thirties who stood out from the others in his lectures on the war. As my father says, "He had served in Russia and told us that it was possible, as a soldier of the Wehrmacht, to refuse to participate in executions of prisoners of war—that struck me."

This teacher got his surprisingly inquisitive student the necessary authorization to borrow the forbidden text from the Mannheim library. Despite his curiosity, Volker had only a limited picture of the Third Reich. "I was repulsed by what I was discovering, and yet I had only seen the tip of the iceberg! Even I didn't realize the scope of the horror and the implications—it was very difficult then to understand." It wasn't easy to get information, because the historiography mainly focused on the way Hitler had managed to come into power, and the priority was to identify the key factors that would protect the new German democracy from taking such a turn. By concentrating on 1933, people sidelined the war and the innumerable Nazi crimes.

From his reading, my father cast a very critical eye on his country's past, which drew some criticism from his classmates who didn't always share his point of view. "They often said, 'You're attacking Germany!' Later, long after getting our high school degrees, I saw their opinions change." I found a report written by his class delegate after a field trip in 1956. It was about "Blacky" (Volker's nickname), "who knew the history of the region better than the teacher." According to the class bulletins that my father kept, he had always excelled in two subjects: history and religion.

Lydia had noticed her son's intellectual curiosity. She was the one to insist that Volker should pursue his secondary school education at the highest level, the Gymnasium, something that Karl was reluctant to do, because of the cost of such schooling and because he liked the idea of having his son work for him at his company. Oma, who often preferred to give way rather than confront her husband's anger, wouldn't let it go this time, and Opa must have read in her determined gaze an unconditional mother's love he was powerless to challenge. The memory of this dispute must have taken root in my father's mind, since he felt an infinite gratitude toward his mother and a certain hostility toward his father, who had proved himself to be capable of risking his son's future so

that he could use him in a mediocre business where he himself
was stagnating. Though Karl cherished Ingrid most of all, she
had already been forced to take a job as a low-paid secretary at
Schwarz & Co., which she always felt was unjust.

My father was an oddity—not only in his age group, but in German
society as a whole, where people who wanted to *know* were rare.
I asked him if he knew how this uncommon interest had taken
hold of him, especially since his parents had taken one of the most
banal positions, neither resisting nor committing criminal acts. "I
don't really know," he says, "but maybe the young teacher who
dared to raise the subject of Nazi crimes in class had something to
do with it." He was also lucky enough to live in a town where the
mayor, the social democrat Hermann Heimerich, moved heaven
and earth to give the Jewish community, which had been reduced
to only 120 members, a new place to pray after the war. Of 6,400
Jews, more than 2,200 were murdered, and those who fled had
absolutely no desire to return to the traces of an annihilated world.
Heimerich also succeeded in erecting a memorial commemorating
both victims of Nazism and of the war, despite opposition from
part of the population and soldiers' associations who objected to
aligning the "heroes" of the Wehrmacht with victims. My father
and I went to see the sculpture recently. In front of a brick wall in
a cobblestone square, an angel of peace whose face is devoured by
huge, empty eyes spreads her arms and wings horizontally, as if to
take flight and watch over humanity, or perhaps in rebuke, since
the inscription reads, *Es mahnen die Toten*, the dead are admon-
ishing. This work by Gerhard Marcks, who was accused of making
"degenerate art" under the Nazis, was inaugurated in 1952 in the
presence of Konrad Adenauer. While the mayor of Mannheim
tried to bring together the victims under the same banner—Jews,
resistance, soldiers, bombed civilians, and the displaced—the head

rabbi declared: "It is different, whether you die in the fight, man to man, whether you are killed in an air raid, or if you find an end in the gas chambers of the East. And it also makes a difference whether you can think of a grave somewhere or whether there is no grave anywhere in this world where loving thoughts can make a pilgrimage."

It was rare for the Jewish community to speak out after the war. Wherever it was based, in Europe or in exile in America, it was wrapped in a silence that would last for decades, petrified by the fear of being disbelieved or of being stigmatized once again, excluded, mistreated. Mixed with that fear was a need to forget, and a certain shame, of having survived while others didn't. Some of them still find talking painful. I had this experience with Ruth Loebmann, wife of Hans, who was the nephew of Julius Löbmann. I had contacted her through the mail, with Lotte Kramer as an intermediary, and she had agreed to let me call her in New York, though she warned me: "Please know, however, I'm not at all sure I'll be able to help you in any way." Hans had changed his name to John when he arrived in New York in the 1950s. Of his past, Ruth knows only that he was saved by a *Kindertransport* that took him to Birmingham with his sister Lore and Lotte Kramer, and that his father had died in Auschwitz. "John didn't tell me about his time in England." And about Mannheim, the city of his childhood and adolescence? "Nothing, he only mentioned the synagogue where his family used to go." She had known her spouse's mother, Irma, who left Strasbourg to join her children in New York. "A wonderful, wise, kind woman, she had a very difficult life during the Shoah." Did she know how Irma had escaped Auschwitz? "I have no idea." I privately wondered—how could it be possible, after sixty years of life together, to know so little about her husband's tragic past? "I am sorry, Géraldine," she said several times. Before clarifying:

"Let me explain something to you. Among folks of my generation, none of us spoke about those days, about the Shoah. John and I lived for the future." And what did she remember about her own childhood in Berlin? Ruth was born there in 1929 and has lovely memories of her childhood. The Nazi flags, the propaganda, her worried loved ones, the discrimination against the Jews have all been erased from her memory. Her family lived in Kreuzberg, on Ritterstrasse—just a few blocks from my own street.

In 1938, her parents sent her to Palestine with her brother while they succeeded in emigrating to the United States, where the family was reunited "with great emotion" after the war. At the beginning of the 1950s, on her own initiative, Ruth traveled to Berlin. "I wanted to walk again the streets I had walked as a child. While I was there, I enjoyed myself. But since then, I've kept asking myself how I could have done such a terrible thing, going back to that horrible city—and liking it. I made a mistake, but I can't undo it." I asked her why it was a mistake. After a short pause, she whispered, "I hate Germany."

At that moment, I was tempted to remind Ruth that I wasn't completely German, but also French. But the shame of that little betrayal stopped me. I contented myself with saying, "Germany has changed a lot, you know . . ." I suddenly understood the courage my father must have had to hitchhike across France at age eighteen, meeting French people who were said to hate Germans. "Some offered me a place to stay, and some threw me out of their cars as soon as I told them I was German, but I understood. It was clear to me that the Reich had deliberately caused the war across Europe, rather than reacting to provocation, that the myth of defensive war had been designed to reduce German guilt." Volker still has some snapshots from that trip, where you can see him in the streets of Paris, in Marseille, in Arles, and at Verdun as well, where he poses before a plaque commemorating the dead from the most murderous battle between the Germans and the French during World War I. On the road he met compatriots eager to reconcile with their European neighbors. It was the beginning of Franco-German reconciliation, and Germans cautiously began to change their attitudes.

An event accelerated this evolution. On Christmas Eve 1959, in Cologne, two young men vandalized a memorial for victims of Nazism with swastikas and scrawled across a newly built synagogue, "Germans won't stand for Jews." In the weeks that followed, the action was copied hundreds of times across the country. You could read: "Down with the Jews! Into the gas chamber!" International opinion was incensed, protests were organized in London and New York, and people called for boycotts of German products. The shameful past returned and swept across international headlines. German politicians were forced to act: the Bundestag passed a vote to make inciting people with hate speech punishable by law, while the regional governments prepared an educational reform that would give the Third Reich a larger place in history courses in schools. In addition, exchange programs with Israeli schools were created. But it was once again Fritz Bauer who would mark a definitive turning point by attacking an unacceptable memory gap: Auschwitz. At the start of the sixties, in Germany and abroad, few people had an idea of what this name stood for. Many knew about concentration camps where political prisoners and members of minority groups were confined in terrible conditions and forced to work, but very little was known about extermination camps, whose specific purpose was to kill. With the help of a team of brave lawyers and the Auschwitz survivor Hermann Langbein, Bauer strove to reveal that German-made invention.

Auschwitz-Birkenau was the only death camp where the SS hadn't had time to make the evidence disappear. A gigantic network of death where more than 1.1 million had perished, mainly Jews, but also Sinti and Roma, political opponents, religious leaders, intellectuals, most of them gassed between 1942 and the end

of 1944, then turned to ash in the crematoriums. The extermination camp was part of a vast complex that made up Auschwitz,
including a concentration camp and a factory for the chemical and
pharmaceutical conglomerate IG Farben, where the detainees
were forced to work like slaves or serve as guinea pigs for often
fatal experiments. In addition, fifty or so annexed camps extended
for sixty miles around, where prisoners worked in mines, on agri-
cultural holdings, on behalf of the state or for German companies
that had come to profit from cheap labor. Some families of camp
and company staff lived outside the complex, in residential areas
with schools, hospitals, and leisure activities. The Reich had even
planned to build a park, a stadium, and a riding club to anchor this
community in its new eastern Lebensraum—the living space the
Germans supposedly needed to survive. In total, over five years,
more than 8,000 people led close to normal lives in this area, side
by side with concentration camps and gas chambers. What did they
know? We'll never be totally sure. But many complained about
the disagreeable odor relentlessly pouring from the chimneys.

In December 1963, a trial started in Frankfurt against twenty-two
staff members from the Auschwitz camp. Fritz Bauer initiated it,
then left the trial to young prosecutors so that detractors would not
have the opportunity to discredit the trial by calling it the "revenge"
of a Jew. The preparations were titanic: sifting through tens of
thousands of archival documents, interrogating hundreds of witnesses, convincing them to talk, researching proof against the executioners and locating them—and all this had to be accomplished
despite the reluctance of the German authorities, especially the
police. The trial was a real event: hundreds of journalists were
invited, an exhibition on the camp opened in Frankfurt, experts
gathered to describe the complex functioning of Auschwitz with
the help of maps and photos projected on the walls.

Among the incriminated were Robert Mulka, second in command at the camp; Wilhelm Boger, head of the "Escape Unit,"
who resorted to the most perverse tortures to uncover alleged
plans to flee; and Josef Klehr, senior paramedic, notorious for his
abspritzen, his lethal injection of inmates. The accused were almost
all from bourgeois families and eight had significant schooling.

More than two hundred witnesses from all over the world followed one another to the stand, propelled by the force of their
courage to describe the unimaginable. One of them said Josef
Klehr "could not be called a human being, and if I wanted to label
him with the name of an animal, then I would have to insult the
animals." Another described how Wilhelm Boger forced him to
swallow five plates of extra-salted smoked herrings before depriving him of water and hanging him up by his feet. There were
also babies who were drowned in basins of cold water or thrown
headfirst against the wall.

For Bauer, the accused were less important than what they
represented: the vastness of German guilt. "The trial should show
the world that a new Germany, a German democracy, is willing to
uphold the dignity of every human being." By trying, as a collective,
people from different ranks of the hierarchy who had occupied various positions in the camp, the prosecutor hoped to get across the
idea that only through everyone's cooperation had such ignominy
been permitted. "Anyone who worked on this murder machine,"
he explained, "was guilty of participating in murder, whatever he
did, provided, of course, that he knew the aim of the machinery,
which, of course, is beyond any doubt for those who were in the
extermination camps or knew about them, from the watch team up
to the top." Everyone in the camp is "guilty of murder, whether he
is a boss at the desk giving the murder order, whether he distributes
the revolvers, whether he attends the scene, whether he shoots
with his own hand, or helps, or whatever tasks he does which are
assigned to him as part of the division of labor."

Almost a hundred former SS members were also called to the stand as witnesses. The gist of their speeches was appalling: they had seen nothing, heard nothing, done nothing. Their solidarity in the lie was sickening, but it allows us to understand the difficult context in which the trial unfolded—a German society unscrupulously bending over backward to deny its crimes. Nonetheless, one man broke the silence: Konrad Morgen, formerly SS-Sturmbannführer, in charge of an investigative commission sent to test the level of corruption in Auschwitz in 1943, where the staff helped themselves to stolen Jewish possessions, including gold tooth fillings. He visited the gas chambers and the crematoriums. Meeting SS who were totally haggard, he learned that they'd had a "heavy night behind them, they had to handle some transports." He realized that while he'd slept peacefully on the train from Berlin to Auschwitz, "thousands of people had been gassed and turned to ashes here, a few trainloads full. Of those thousands of people, not even a speck of dust was left on an oven faucet," he gasped to the court before collapsing.

With the exception of Morgen, the accused denied everything, even Robert Mulka, number two in the camp, who had the indecency to say he had never heard of the gas chambers. Thanks to the German penchant for bureaucracy, however, many steps of the extermination had been documented: the transport of Zyklon B from Dessau to Auschwitz, the radio messages with Berlin, the total number of Jews at their arrival and those who had received *Sonderbehandlung* (special treatment), which in Nazi jargon meant gassed. "I think Germany would breathe a sigh of relief, and the whole world, and the survivors of those who died in Auschwitz, and the air would be purified once a humane word was finally spoken," said Fritz Bauer during a television broadcast. But that humane word "was not spoken, and it will not be spoken." Of all the accused, only the youngest, Hans Stark, head of the reception department at Auschwitz, voiced a regret: "I regret my mistake very much but I cannot undo it." At the camp, this motto hung over his desk: "Pity is weakness." Despite the solidity of proof and testimony, the outcome of the trial was disappointing: Robert Mulka, the vice-commander of the camp, escaped life in prison, three of the accused were acquitted, and only six were found guilty of murder. The others were considered to be only accessories because they hadn't killed with their own hands.

The idea that the men had acted under orders continued to be an attenuating circumstance, even if the experts proved that the SS did not risk death if they refused to obey an extermination order. But unconditional obedience to orders and laws was still considered a virtue in the federal republic of the sixties. This blind automatism of bureaucrats and soldiers was exactly what Fritz Bauer wanted to inoculate young people against when he declared: "Nobody is allowed to execute an order that contains a criminal offense. In life, there are limits beyond which we have the duty to stop participating. . . . Every ethical system is based on that, and every law is based on that." During this period, the insults and threats, often anti-Semitic, continued to multiply on the prosecutor's desk, and he sometimes courted despair in his solitary fight. He was embittered by the persistent bias of German officials in favor of former Nazi criminals, and by the slowness of the investigations. In reality, his determination had produced crucial progress: the word *Auschwitz* had burst into the comfortable lives of Germany's economic miracle. In total, about 20,000 people, including many students and hundreds of journalists, had come to watch the proceedings; 80,000 people had seen the exhibition on the camp, which toured the country. In 1965, a play by Peter Weiss called *The Investigation* used the trial as its theme and caused an uproar in theaters. A return to amnesia was unthinkable.

❖   ❖   ❖

On July 1, 1968, Fritz Bauer was found dead in his bathtub in Frankfurt. He was a heavy smoker in fragile health, and his heart had given out after a large dose of sleeping pills. To this day, the circumstances of his death have produced speculation about suicide, if not murder. Shunned by lawyers, he was beloved by the younger generation. One day, to the young people gathered around a table during a German television program, he said: "We've done some things, a democracy, the separation of powers . . . you can write paragraphs, draft articles, imagine the best fundamental laws. What matters is that the people are fair." He died too early to be able to witness what he'd helped to unleash: the rise of a new generation who had been enlightened by people like him, a generation that would demand a radical change in German attitudes toward the past.

VII

From Amnesia to Obsession

My father first experienced a substantial change in the attitude of his country's institutions during his military service from 1963 to 1965. The creation of the Bundeswehr, the new federal armed forces, in November 1955 didn't generate much enthusiasm among the German people, who were still traumatized by the war, and international opinion remained suspicious. The new army was under pressure to avoid any missteps. Inevitably, the majority of its members had served in the Wehrmacht, some even in the Waffen SS, but a personnel review panel had been created to examine candidates' backgrounds, excluding those whose histories were too troubled. This step didn't prevent an embarrassing slip-up in 1956, when a marine officer publicly described Erich Raeder and Karl Dönitz, the high admirals of the Reich who had been condemned at Nuremberg, as martyrs who had been "clean, decent, and honorable" in fulfilling their duties. Not only had these two men played a major role in the Reich's destructive war, but Dönitz had also been the executor of Hitler's will, and Hitler had recognized this anti-Semitic sailor as a sort of alter ego. After this scandal, army personnel were strongly advised against any expressions of nostalgia for the Third Reich. "I never heard officers make excuses for National Socialism," Volker says. "It wasn't that they didn't want to, but it was nonetheless looked down upon, and that alone was a small revolution." With little inclination for physical exercise, my father was quickly elected "ombudsman" by the soldiers, thanks to his verbal agility and his level of education. In this role, he was responsible for communication between the soldiers and the officers, but he also had to encourage his comrades to reflect on their mission. He had a large blackboard at his disposal where he put up texts and articles of his choosing to be read by the young recruits. He was given an astonishing amount of freedom. "I always chose antiwar texts. I remember, for example, putting up an article from *Paris Match* on 'the butchery of Verdun,' and they let me do it! At the time, in the new German army, the soldiers had more rights than, say, in France." It can't have been easy to build an army in a country that had been shaken by the fatal consequences of unconditional obedience. They had to teach the soldiers loyalty and discipline while still inviting critique and independence of spirit. My father took up the latter. "We felt that the officers were torn, that at heart they remained very conservative. But they had no choice, they had to adapt to the spirit of the times."

The birth of the Bundeswehr was accompanied by a new antimilitary and antinuclear movement that was particularly popular with young people. Rudi Dutschke, the future leader of the student uprising, belonged to the movement, as did the journalist Ulrike Meinhof. The Nazi past haunted Meinhof, whose father was an art historian who had joined the NSDAP in 1933 before participating in the censure of certain works as "degenerate art." The sworn enemy of the antinuclear movement was the minister of nuclear research, Franz Josef Strauss, who went on to become minister of defense and who wanted to provide Germany with nuclear

arms. In 1958, Meinhof justified her battle against atomic armament in these terms: "We do not want to once again plead guilty
to crimes against humanity before God and mankind." After she
compared him to Hitler in an article, the minister filed a complaint,
but instead of winning his case, he allowed this young woman to
become one of the most famous journalists in the country. Strauss
was a demagogue who passed off the need for remembrance as a
sadomasochistic perversion of "German atonement." His ambiguous relationship to democracy emerged in broad daylight when,
in 1962, he had the editor in chief and some journalists from *Der
Spiegel* arrested for supposed high treason after they reported
that the Bundeswehr was poorly prepared for war with the Soviet
Union. The public swiftly protested, leading to Strauss's forced
resignation and a reorganization of the government.

In the wake of this major crisis, which helped liberalize and
democratize Germany, transparency became a required principle
of the Bundeswehr. My father remembers that they held a "Current Events Hour" each week where an officer would communicate
the latest news—political, military, and otherwise. The soldiers
were allowed to openly react, to argue, and to demand clarifica-
tions. My father never missed an opportunity to do so. "The officers
didn't like it when I said, 'Hitler's war was a war of aggression!' In
general it was frowned upon to attack the Wehrmacht, which they
fought tooth and nail to defend, as if it had been a spotless army
that had nothing to do with the crimes of the SS. There was even
a pastor for the Bundeswehr who used his sermons to lecture us,
saying that it wasn't right to accuse the Wehrmacht." My father also
sometimes contradicted his superiors on the genocide of the Jews.
"Some of them would say: 'It wasn't six million Jews, it was only
three million!' I could tell them directly what I was thinking—none
of them would have risked punishing the ombudsman. It was real
progress, but, at the same time, I think it may have had something
to do with why I was never promoted."

✦   ✦   ✦

A political transformation was also beginning. A central event in this evolution was the sharp debate, in 1965, around the Bundestag vote on lengthening the statute of limitations for murder, which was fixed at twenty years. This decision was very important because it concerned Nazi crimes, dated officially from May 8, 1945, and which were therefore about to expire according to the law.

The day before the debate, *Der Spiegel* published a long interview with the philosopher Karl Jaspers with the suggestive title "There Is No Statute of Limitations for Genocide." Jaspers believed that this vote was decisive for the future of the country, since it would measure the degree of consensus among Germans about whether the Third Reich was a criminal state that had committed crimes of a degree unprecedented in the history of humankind. One by one, the internationally renowned philosopher dismantled the numerous German arguments aimed at lessening Nazi crimes. He emphasized that there was a "radical difference" between "war crimes," which were also committed by other countries, and "crimes against humanity." "Crimes against humanity claim to decide which groups of people may or may not live on earth, and to carry out these claims through extermination." Jaspers dismissed the mitigating circumstance of obeying orders, since, he said, the only risk people took in refusing to kill on command was to damage their careers and eventually be sent to the front. The fact of having acted from within the ranks of an arm of the governing body was never an attenuating circumstance of guilt, the philosopher reasoned. "Everyone knew: it was criminal. It must have been evident that the state was criminal at the very moment it gave the order to commit a crime. The excuse of acting under orders is not legitimate. He who aided and abetted was an accomplice of a criminal state." Jaspers and Rudolf Augstein of *Der Spiegel* wholeheartedly denounced the "nasty" attitude of the

German government since the founding of the republic, which was uniquely preoccupied with making a "clean break" with the past, and had given important positions to former Nazis. "Parliament is the last hope," the philosopher concluded.

Jaspers had seen the truth. The day of the Bundestag debate, March 10, 1965, loud voices from all parties were calling for an end to silence and impunity. Even in the conservative party, which was traditionally in favor of the "clean break," 180 out of 217 delegates voted for extending the statute. The social democrats approved the extension en masse, including people like Adolf Arndt, who had called for an end to the "manhunt" ten years earlier. He had since changed his mind: "I myself am guilty. Because you see, I did not go out on the street and scream when I saw Jews from our midst being transported. I did not staple the yellow star and say: Me too! . . . One cannot say: I was not born yet, this heritage is none of my business." The vast majority of deputies voted to extend the statute, allowing parliament to demonstrate the importance of its function in a democratic state. Faced with a government that had failed to seize the opportunity to end the country's ambivalence to its Nazi past, parliament had sent a clear message to the people: rejecting National Socialism was the bedrock of the new republic.

After he left the army in 1965, my father began his studies in business management at the University of Mannheim, where he got involved with several students' associations and became a member of Asta, a sort of "student government" that mainly exists in German universities. His activities earned him a little pocket money, which was enough to pay for classes at the riding club and pints of beer at Mannheim's numerous bars. "We talked about politics, economics, capitalism, the war in Vietnam, and we had the impression of learning much more at the bar than we did in class. Our eyes were fixed on the United States, where a

protest movement was developing in the universities." This revolution had created a deep intergenerational divide in American
culture and society, and the new counterculture combined music,
drugs, and sexual freedom with promoting civil disobedience,
equality between races and sexes, the rejection of imperialism,
and a refusal to participate in consumer culture. Little by little,
similar movements emerged all over the world, and Germany
was no exception. Volker didn't belong to the leading group, the
German Federation of Socialist Students (SDS), nonetheless he
got involved. Especially after June 2, 1967, when the twenty-six-
year-old pacifist student Benno Ohnesorg was killed by a German
police officer who targeted the back of his head from five feet
away, for no apparent reason except his participation in student
protests in West Berlin against the tyrannical Shah of Iran Reza
Pahlavi's state visit. "Everyone was shocked by it," my father says,
"it was the first time a policeman had killed a civilian since the
war, I think." Attempts by the authorities to make people think
it was an accident only made the younger generation angrier. As
a member of Asta, my father received a telephone call from his
counterpart at the Free University of Berlin: "My colleague said
to me, 'We have to organize actions immediately. The universities must work together.'" Volker went to the city center, to the
Union House, where he met with the "forces of progress" and
helped to organize a demonstration in Mannheim. In addition to
Benno Ohnesorg's death, the war in Vietnam fed student anger
as the United States displayed increasing brutality. On February
18, 1968, more than 10,000 people flooded the streets of Berlin to
demonstrate against the war in Vietnam. SDS membership grew,
and protests multiplied all over the country.

The dissenting students questioned what they saw as the bourgeois
order: militarism, authority, hierarchy, consumerism, capitalism.

They were inspired by the thinkers of the Frankfurt school, an "Institute for Social Research" that had opened in 1924 and had drawn intellectuals from many different backgrounds, such as the economist Friedrich Pollock, the psychoanalyst Erich Fromm, and the philosophers Max Horkheimer, Theodor W. Adorno, Walter Benjamin, and Herbert Marcuse. Confronted with the failure of the Communist revolution in Germany after World War I, and with the totalitarian drift of the Soviet Union, these intellectuals proposed a new way of critiquing capitalism and the bourgeoisie, far from the dogma of Communist parties aligned with Moscow. Baptized *critical theory*, this new approach proposed that on its own, Karl Marx's method was not enough to analyze capitalist society; these theorists advocated an interdisciplinary approach that included other thinkers, notably the psychoanalytic work of Sigmund Freud and the sociology of Max Weber. In 1933, the institute was closed by the National Socialists and moved to Columbia University in New York. In 1944, Adorno and Horkheimer published one of their major works, *Dialectic of Enlightenment*. There, they described fascism as a perversion of the eighteenth century Enlightenment's ideas, centered on reason, liberty, and scientific progress: the outrageous rationalization of technology and bureaucracy that had been weaponized to subjugate man himself and the natural world. These powers had reduced people to disciplined robots, performance fanatics, stripped of feeling and capable of horrors. "Administrative murder" under the Third Reich was the most terrible enactment of this transformation: the organization of massacres from desks, coldly, following procedures that were parceled into a multitude of steps designed to keep each person from thinking of the goal of his work. The codified vocabulary also helped people ignore the crimes: *Sonderzug* (special train), *Sonderbehandlung* (special treatment), *Himmelsweg* (path to heaven), *Gesundpille* (health pill) . . . The method used for the killing machines in the extermination camps had something in common with the assembly line of the industrial era. The executioners were real machines, plunged into the precise task, timed, repetitive, and limited, of killing masses of dehumanized people in record time, turning them into numbers, a product that had to be reduced to ashes in a few hours.

After the war, Horkheimer, Adorno, and Pollock decided to return to Germany to reopen the institute in Frankfurt to help with the democratization of Germany. The institute rapidly became the epicenter of serious thinking about capitalist society and fascism. There was still much to be done. In the fifties, according to a study by the Frankfurt School, two thirds of the population declared they had reservations about the democratic model. But in time, Frankfurt thinking would very strongly influence the way people reflected on the Nazi past, relayed by intellectuals like Jürgen Habermas. At the start, the institute expressed sympathy for the student movement, but later rejected it, seeing it not as a revolutionary uprising, but as an attempt destined to fail, without guiding principles.

"We got together in the lecture halls to talk about the poor division of wealth in the world or the absurdity of having dozens of brands of toothpaste when two would suffice," Volker remembers. "I was interested in these questions, but I wasn't an anticapitalist. I studied economics and I admired Ludwig Erhard, the father of the economic miracle, who brought Germany out of ruin with impressive speed." "Behind their anticapitalism," my father explains, "certain students were in fact attacking the paternal figure who had been part of an economic miracle. That was never my problem, I would have had trouble identifying my father with that."

When I talked to my aunt, I wondered if the setbacks in Karl Schwarz's business hadn't encouraged his son to later make a career in the field of industry, as a reaction to his father's failure. Each year, Opa had to dish out large sums for the mortgage he had taken out to pay Julius Löbmann and Max Schmidt, his former partner. He also had to pay a yearly tax designed to support Germans whose property had been completely destroyed during the war. According to my aunt Ingrid, "My mother said that we would have been better off if the house had been destroyed, thanks to that money!" Since leaving school, she was the one who took care of the wire transfers as well as many other aspects of his business. "With stones from the ruins of the war, my father built a new building to replace the one that had been destroyed in 1943. But it was poorly insulated and so damp that you could watch the paint peeling. When a client called we made it seem like we were a big business. I would pretend to be his secretary and say: 'You've reached the reception of Schwarz and Company . . . stay on the line, I'll transfer your call to Mr. Schwarz's office.' In truth, he would be sitting right next to me and I would pass him the receiver." There were also hundreds of business cards with elegant italic writing that piled up without any clients to receive them. When I was little, I found them everywhere, lingering in drawers at Chamissostrasse, yellowed with age. In the middle of the sixties, when he was just beginning to bounce back, Opa had to face new woes. "Big oil companies like Esso offered to lower their prices if clients agreed to buy everything from them." These aggressive tactics were the death knell for small businesses like Schwarz & Co. "Two or three clients with empathy who valued my father agreed to a scheme where he would continue to deliver several barrels to them in addition to what they bought from the big oil company," my aunt continued. "He had to paint his own barrels the colors of their principal supplier so that they wouldn't find out when they visited their clients' warehouses." During his studies, my father spent quite a few Saturdays repainting Karl Schwarz's barrels; then, since he'd acquired some tips on accounting thanks to his economics courses, he offered to balance the books. "It was a disaster," Volker says. "My father had no accounting skills, it wasn't profitable at all. He wasn't gifted in business. I tried to save what I could." At that time, Volker didn't confront his father about the past anymore—it was pointless—so he taught himself by reading books.

Volker on a trip in France, 1960.

But for many young Germans, a central, specific point of the student uprising was to confront the roles their own parents had played under the Third Reich. They asked the question they'd never thought or dared to ask before: and you, what did you do when Hitler was in power? It was no longer about accusing the worst Nazi criminals, the leaders and the monsters, but about lifting the veil that had concealed all the others, those tens of millions of *Mitläufer* who since the end of the war had profited from the taboo surrounding the fact that the majority of the population had been supportive of the Führer. The students accused the "economic miracle" generation of having buried the crimes of the past under a mountain of material comfort. Young people also demanded the truth from their teachers, whom they accused of sugarcoating the past. A new generation of educators agreed with them, disputing in their own right the way their elders had taught the Hitler years. Lecture series were organized to recount the positions universities had taken under National Socialism. Throwing light on the shadows of the past became an imperative of the German student movement, summarized in its main slogan: *Unter den Talaren—Muff von 1,000 Jahren* (Under the togas, whiffs of 1,000 years), a reproach of the complacency of professors toward the Third Reich, which had presented itself as the Thousand-Year Reich.

In general, the students called into question the legitimacy of a political establishment that counted persecutors among its ranks and had protected murderers instead of standing with the victims. The critique was forceful because it no longer came from abroad, but from within the country, from the very children who would one day control the political landscape. Tens of thousands of students descended on the streets of Bonn in May 1968 to protest the emergency measures that introduced into the constitution an emergency law to ensure the ability of the state to act in crisis situations, at the cost of undermining basic laws. The demonstrators were quick to catch the drift, calling these measures "Nazi laws" and brandishing signs that warned "No Second 1933." Several months later, on November 7, 1968, during the Christian Democratic Union (CDU) congress in West Berlin, a young woman approached the podium and slapped the chancellor, Kurt Kiesinger, in front of the cameras, shouting, "Nazi, Nazi!" The young woman was Beate Klarsfeld. She became a celebrated anti-Nazi militant along with her husband, Serge Klarsfeld, a French Jewish lawyer who had lost his father to Auschwitz. The choice of Kiesinger as Konrad

Adenauer's successor in 1966 had caused controversies due to Kiesinger's membership in the NSDAP as early as 1933 and his tenure as vice-president of the Radio Division of the Reich. Before his nomination, the writers Günter Grass and Heinrich Böll wrote an open letter to the daily *Frankfurter Allgemeine Zeitung* begging him to renounce his attempt at the chancellorship because of his past, and the philosopher Karl Jaspers and his spouse turned in their German passports in protest. In the wake of Beate Klarsfeld, students circulated a tract that argued: "finally a true denazification . . . Let's finally stop letting the Nazi racial agitators, the murderers of Jews, the killers of Slavs, the butchers of socialists, all of yesterday's Nazi shit, keep on spreading their stench over our generation. Let's make up for what was neglected in 1945: Let's drive this Nazi plague out of our city." In 1969, for the first time since the creation of the Federal Republic, the social democrat party rose to power with Willy Brandt at its head as chancellor. Brandt announced from the start that he considered himself "the chancellor of not a defeated but a liberated Germany." During a state visit in Poland, he kneeled before the monument to the heroes of the Warsaw Ghetto to express his desire to put an end to the ambiguity his predecessors had shown toward the past.

"It was a good time," my father remembers. "Horizons were expanding at an overwhelming rate. We felt close to young people from all over the world, through travel, pop music, new clothing styles from abroad which had an atmosphere of celebration and tolerance." This was a way of abolishing those borders which fueled twentieth-century nationalist fantasies. Thanks to exchange programs, Volker left to discover Europe, Lisbon and especially France: Lille, Lyon. During a placement in Paris, he became friends with an Israeli woman, Ilana, and left to explore Spain along with her and two other Germans. "There was no tension, maybe because it was clear to her that we condemned Nazism. She didn't speak about her family's past, like many of the Israelis

I met," he remembers. "We wanted a community of people, to break the old patriotic and conservative values. Everything was overturned, the idea of a family, marriage, education, teaching, everything seemed possible . . ." Volker hadn't lacked freedom in his teenage years. However authoritarian Karl Schwarz was, he had allowed his son to be the master of his own movements. At the age of fourteen, he'd moved out of the family apartment into a maid's room under the eaves of the Chamissostrasse roof, where he could do pretty much as he pleased. Since he valued it so highly, Opa had a certain respect for liberty, especially in sexual matters. "He didn't much like the new ways of the sixties, except for the contraceptive pill. He said to me: 'With that, you can be careful not to get a girl pregnant, and avoid paying as much as you would for a Porsche.'" In the sixties, it was still illegal in Germany to rent an apartment or a hotel room to an unmarried couple. And so "my father forbade me to bring girls back to my maid's room, not for moral reasons but because he could go to prison and have to pay a fine! Sometimes he would burst into my room. One time he found a girl there, but he never said anything." Karl was often away, making the rounds in his van to deliver barrels to his clients or else on vacations where he liked to practice nudism on the Adriatic Coast. It was Lydia who cared for her son, and she looked after him with an infinite benevolence, tolerating his escapades. All the same, the changes in society surpassed her. "My mother was very much shocked by this new freedom of speech young people practiced towards parents, professors, leading politicians. If we heard a comedy sketch about the German chancellor, she would say, 'It is indecent to talk like that about the Führer!'"

In spring 1968, my father went to West Berlin to spend two weeks in one of the many communal apartments in Kreuzberg, an alternative neighborhood that housed many militants on the left. Shortly

before that, on April 11, 1968, in front of the Berlin office of the
German Federation of Socialist Students (SDS), a neo-Nazi fired
three times at Rudi Dutschke, the leader of the student movement,
gravely wounding him in the head. The SDS, which was already
on its way to radicalization, took an even harder line. "The young
people I met in Berlin were much more extreme than those in
Mannheim. They had drifted towards anarchy. I didn't see myself
in these groups that had become so rigid in their dogma that, in
my opinion, they had come to resemble the people they critiqued."
These groups were criticized for "leftist fascism" by a segment of
German society, including liberals like Habermas, who expressed
fear at this tyrannical drift in the methods and discourse of protest.
Under the banner of antifascism, the students' circle of targets
only continued to grow. In 1968, Rudi Dutschke said, "The new
form of fascism is no longer found in a party or in a person, but is
present in all institutions of late capitalism." This definition of fascism presented a problem—of minimizing the crimes of National
Socialism by comparing the Third Reich to the Federal Republic.
Volker stopped getting involved in the student uprising, which had
begun to take a turn that corresponded with neither his political
leanings nor his independent character.

On the other side, the state and certain media groups started to
become paranoid, perceiving these young people as Communists
sowing disorder and having potential links with East Berlin and
Moscow. In truth, the students held several views in common with
East Germany. Their critique of capitalism, of course, but also their
denunciation of the continuities between the Third Reich and the
Federal Republic. Calling out criminal impunity was at the heart
of East Berlin's anti-Western propaganda. In 1965, East Berlin
had presented the international press with a *Brown Book*, which
listed 1,800 leaders in the political, economic, military, justice,
and scientific sectors in West Germany who had been members of
the SS or the Nazi Party. The West German authorities seized the

book and labeled it an instrument of propaganda. In fact, much of the information was correct. Even if East Germany had been motivated more by political calculation than moral imperative, its actions had the positive effect of forcing the Federal Republic to confront its past. Nonetheless, these convergences were harmful for the student movement, since in the middle of the Cold War, being suspected of conspiring with communism was dangerous, especially in West Germany, where the KPD Communist party had been banned in 1956, a measure that has remained controversial.

Axel Springer, a very powerful media group that edits *Bild Zeitung*, Germany's most-read daily, led a violent campaign against the students, who were presented as "ringleaders" charged with destabilizing the republic. It called for its readers to "Stop the terror of the red youth," adding, "We must not leave all the dirty work to the police and their water cannons"—a semi-incitement to violence. The newspaper was accused of being indirectly responsible for the assassination attempt on Rudi Dutschke. On April 11, 1968, several thousand people attacked the general headquarters of Axel Springer in West Berlin, and Molotov cocktails were thrown at newspaper delivery vehicles. Forty years later, documents revealed that these were handed out by an agent provocateur for the German intelligence services, which hoped to unleash violence to justify arrests.

The rupture between the student movement and the state passed the point of no return when a small minority of young extremists decided to impose their vision through violence at the beginning of the seventies. Terrorist organizations sprang up like mushrooms. In certain ways, they saw themselves as acting "in compensation" for the opportunities they had missed under the Third Reich. It's no coincidence that the only other countries where student protests developed into terrorism were also former allies of the Reich: Italy with its Red Brigades and Japan with its Red Army. The most important terrorist group in Germany was the Red Army Faction, RAF. Its two main leaders were Andreas Baader, a young delinquent who recycled himself into an anti-capitalist rebel, and the famous journalist and brilliant intellectual Ulrike Meinhof, who suddenly slipped into terrorism. The journalist's transformation fueled all kinds of allegations, and some even speculated that a brain surgery she'd undergone in 1962 had affected her mental stability. Her actions can perhaps be explained by her 1968 paraphrase in *Konkret* of a declaration from a member of the Black Panther Party: "Protest is when I say I don't like this and that. Resistance is when I see to it that things that I don't like no longer occur. Protest is when I say I will no longer go along with it. Resistance is when I see to it that no one else goes along with it anymore either." Ulrike Meinhof's decision to join the RAF lent a decisive intellectual credibility to the terrorism of the extreme left. On June 5, 1970, she published "Building the Red Army," a foundational text of the RAF. Addressed to "potential revolutionary sectors of the people," it called for the "end of the censorship" and the start of "armed resistance" to prepare the proletariat for class warfare. In April 1971, in an article titled "The Concept of the Urban Guerrilla," she declared war on American and German imperialism. The FRG designated Ulrike Meinhof "public enemy number one." Many former militants from the student uprising and intellectuals on the left were seduced by the intransigence of these movements and heeded their warnings about the "new fascism" they claimed was emerging in the Federal Republic. Some were even prepared to help the terrorists by putting apartments, hiding places, or cars at their disposal. Paradoxically, the way the authorities reacted seemed to justify suspicions that Germany was becoming a police state. The young state was completely unprepared, and reacted with an outrageous level of police-enforced repression. I wasn't alive to witness that decade, but in the eighties, when I took the train in Germany with my mother, there were huge posters in the stations. One word in bold letters immediately caught my attention: *Terroristen*. Upon closer inspection, you could see a mosaic of photos in black and white, portraits of men and women with captions specifying their names, age, height, eye color, and other physical characteristics that would help to identify them. At the bottom a warning read: *Armed and dangerous!* And in very small print, 50,000 DM was offered as a reward for any information leading to the capture of one of these terrorists. As a little girl, this poster seemed to me to have emerged straight from the set of a Western or *Lucky Luke*, like the *WANTED!* notice stuck on the saloon entrance promising a shower of money to anyone who would help to find the man in the sketch. In truth, the men and women on the poster represented one of the most arduous challenges faced by the young German republic.

"I was living in France, but I remember when I visited Germany, I was shocked to see so many armed police officers at the airport," my father says. "It created quite an impression." The state turned to strong-arm tactics, which culminated in an unofficial state of emergency. It began strict surveillance of the territory and its citizens, emphasizing the presence of law and order, conducting searches at the slightest suspicion, and creating dossiers that violated citizens' rights to privacy. The tabloids, particularly *Bild Zeitung*, sowed hate and suspicion everywhere, destroying the lives of mere suspects and dragging public personalities through the mud if they refused to side unconditionally with the authorities.

The media and the authorities felt they were surrounded by terrorist "sympathizers," and the search for perpetrators took on serious proportions. In June 1972, police encircled Heinrich Böll's country house and demanded that two of his guests identify themselves. The Nobel laureate had been under surveillance since he'd published an open letter in *Der Spiegel* addressed to *Bild*, which he accused of calling for violence and violating the presumption of innocence: "This is no longer crypto-fascist, no longer fascistic, this is naked fascism. Hate, lies, dirt." He denounced the general hysteria in this "war" pitting "6 against 60 million" and compared the fate of former Nazis, "who have so easily and painlessly transitioned from fascism to the liberal democratic constitution," to that of Ulrike Meinhof, who must reckon with "being at the mercy of total mercilessness." Many prominent people were opposed to Heinrich Böll's argument, accusing him of apologizing for terrorism and of dipping into the same rhetoric as the RAF, which used the term *fascism* every chance they got. But the writer had support from another part of society that, after a long postwar amnesia, was also on the hunt for "fascists," which it believed were lurking everywhere: behind capitalism, banks, temples of consumerism, the army, the media, and even the parliamentary democracy. "Nazi" became a way to denounce anything and everything, all over the world. A habit that was quite counterproductive for coming to terms with the actual Nazi past.

In May 1972, the RAF suddenly picked up speed. In just one month, it committed six attacks, killing four people and seriously injuring seventy more. The bombs had targeted American troops, police buildings, a judge's car, and a printing facility owned by Axel Springer. The German police mobilized like never before, and by the end of June, all the leaders of the RAF had been arrested and transferred to Stammheim Prison, near Stuttgart, a brand-new fortress that was supposed to be impermeable. Instead of putting an end to the movement, these arrests gave new life to the RAF, which developed very effective ways of communicating thanks to outside supporters. The group's aura surpassed German borders. By way of the Italian Red Brigades and Action Direct in France, it had contacts in many international terrorist movements such as the Irish IRA and the Basque ETA, based in

Spain, but their closest collaboration was with Palestinian terrorists. And so, on September 5, 1972, at the Munich Olympic Games, when a commando unit of the Palestinian terrorist group Black September took nine members of the Israeli team hostage, the perpetrators demanded not only the liberation of more than two hundred Palestinian militants who had been detained in Israel, but also the release of Ulrike Meinhof and Andreas Baader. After a day of negotiations between the commandos and the German authorities, the situation spiraled out of control and all the hostages were killed. From prison, Ulrike Meinhof congratulated the terrorists and accused Israel of "burning down its athletes like the Nazis did the Jews—fuel for the imperialist extermination policy." Shortly after, during a trial, she went even further: "Auschwitz meant that six million Jews were murdered and dumped on the rubbish heap of Europe for the way they were seen—as money Jews. Anti-Semitism was essentially anticapitalist in nature." This anti-Semitic rhetoric wasn't uncommon in the anti-Zionist circles of the extreme left, and it wasn't the only contradiction within the RAF regarding its relationship to the Nazi past. The group didn't hesitate, in justifying their attacks on American troops in Germany, to give equal footing to Auschwitz on one hand and the Allied bombing of Dresden or the American intervention in Vietnam on the other. Despite these positions, sympathy for the detainees continued to grow among militants and intellectuals on the left. In 1974, Heinrich Böll published *The Lost Honor of Katharina Blum*, a novel about the critical relationship between the extreme left and the mass media, which the directors Volker Schlöndorff and Margarethe von Trotta turned into a splendid, daring film.

Böll wasn't the only intellectual to be alarmed by the new methods Germany adopted, to the point of sometimes taking an ambiguous attitude toward terrorism. But no one crossed the line more than the French philosopher Jean-Paul Sartre, who openly justified the actions of the RAF. In December 1974, he visited Andreas

Baader in prison to see for himself the conditions in which he was held, after the prisoner's lawyer Klaus Croissant had attested that he lived in "isolation torture." Sartre spoke to Baader for about half an hour and when he emerged he declared to the press that the RAF detainees were kept in isolated cells, soundproofed, and subjected to constant light. This was not "torture like the Nazis," he said, but "another torture, a torture that can cause mental disorders." These accusations were false. Sartre never saw Baader's cell, and the RAF detainees were not in solitary confinement. They could visit one another, even if they were members of the opposite sex, which was a privilege. They had record players at their disposal, televisions, hundreds of books, and they regularly got newspapers.

A few years ago, *Der Spiegel* got a hold of the official transcript of the conversation between Jean-Paul Sartre and Andreas Baader in prison. In a rather tense atmosphere, the philosopher criticized the prisoner: "the RAF has taken clear action that the people did not agree with," and tried to persuade him not to resort to murder. The detainee robotically repeated the axioms of his organization, without managing to deepen them, when the French intellectual questioned him. "What an idiot that Baader is," Sartre said after the meeting, according to his interpreter, Daniel Cohn-Bendit, who was the leader of May '68 in France. Why did this philosopher, who seemed to disagree with the RAF in private, support it in public?

These criticisms, from a man with great influence in the world, painted a disastrous picture of West Germany, which many suspected of not being cured of Nazism, and treating its prisoners like they had treated them not so long ago in the Nazi camps. But above all, by presenting Andreas Baader as a victim, the philosopher legitimized the dangerous parallels between terrorism on the extreme left and the fight against fascism. In hindsight, it seems that beyond a certain intellectual dishonesty, Sartre, like other leftist intellectuals, hadn't perceived the danger of a completely new form of terrorism, like a powerful international conglomerate, with offshoots throughout the whole world and causes that seemed to melt together into a jumbled slurry.

The evolution of the RAF after 1975 would confirm the dangerous character of the movement. Since the trials of these terrorists still hadn't begun, a second generation took up the mantle even more violently, out of a desire to exert maximum pressure to release the prisoners. They kicked off the new era by taking the occupants of the German Embassy in Stockholm hostage and killing two diplomats. On April 1977, a biker and his rider fired machine guns at the car of the attorney general, Siegfried Buback, who had once been a member of the NSDAP under the Reich. He was killed along with his chauffeur and one of his employees. Two months later, the president of the Dresden Bank, Jürgen Ponto, was waiting for his goddaughter's sister, Suzanne Albrecht, who had planned to visit him at his house for tea, when she arrived at the head of an RAF commando that had come to kidnap him. Faced with his resistance, they killed him. In September, it was Hanns Martin Schleyer, president of the Employers Federation, who had joined the SS in 1933 and the NSDAP in 1937, who was kidnapped by a group that killed his four companions and demanded the release of RAF prisoners.

Helmut Schmidt, the German chancellor, convened his crisis unit and spent weeks smoking cigarette after cigarette, torn between his desire to avoid giving in to the perpetrators' demands and the human desire to save the hostage's life. On October 13, 1977, while Schleyer languished in his hole, a Lufthansa plane from Palma de Mallorca to Frankfurt disappeared from radar. From the cockpit, a man announced that the PFLP, the Popular Front for the Liberation of Palestine, had diverted the plane to Mogadishu with its eighty-seven passengers and crew, and threatened to kill them if the

RAF prisoners and the other Palestinian detainees weren't released immediately. Five days later, German special forces launched a counterassault on the grounded plane and rescued the hostages. At this news, Andreas Baader and another RAF member shot themselves in the head with weapons that had been smuggled into the prison, and Baader's companion, Gudrun Ensslin, hung herself with a cable from the ceiling. A year and a half earlier, Ulrike Meinhof had already hung herself from a window with a strip of fabric. On October 19, Schleyer's kidnappers sent a message to the French newspaper *Libération* stating that his body could be found in the trunk of a car in Mulhouse. The RAF continued to operate for a dozen years, but it had lost its leaders and all popular support.

In France, on the other hand, intellectuals and journalists on the left continued to defend the RAF. German newspapers returned fire by calling the French left "chauvinist" and "anti-German." A media war began between the two countries. The solidarity certain French intellectuals and media outlets felt for the terrorists doubled in July 1977, when Klaus Croissant, lawyer for the RAF, was arrested in Germany for transmitting instructions from the detainees to their supporters on the outside. He fled to France, where he was denied political asylum by the authorities and arrested. A campaign against his imprisonment began with the support of philosophers such as Michel Foucault and Jean-Paul Sartre. Gilles Deleuze and Félix Guattari penned an opinion piece in *Le Monde* in November 1977, where they denounced a society where "many men on the German left, through an organized system of denouncements, are watching their lives become intolerable in Germany." They warned against "the prospect that all of Europe falls under the type of control Germany demands." Croissant was finally extradited to West Germany, where he was condemned to two years in prison for supporting a terrorist organization.

❅   ❅   ❅

The violent Germanophobia and references to the unchangeable Nazi "character" of the Germans were a long-running trope in France, where some feared that Germany might fall back into old patterns. In fact, by coming back from the perilous challenges of the seventies, West Germany had proved that its democracy was stronger than some had predicted. Slowly but surely, its memory work had begun to bear fruit. At the same time, France was only waking up from its own thirty years of amnesia.

VIII

Sweet France . . .

My mother, Josiane, was a brilliant student, one of the few pupils from her teacher's college to go to the Sorbonne on a scholarship, the pride of her policeman father and her homemaker mother, with whom she lived in a little apartment in the Paris suburb of Le Blanc-Mesnil. She had chosen to study English after visiting Le Blanc-Mesnil's sister town in England, where she had found the English "exotic." She had practically never been outside of France.

It was a long commute each day to the university and back, and to make up for the lost studying time, Josiane would pore over her books in the evenings instead of going out with other Sorbonne students, bourgeois sons of doctors and lawyers who never made her feel at ease. For all that, Josiane didn't live a monastic life—her scholarship allowed her to go on ski vacations, visit Brittany, and see the Mediterranean, where the photos often show her surrounded by boys. She was a pretty girl with dark hair, quick to smile, and she dressed with much care, a coquetry she'd inherited from her mother, who was an expert dressmaker. "I never thought about the war, I was young, I wanted lightheartedness. Besides, I don't think it was much in people's minds, either in the media or at the university. When I heard stories, it was usually about the resistance or monstrous accounts like that of Dr. Marcel Petiot . . ." This Parisian doctor had exploited the desperation of persecuted Jews by making them believe he could help them flee to Argentina. He would invite them to come to his office with all of their valuables before robbing them, killing them, and burning their bodies. Sometimes entire families fell into his hands. This affair fascinated France. Like Josef Mengele in Germany and all the other figures who were considered "pure evil," Petiot provided a distraction from another evil that was less sensational, subtler, and more frightening because it was also much more common: the attitude of many French citizens under the German Occupation.

Each day, to get to the university by bus, Josiane crossed the village adjacent to Drancy, where, during the war, the vast majority of the 76,000 Jews deported from France—who were mainly foreign citizens, but also some French—had been detained in very poor conditions before the Germans sent them to death camps. Even though it was under the authority of the Gestapo, the Drancy camp, established in a large modern complex at the Cité de la Muette, was administered until 1943 by the Prefecture of Paris, which had offered the use of French police officers as guards. "I had no idea what Drancy was," my mother says, with a slightly guilty air. "Not in the fifties, and not in the sixties either." I wonder how she managed to be unaware that one of the biggest Vichy dramas had taken place right next to where she was living, just a few years before her family moved to the area.

In fact, no one in France was interested in Drancy at the time. After the war, associations for the victims and religious groups began to organize discreet ceremonies at the site, then, in the early sixties, commemorative plaques were placed. It was only starting in the seventies that the site was very gradually turned into a memorial.

So it's not completely surprising that my mother didn't hear about it until so late. However, in the course of my research, I discovered that some of the large towers in the Cité de la Muette had continued to serve as a barracks for the camp's police officers. And Josiane's family lived at a barracks in Le Blanc-Mesnil where police officers, like her father, Lucien, would certainly have been in touch with their colleagues in the nearby Cité de la Muette. When her father Lucien rubbed shoulders with the former Drancy staff, is it possible that they never spoke among themselves, that they never let slip a comment, a question, an anecdote, a mean remark, a regret? The camp was close to the center of town, and there was even a hotel across the street where the owner charged exorbitant prices for rooms on the upper floors so that family members could glimpse their detained loved ones inside the walls for a few moments and wave. As for the Bourget-Drancy station, the point of departure for forty-two convoys between March 1942 and June 1943, it was located exactly on the line between Drancy and Le Bourget, a high-traffic area because the second-largest airport in Europe was also located there. After July 1943, the convoys began to leave from Bobigny train station, a bit farther away, for logistical reasons, and out of discretion. Just before the liberation of Paris in August 1944, two transports were sent to Auschwitz and Buchenwald at the last minute, under the orders of the Drancy commander, SS-Hauptsturmführer Alois Brunner, who had rushed to arrest another 1,327 Jewish children in Paris at the end of July.

The inhabitants must have seen these men, women, and children packed by the hundreds onto cattle cars with straw wet from urine, furnished only with a bucket of rain and a washtub as a toilet. Did they never bring up these events after the war, at the counter of a café, in church, or at the store? That seems unimaginable to me, but I probably underestimate the rule of silence in France. "We didn't talk about the past at home," my mother says. "I got along well with my father, but he almost never told me anything."

Yet Papi had been a policeman under Vichy orders during the occupation.

During the war, Papi was serving in Mont-Saint-Vincent, a village of a few hundred inhabitants, situated in the so-called free zone. After the crushing defeat against Nazi Germany in June 1940, France signed an armistice dividing the country in two: the northern zone was occupied by the Germans, and the southern zone was called "free" and placed under the authority of a government in Vichy led by Marshal Pétain. Papi liked to tell one story from that time, and only one, but he repeated it over and over. In November 1942, the Germans invaded the free zone in part so they could control the Mediterranean coast and face the Americans and British who had disembarked in North Africa. The area around Mont-Saint-Vincent found itself occupied by the Germans, who demanded that the police give up their arms, but in a fit of courage, Lucien and his colleagues kept a few, which they hid.

One day, after a resistance attack, the Germans barged madly into the surrounding barracks and promised to execute hostages if they found a single weapon. My grandfather had a bad fifteen minutes while they rifled through his barracks, but strangely, they didn't think of something as simple as a hiding place against the wall behind the cupboard. If they had, they would probably have sacked the village, perhaps even burning it and killing hostages, to cut off the inhabitants from the resistance, as they did at Oradour-sur-Glane on June 10, 1944. This village was totally destroyed and most of its six hundred residents were killed with stark brutality by an SS company that was out to get revenge for attacks by partisans. This massacre was one of the worst committed against non-Jewish civilians during World War II.

Papi died when I was ten years old, and unfortunately, I didn't have the chance to learn more. But a family friend named Claude, who was born in 1929, offered to tell me how he had lived during that time of war and occupation. Claude grew up in a family that was much more comfortable than my mother's, in a house with a large garden and a garage for the car, located only twenty minutes from Paris. His family was very anti-German. His grandfather had already mobilized twice against German invasions of France, in 1870 and 1914, and three of his uncles had been drafted in World War I. Like many of their comrades, they never talked about what they had been through in the trenches, those lines of defense hollowed out of the ground and linked together over hundreds of miles, where soldiers on both sides waited for death to come over them at any moment, from any direction. France had been greatly weakened by the war, morally, demographically, and economically. People cried "Never again!" and called it "the war to end all wars!"

Twenty years later, Europe was back at it. "I definitely felt the war coming," said Claude, who was ten in 1939. "There were mobilization posters everywhere, and we stuck strips of paper to the windows to muffle vibrations from the bombings. At school, they distributed gas masks, which made an impression on me." In the end, the area where he lived was mostly spared by bombs, but one of his friends who lived in Paris told him about the dead and wounded who lined the streets. "In May 1940, as the Wehr-macht approached, my parents decided to flee, we closed the house, leaving the cat and the dog. The roads were very crowded, everyone was afraid of the Germans and fled." They took refuge in a relative's beautiful villa at the mouth of the Loire. One month later, German officers requisitioned the attic of the house. "They were perfectly well behaved. This attitude was very reassuring to the French, and most people who had fled went back home, as did my family."

Confronted with the complete rout of the French army, which was considered one of the strongest in the world, the French state called on Marshal Philippe Pétain, a World War I military hero, to come to the rescue. Pétain called for surrender. In response, General de Gaulle broadcast his legendary "Appeal of 18 June" from the BBC in London, calling on French people to continue the fight, cementing this act as the foundation of the resistance movement, the Free French Forces. Four days later, Pétain signed an armistice with Adolf Hitler that arranged for France to be divided in two. The French had to pay for the cost of the German Occupation, and agreed, in a first step toward losing the country's moral integrity, to "deliver any German and Austrian political refugees present on its land." The new French government left Paris and moved to Vichy in the southern "free zone." On June 24, France signed an armistice with Italy, an ally of the Reich, giving it a small occupied zone along the Italian border on the Côte d'Azur and in the Maritime Alps, which was later expanded.

"When I returned from the Loire," Claude continued, "I started going door to door with my friends from high school, selling portraits of Pétain to benefit Secours Populaire. I don't remember a single person slamming the door in my face. At that time, the marshal had a very good reputation, people thought: 'Here's a fellow who can save something from the wreckage!'" Pétain had enormous prestige. The French were grateful to him for having spared them another bloodbath, and they reassured themselves by thinking that Hitler was the best defense against the much-feared Bolsheviks. The parliament voted in an overwhelming majority to assign full powers to the marshal, who was charged with drafting a new constitution. It was the death of the Third Republic and its parliamentarianism, which was blamed for weakening the country in economic, military, and diplomatic terms. Its collapse into an authoritarian regime whose values were the antithesis of the republic didn't seem to bother the French, who remained stony while Gaullists and former leaders of the Third Republic were imprisoned.

*   *   *

On October 24, 1940, while the Führer crossed France by train on his way back from meeting the fascist-friendly Spanish dictator Francisco Franco, the old marshal came to meet him at a remote train station in the countryside for a much-publicized handshake celebrating France's official entry into the "path of collaboration." "That handshake changed everything for me," explains Claude. "I stopped selling portraits of Pétain." A new chapter was beginning as France was trapped by the collaboration, becoming actively complicit in the Reich's crimes against Jews and members of the resistance. Vichy misjudged the situation, and despite its goodwill, the Germans didn't really treat France any better than the other occupied western territories, and economically drained the country. The Reich requisitioned enormous amounts of money, food, and raw materials, strangling the nation. In Paris, where Claude went to the lycée each day, "tons of stores were closed and there were long lines in front of the ones that were still open." Many inhabitants lived on fewer than 1,500 calories a day, electricity was rationed, coal for heating was rare, and the lack of gasoline made getting around almost impossible. But in the country, life was easier than in town. "We didn't suffer as much, thanks to our fruit trees, our vegetable garden, our chicken coop, and a family acquaintance close to a grocer, and a little bartering allowed us to have coal to heat two rooms in winter," Claude says.

"But there was a very strong feeling that we were adrift, on a ship without a commander. In my region, for example, the mayor of my village was never and nowhere to be seen," Claude remembers. In the "free zone" in the south, the French authorities made their presence felt, but in a bad way. The Vichy regime had moved from an initial charm offensive to repression. After Germany attacked the Soviet Union in June 1941, in violation of the nonaggression pact signed by the two countries in August 1939, the French

Communists abandoned their neutrality and increased the number of attacks, instances of sabotage, and assassinations, at first on their own and then in partnership with the Gaullists. The Germans counterattacked by executing prisoners by the dozens, picked off almost at random in the prisons. Pétain tried to intervene. But the only thing Vichy got out of it was responsibility for carrying out the dirty task of persecuting members of the resistance and executing French hostages.

As for the Germans, even in the occupied zone, their presence was inconsistent. "I rarely saw Germans, there were none in my village. We lived in a bubble, as other French did, too. Yet those who lived in Paris were confronted with the occupation. I even had a friend whose parents were interrogated by the Gestapo because they knew Paul Éluard." This poet and pillar of surrealism lent his incendiary pen to the resistance efforts—"I am born again to know you / And to name you / Liberty." Claude knew nothing of the resistance aside from posters of those who had been shot, put up in trains by the Germans to dissuade anyone who might have been tempted to join. But his father, who was an Anglophile, listened to the BBC, which had a broadcast in French. "He had taken out a big map of Europe, and depending on what news he heard, he would make pawns advance or retreat." After November 1942, when the Reich invaded the free zone, the popularity of the Vichy regime rapidly declined. The promised peace was still far away, while deprivation, and the pressure to send French people to work in Germany, became unbearable. Even if it was hard for everyone, living through the occupation had many different faces depending on what acquaintances you had, if you were political or not, if you lived in the free or the occupied zone, in the country or the city, if you had members of the resistance, collaborators, or prisoners in your family. On June 6, 1944, the Allies stormed the beaches at Normandy. At the end of August, Paris was liberated.

✻   ✻   ✻

Like the majority of her compatriots, my mother was comforted after the war by the lingering official story that her country had mainly resisted the Germans and had liberated itself through fighting off the yoke. But in their hearts, did the French really believe this version of history? Among Claude's group of friends, who were students after the liberation, "we were well aware that there was nothing very glorious about this episode, and we preferred to avoid talking about it." Never mind that the official myth took hold from the first hours of the liberation of Paris on August 25, 1944, when General de Gaulle exclaimed: "But Paris liberated! Liberated by itself, liberated by its people with the help of the French armies, with the support and the help of all France, of the France that fights, of the only France, of the real France, of the eternal France!" In truth, Paris had not been liberated by the resistance, which had certainly put up a brave fight but was too hard-hit for such a challenge; however, the American army had permitted de Gaulle to allow General Leclerc's French division to be the first to enter the city.

The American president, Franklin D. Roosevelt, and other Allied leaders doubted that France could become a faithful and democratic ally after not only giving up the fight and abandoning Great Britain to face Nazi Germany alone, but also collaborating closely with the enemy. At the same time, thanks to the resistance fighters, and especially thanks to the stubbornness of de Gaulle, Roosevelt finally accepted the idea of associating France with the victory over Nazi Germany. This way, France avoided the humiliation of being treated like a conquered country, and even if it wasn't considered a victor of the first order, and wasn't invited to the Allied conferences on the fate of the vanquished Reich, France paradoxically obtained a small zone of occupation in Germany and a permanent seat on the UN Security Council.

❀   ❀   ❀

The myth of "resistant France" would be built on top of the fiction of "victorious France." General de Gaulle, who took charge of the country after the liberation, decreed the Vichy government "null and void," considering that it had never represented France, as "the Republic had never ceased to be," since it had been represented by "the Free French, the fighting French, and the French committee for national liberation" that made up the resistance. This logic formed the story that the French state would shelter behind for the next fifty years. France got rid of its encumbering limb, as if Vichy had been forcibly imposed by a small group of criminals on a population that was fiercely opposed. Even the national police were celebrated as "resisting" although they had participated in Jewish raids and surveillance of the camps. "All of a sudden, hundreds of so-called members of the resistance came out of the woodwork," Claude said. "We thought they were fakes." Opportunism reigned. People fought over the cards identifying them as Voluntary Combatants of the Resistance. Between 220,000 and 300,000 of them were distributed, sometimes recognizing not so much a pledge to fight to the death but rather a talent for passing yourself off as something you never were. The vague notion of "services rendered to the resistance" was exploited to guarantee immunity to collaborators who had been last-minute converts to the resistance. Even among those who had truly taken up arms against the Germans, people inflated their own roles in the resistance effort.

General de Gaulle's party was in competition with the Communist party, which defined itself as the "party of 75,000 martyrs," an allusion to the supposed number of Communists who had sacrificed their lives, a figure that is quite exaggerated according to historians. The party glorified the great antifascist family, giving itself pride of place, and mined this vein to deliver a spectacular electoral performance, making it the leading party in France. It is true that the Communists played a central role in the resistance, but they seemed to have forgotten that, out of obedience to Stalin, they waited until the summer of 1941 to get involved, when the resistance could have used the strength of their numerous networks and sympathizers from the start. Nonetheless, at the liberation the Communist party had the grace to honor all the victims together—prisoners of war, veterans, Jews, civilians, forced laborers—while de Gaulle preferred to focus on a few heroes of the resistance to sell an image of fighting France and make people forget that she had surrendered. Movies were a marvelous vehicle for this propaganda. From 1944 on, the Committee for the Liberation of French Cinema, which was created by film artists worldwide, was encouraged by the authorities to reinforce a "positive" national identity; in other words to sublimate the resistance and leave the collaboration in the shadows. *The Battle of the Rails* by René Clément, which came out in 1946, is emblematic of this mission, as it pays homage to the sabotage efforts of French railway workers to disrupt train traffic during the Nazi occupation.

Sugarcoating the French role in the war was welcome, since the French had suffered harsh consequences: infrastructure and towns reduced to rubble, food rationing, a lack of coal. On top of all this, the social atmosphere was poisonous, with people settling scores over collaboration, and waiting to find out who would be the denouncer, and who the denounced. After the liberation, tens of thousands of French people were destroyed in the court of public opinion when the desire for justice and vengeance overlapped with getting even in other areas. Profiteers would manufacture evidence to get rid of a competitor or seize coveted goods, and people could be dragged through the mud over the slightest suspicion. Around nine thousand people were summarily executed. Twenty thousand

women accused of "horizontal collaboration," meaning they had
slept with Germans, had their heads shaved in the middle of the
street before being dragged in a procession before a hateful crowd,
hostages of an archaic vision of manhood that required women's
bodies to belong to the nation. "Near the village where she grew
up, my mother knew a woman who was shaved with the others
in the central square for having 'frequented' Germans," Josiane
remembers. "My mother went to visit her, openly disapproving of
her behavior even ten years later, but all the same, she still thought
the sentence had been too rough."

The violence of this spontaneous cleansing made it urgent to
organize legal processes. A new crime, "national unworthiness,"
was created, for those who had contributed to the "national deg-
radation" by participating in the regime's activities, organizations,
and propaganda. Approximately 100,000 people were sentenced
for this crime, suddenly losing their civil rights and being barred
from practicing certain professions. According to Henry Rousso,
a specialist in this period, 50 ministers or very high officials were
condemned to serve time in prison. In total, some 7,000 death
sentences were pronounced, and 1,600 were executed, which was
more than in other countries, and seven times more than in all of
Germany. Sanctions were imposed on thousands of bureaucrats
and employees, in the church, the army, the economy, and the
media. But many major players remained unpunished: magistrates,
who had made large contributions to carrying out the laws of Vichy;
the larger state corps of engineers, and businessmen, apart from
Louis Renault, who died in prison before he was tried.

The hardest hit were the journalists and intellectuals who had
been close to collaborationist circles. The writer Louis-Ferdinand
Céline, the author of the antiwar novel *Journey to the End of Night*
and of anti-Semitic pamphlets, fled to Denmark and returned
in 1951 after he had been pardoned. Pierre Drieu la Rochelle,
dandy-novelist, friend of the Dadaists and the Surrealists before

becoming a supporter of a kind of "fascistic socialism," killed himself. Several journalists were executed, including the influential writer and film critic Robert Brasillach, editor in chief of the collaborationist and anti-Semitic newspaper *Je Suis Partout*. Many writers sprang into action to demand a stay on his execution from de Gaulle. "Talent confers responsibility," reasoned the head of state, arguing that talent becomes an aggravating circumstance, since it causes a writer's influence to grow. Brasillach's death at the age of thirty-five made him into a martyr on the far right.

Everyone was impatiently awaiting the trial of the principal actors. In July 1945, Marshal Philippe Pétain's trial opened. At the age of eighty-nine, he put forward a line of defense that was, if nothing else, audacious: "With this power, I worked like a shield to protect the French people . . . Each day, a knife at my throat, I fought the enemy's demands. History will tell how much I have spared you, when my adversaries only think of criticizing me for the inevitable. . . . While General de Gaulle, outside our borders, pursued his fight, I paved the way for the liberation by keeping France unhappy but alive." His lawyers went so far as to claim that because of his great age, the leader of Vichy had been deceived by the second most important person in the regime, Pierre Laval, who would have dragged him into an even greater collaboration. The marshal was condemned to death, but General de Gaulle commuted his sentence to life in prison. To keep the peace in France, it was much better to avoid upsetting the former Pétain-ists, who were many.

But someone had to pay. It was Pierre Laval who, on June 22, 1942, during a speech over the radio, had pronounced a shocking sentence: "I hope for a German victory, because otherwise, Bolshevism will be everywhere, overnight." During his trial, Pétain admitted his disgust at this declaration. In truth, as the historian Marc Ferro has revealed, the marshal had fully endorsed it, and had even replaced the first version, "I believe in a German victory," with "I hope for a German victory." Laval's trial was a disaster. Constantly booed by the public, threatened by a biased jury, severely attacked in the press, he was finally condemned to death for high treason, and executed a week later after refusing to request an appeal. In *The Complete War Memoirs*, de Gaulle wrote: "Laval had played. He had lost. He had the courage to admit that he must answer for the consequences."

Only a few years after the liberation and the French people's great anger at collaborators, the storm suddenly blew over, leaving a door open for what historians have called "depurification." France could not deprive itself of all its top bureaucrats, and many members of the resistance were not prepared to fulfill these specialized technical positions at the center of state operations. The massive reintegration of Vichy bureaucrats and the pardoning of the condemned took place with disconcerting ease, in an atmosphere of general indifference, perhaps made simpler by General de Gaulle's absence—he had stepped down from the country's leadership in 1946.

By December 1948, 69 percent of the condemned had been pardoned. In 1953, a new amnesty law managed to legalize impunity, allowing the great majority of remaining prisoners to be freed. Former collaborators and leaders of the Vichy regime entered the government and the Assemblée Nationale. The continuity between the two regimes was even stronger outside of the spotlight, where between two thirds and 98 percent of administrative functionaries and major legislative bodies had held their posts under Vichy.

"At school, we almost never spoke of the war," my mother confirms. "They taught us about antiquity, the Middle Ages, and especially France's glorious eras: Louis the Fourteenth reviewed and revisited countless times, the French Revolution, Napoleon, then the colonial expansion of benevolent France, bringing civilization; we were proud to see everything we possessed across the globe." Claude, who studied at an elite Parisian school aimed in particular at training future high-ranking officials, was equally emphatic: "The classes stopped at 1939, and once again—all the problems of the war and even the immediate prewar period were not included in the order of the day. Yet we talked a lot about communism, we were afraid that Europe would be invaded." Very soon, news of another kind would monopolize the attention of the French people: the loss of the colonial empire, where emancipation movements had been developing, helped along by the weakening of French colonial power during the war. In a few years the French would have to let go of Indochina—after an arduous war—then Tunisia, Morocco, and the territories in sub-Saharan Africa. But the most traumatic loss for France was that of Algeria, which held the status of a French Department, and was therefore seen as a natural extension of France across the Mediterranean. War broke out in 1954, when advocates for Algerian independence in the Front de Libération National (FLN) took up arms to free themselves from the colonial yoke. "French men trembled, fearing the draft," my mother says. "I remember the day they came to recruit young men in Le Blanc-Mesnil to send them to fight over there. Everyone said they would never return."

In 1958, while France was going through a major crisis due to the war in Algeria, several French leaders launched an appeal to General de Gaulle to return to government. De Gaulle, after a decade of "crossing the desert," accepted the mantle of power. He confirmed by referendum the constitution of the Fifth Republic, then was elected president of that republic. He opened the way for Algerian independence, provoking ire from the Pieds-Noirs, the French living in Algeria, 800,000 of whom were quickly forced to flee the land where they'd lived for generations. They were unwelcome in France—a country they barely knew. The Algerian conflict also undermined the belief that France was respectful of human rights, as it was revealed that the French army had systematically used torture to extract information from prisoners. Former members of the resistance and intellectuals like Jean-Paul Sartre and his companion, the feminist writer Simone de Beauvoir, compared these practices to the Gestapo and the Nazis. The image of France as supposedly inoculated against such cruelty, in opposition to Nazi barbarism, had suddenly faltered.

But de Gaulle held on to his national myth. Once in power, he saw that the "Fighting French" had been somewhat forgotten and hurried to resurrect their memory. He inaugurated a huge memorial for them and moved the ashes of one of their main leaders, Jean Moulin, who was tortured to death by the Gestapo, to the Pantheon in Paris—among the tombs of the "great men" of France. Under the general's presidency, resistance films returned in force, with *The Line of Demarcation* by Claude Chabrol (1966) and *Army of Shadows* by Jean-Pierre Melville (1969), among others. They celebrated the competence and the sacrifices of these heroes without ever challenging the accepted image of a France unified around its resistance.

In 1962, while she was picnicking with her friend Françoise on the impeccable lawns of St. James's Park in London, Josiane was approached by a lanky young man with hair blonder than wheat and a gaze that was overwhelmingly blue. In hesitant yet charming French, he asked them if he might join their feast. It was Volker, who, having recognized the spread of cheese, saucisson, and wine on their blanket, understood that these were Frenchwomen who, in a country whose gastronomic reputation was pitiful, had taken the precaution of bringing provisions from home. In retrospect, no one can say which of these pleasures won my father over, but when he took his leave of the girls, he had Josiane's address in his pocket. Two years later, passing through Paris, he contacted her, and when they met, he gave her a bouquet of violets and kissed her.

In 1966, the first time she visited Volker in Mannheim, at the wheel of her Citroën 2CV, Josiane was impressed by the infra-structure of the roads, the "green wave" that allowed drivers to string together green lights while still respecting the speed limit, the complex intersections, the big, modern bridges, and of course, the highways. The economic miracle in Germany had preceded any such progress in France. "It was overwhelming, everything was more modern than it was back at home. And also, having the deutsche mark in your hand, that meant something compared to the franc, which was always being devalued." Right away, my mother felt good in Germany. "I never had the reflex of seeing a Nazi behind every German. As young people, we were mainly optimistic, and from then on there was the European Economic Community, everything was forgotten and we were all starting over together, trusting in the future and in solidarity." It's also true that Josiane already knew the country a little. Between 1947 and 1949, she had lived in Lindau, a pretty town in the southern, French-occupied zone, where her father had been transferred. The family lived in an apartment that had been requisitioned by the French, and whose German occupant was reduced to serving as their maid, even though my French grandmother, who wasn't used to having staff, preferred to take care of the household herself. But Josiane remembered parties, fireworks, and plenty of food at a moment when the Germans were fighting to keep their heads above water.

My mother appreciated the kindness of her fiancé's family in Mannheim, especially because she could exchange a few snippets of conversation with them. When she returned from Lindau at age eight, her French teacher had convinced her parents to pay for special courses in German for her, which was unusual at a time of marked hostility to Germany. "These expenses put quite a strain on the already modest family budget, but my parents always tightened their belts to give us the education they never had." Karl Schwarz was proud to stroll around town with this brunette beauty, and

Lydia Schwarz was glad to have another fan of her legendary cakes. However, Oma was a little upset when her son announced his plan to get engaged to a "Catholic French girl." She told him, "With all the honorable girls we have in Germany, couldn't you have found one of them?" My mother's religion, more than her nationality, was difficult for Oma to accept, since as a devoted Protestant, she viewed Catholicism's pageantry—its bishops decked out in rich colors and golden thread, its masses clouded with incense, and its ornate rituals in which the priest plunged his lips into a chalice of wine—like a "cult" whose members she strongly doubted would be allowed entrance to Paradise. As a consolation, she made sure that the marriage, to take place in France, would be celebrated in a Protestant church. My parents had to prepare for months in advance, going through endless prayer meetings with a Pietist pastor from a very severe branch of Protestantism. But what saddened Oma most was to see her son, her "god on earth," in an unfamiliar country, where her grandchildren would grow up without her.

For New Year's Eve in 1971, it was decided that Volker would come to Paris with his mother and sister to meet Josiane's father and his new wife, Geneviève, so they could talk about the wedding preparations together. Josiane's mother had died several years earlier, without meeting Volker. They would travel by car from Mannheim, and Oma, who knew the quality of the German highways, set out without any concerns. But once they crossed the border, they had to contend with Route Nationale 3, linking Metz and Paris, a dangerous two-lane road crowded with trucks and covered with black ice and snow at that time of year. They crossed a deserted Champagne, devoid of infrastructure, where they nearly ran out of gas, before arriving in Paris ten hours later, exhausted, starving, and thirsty. Oma was appalled at the roads full of potholes, the lack of restaurants and public toilets on the route, and the Champagne countryside with no traces of buildings on the horizon, a sharp contrast with the urban density of the

Mannheim region. She certainly missed the *Autobahn*, since in that respect, there was no contest—the Germans were leagues ahead of the French, and thanks to whom? It was too bad Hitler hadn't had a chance to help out with French infrastructure during the occupation!

In Paris, Volker took his mother and sister on a drive to show them the Sorbonne, that noble building where his fiancée had studied. All of a sudden, Oma exclaimed, "These French people are harlots, they have no modesty!" From the car, she had noticed the acronym for the Presses Universitaires de France, PUF, on a window, and she hadn't seen what the building contained. She thought it was a "puff," a brothel, and concluded that, at the foot of the Sorbonne, a house of carnal pleasures sat right there in the open so that students could amuse themselves in between lectures. For a moment, this image bolstered her idea of a Catholic country with disgraceful morals.

On New Year's Eve, my mother, Papi, and his new wife bent over backward to prepare a meal worthy of a king. They waited to serve it until 10 p.m. so that the dessert would arrive smack-dab at midnight. Ingrid and her mother, who were used to eating at 6:30, had to console themselves with cocktail-hour cake. When the dinner hour finally arrived, they had to bravely confront servings of oysters and snails, which was the equivalent of asking a French person to eat a fried spider in Cambodia. They didn't say anything that night, but afterward they didn't hesitate to criticize my mother's cooking, since they thought it was far below German standards. At the beginning, Josiane brought her mother-in-law to the French markets, but this culinary tourism was cut short, since she hadn't considered the discomfort a noninitiated person might face at seeing the open-air meat stalls in the market, the beef tongues hanging from hooks, the lamb brains in tubs, the kidneys bathing in their blood. Curiously, it was mainly the vegetables that upset Oma, piled on newspapers or on the ground with the earth still clinging to them. "A German would never eat that dirty spinach!"

My mother didn't ask what her fiancé's father had done during the war. Volker had assured her that he wasn't a Nazi. "If I had known then that he'd been in the party, it wouldn't have changed my decision, but it would have bothered me some . . . The son of a Nazi . . ." she says today. Lucien didn't ask questions either, but it didn't stop him from making unpleasant remarks about Volker. "My father said to me: 'What's this you're bringing us? Aren't there enough French boys here? A rough-looking boy, with no neck, like all the Germans. I wonder what you see in him.' Eventually he started to appreciate him, he thought he was intelligent."

Elsewhere in Josiane's family, the welcome was rather icy, as some French had suffered terribly from the brutality of the Germans. In order to announce their marriage, Josiane and Volker traveled in the 2CV as far as the Jura, where Lucien was from, to visit his brother Prosper and his wife, Madeleine. During the war, the Germans had burst into her farmhouse searching for her brother, a member of the resistance who had been denounced and fled to join the Maquis, who were powerful in that mountain region, where the forests were conducive to camouflage. While they turned the house upside down, Madeleine feared that they would stumble on traces of a British parachute that they had discovered in a nearby field and brought home to make sheets—a precious find for these poor peasants. Furious that the brother had escaped them, the Germans torched the whole farm. If they had recognized the parachute fabric among the sheets, they probably would have gathered that they were dealing with a family in the resistance. They might have shot them on the spot. And so, when Josiane sat in their living room with Volker and his strong German accent, Madeleine and Prosper tensed. Though they were usually so welcoming to their niece, this time they withheld their hospitality.

The next step had to be Bellegarde-en-Forez, an idyllic little village not far from Lyon where Josiane's mother was from and where she had an aunt she was very close to, having spent all the school vacations at her house. When I was little, we stayed with her on our way south. She didn't have a bathroom and didn't ever wash our glasses, but she compensated for this with a barnyard and a huge cage full of canaries, a balance that perfectly suited my sister Natalie and me. "Tante Jeanne never said 'German,' she always said 'Boche' or 'Kraut.' When I told her I was marrying a German, she said: 'That's the last straw! And if your mother was here . . .'" In fact, Aunt Jeanne said much more than that, even writing a letter that Josiane had forgotten. I found it, and when I read it to my mother and her brother, it was so saturated with hate that they thought it was fake. Here is a part of it: "What's this I've just heard, that you're marrying a Boche, it's a dishonor to your family. I knew there were simpletons in this family but I didn't know there was a crazy person, your father is just as crazy as you are, you've really lost your mind, I should think there's enough French boys, you don't have to marry that dirty race. . . . If your poor mother were alive what would she say, she knew what the wars were like, she dealt with so much, survived hunger and everything, and you, you put yourself out to pasture with these hulans." I didn't know that last word, one that she'd misspelled in place of *Uhlan*, which means "a cavalryman armed with a lance as a member of Slavic or Germanic armies." Tante Jeanne concluded: "I remove you from my family like a pestilence. . . . Find yourself a French boy, even if he's only a shepherd, he'll be French."

Tante Jeanne had not, however, particularly suffered under the occupation in the quiet village of Bellegarde-en-Forez, but after the Germans left, she was among the French who displayed a ferocious hate toward those she suspected of being in cahoots with the enemy. "She would tell us much more about the war than my father, she would drill us on the fates of collaborators, especially the women in the area who had slept with the occupier."

In the seventies, the mythology that the French tried to maintain about their role during the war came clattering down. A documentary film opened the breach—*The Sorrow and the Pity* by Marcel Ophuls—revealing the ambiguous position the French had taken toward the Germans under Vichy. It used the example of a French town, Clermont-Ferrand, where the director had interviewed inhabitants and former German soldiers who had been garrisoned there. The film was censored by the French State Office of Radio Broadcasting and Television (ORTF) and had to wait until the end of 1971 to come out in a little cinema in Paris, but the censure and the surrounding polemic brought the film a lot of publicity. Ophuls told the story of how the ORTF's general director, who had been favorable at first, went to see the retired General de Gaulle to ask his advice about this film that told "disagreeable truths." De Gaulle responded: "France doesn't need truth; France needs hope."

General de Gaulle was more aware than anyone of how, in the summer of 1940, only a few thousand Frenchmen had responded to his call to arms, and how the resistance had only begun to seriously come together at the end of 1942, when people were mainly looking to escape forced labor in Germany. The general died before the collapse of the myth he'd helped to build. The upset continued in 1973, with the French publication of *Vichy France: Old Guard and New Order*, a book by the American historian Robert O. Paxton, who, with the help of German and American archives, created a remarkable and unsparing portrait of WWII France, though within France itself, the records were still sealed. One by one, he took apart the legends that had accumulated after the war. He revealed that the active resistance had never mustered more than 2 percent of the French adult population, fighters with often exemplary courage who paid a heavy price to counter Vichy forces and the German army. Most historians estimate the number of active members of the resistance at 200,000–300,000. Along with them were sympathizers from within the population, about 10 percent of the French people by Paxon's estimate, who were ready to take large and small risks to relay messages, bring logistical aid, lie to the Germans, or hide people who were fleeing pursuit.

Paxton proved that collaboration was Vichy's idea, since they believed that the Germans would win and wanted to assure themselves a place in the future of Hitler's Europe, while Germany had hesitated, at least at the start, with Hitler considering France as a source of loot and a military base against Great Britain, rather than a potential ally. The historian described how, instead of limiting itself to the clauses of the armistice, which required a simple administration of the territory, the government's decision to take an active role in the Reich had greatly increased French complicity in criminal measures and actions, and had even allowed the Germans to carry out their projects much more easily: stealing food and wealth, forcing the exile of labor and manpower to Germany, and especially the bloody repression of the resistance and the deportation of 76,000 Jews from France. With their lack of troops and personnel, the Germans would have had trouble controlling such a large, well-developed country.

In another essential point, Paxton explained that Vichy's politics hadn't only been a pragmatic reaction to the German occupation— and one that would turn out badly—but also a political, or even ideological, aspiration on the part of some French people. The historian dismantled the myth that the Germans had tried to impose their ideology on France. In truth, Pétain had tried to associate himself with the new Nazi order through his National Revolution project, which had points in common with fascism and National Socialism: rejecting parliamentarianism and the republic; shunning

cultural modernism and intellectual and urban elites; suppress-
ing unions and forbidding the right to strike; glorifying the traditional values of *Work, Family, Country*; endorsing state-sponsored
anti-Semitism; and creating a cult of personality around the leader.
The image of the marshal was everywhere—on currency, stamps,
walls, public buildings, as a bust—while the famous *Marshal, here
we are!* became the official national anthem.

From the beginning, the National Revolution project generated
much enthusiasm among political families, whose fight against the
republic had begun long before the arrival of Vichy. At the start of
the 1930s, faced with the powerlessness of successive republican
governments and the growing influence of Bolshevism, political
organizations with a paramilitary bent began to multiply. These
"leagues" were nationalist or fascist and largely composed of former
combatants. One of the most influential was Action Française, carried by the charisma of the writer Charles Maurras, a pro-clerical
royalist opposed to the liberal forces he felt were assimilating the
Jews he wanted to exclude from France. On February 6, 1934,
the leagues formed the opening ranks of a demonstration against
parliament that had gathered about 40,000 people. Some thought
they could topple the republic. But the demonstration devolved
into fatal fighting in the streets, and two years later, the leagues
were dissolved. Vichy marked the triumph of their ideas.

Paxton's book rattled French society. At the movies, the resistance lost its untouchable cult status. In *Lacombe, Lucien* (1974),
Louis Malle dared to paint the portrait of a rather crude young peasant who, after being rejected from the local resistance, becomes a
collaborator out of spite and commits brutalities before falling in
love with a Jewish woman and running off with her. The director
raised a new question for the French: in 1940, which side would
I have chosen?

✿   ✿   ✿

When Josiane and Volker's marriage was celebrated in May 1971 with a river of champagne and wine, everyone understood one another perfectly once again: my father's many friends who had come without their wives and who impressed Papi by drinking his whole store of Ricard without water, as if it were schnapps; the Schwarz family; the family of Lucien's former wife; and that of his new spouse. This explosive mixture ended with a huge stampede, where everyone was dancing on top of and lying under the tables, laughing, making faces, and gesticulating to try to make themselves understood to their neighbors who didn't speak the same language. "We felt a little like we were breaking the rules, braving the old hatreds," my mother remembers. "It was a slight provocation, the sign of a new European spirit, it was exultant."

My parents, Josiane and Volker Schwarz, on their wedding day in Antony, in the Paris suburbs, 1971.

Papi invited Oma to dance, and she found him charming. I don't think he told her about his years with the French occupation forces in Lindau. And I don't believe she repeated what she had shouted at Josiane one day when her future daughter-in-law had invited her to a restaurant in the French Alsace-Lorraine region: "This was ours, you took this from us when we, we had such a need for this space!" The old Hitlerian phobia about a lack of *Lebensraum* (living space) had left its mark.

IX

The Holocaust? Never Heard of It.

At Oma's house, the dining room always impressed me most. With its heavy furniture carved from dark wood, it had an intimidating nobility that was unlike the rest of the apartment. An imposing sideboard that was close to ten feet long, whose doors were decorated with a labyrinth of fine, flowering curlicues sat facing a claw-footed display cabinet cut from similarly embossed wood. This was where Oma exhibited her fine porcelain treasures, objects of delicious fascination, which I succumbed to every time I entered that room. She had begun collecting in the thirties, when the fashion for chinoiserie was at its height, and women were snapping up rare pieces at auction. I like to imagine the feverish uproar and the frenzied tapping of umbrellas and high heels provoked by a delicately painted miniature.

My grandmother must have done very well, since her cabinet was filled with a fabulous variety of cups, in different sizes and forms: half spheres, hexagons, or cylinders whose handles also varied, seeming to follow the calligraphic curves of a mysterious alphabet. What made these objects so outlandish were the scenes painted on the porcelain surface with the minutiae of fairies—a voyage in a gondola on a stream swollen with fish like dragons, a

rice paddy under a brilliant sun. And the figures! How skillfully
their ample, embroidered outfits were drawn, and the rouged
faces that emerged from them like masks.

Sunday afternoon was the celebratory moment when the cups
came out, when Oma invited the family and her friends for *Kaffee und Kuchen*, coffee and cake, an event she prepared from
Saturday morning on, with the confection of cakes by the plat-
terful, transforming the kitchen into a battlefield where a wrong
step could mire your feet in crystalized sugar or plum compote.
My mother, who was always fanatical about cleaning, would flee
the house at dawn, returning long after the conventional lunch
hour in Germany, to the great distress of my grandmother, who
lamented having a "liberated" daughter-in-law who would "let
her little children starve to death." I remember several of these
Sundays when we were gathered around the big oval table carved
from the same wood as the rest of the dining room, a table that
distinguished itself with lion-clawed feet and a tabletop so high
that even very tall Germans had to sit up straight so as to avoid
dipping their chins in cream cake. Lydia's older lady friends would
be freshly coiffed for the occasion, with necklaces around their
throats, guffawing over the latest gossip, while several old men
smoked their pipes in silence and I alleviated the boredom of
these adult rituals by inspecting, up close, the china treasures
that Oma had brought out of their case, treasures finally in reach
on the table. You had to wait for them to empty to appreciate
their infinite elegance, since the cups harbored an ultimate secret
on the inside—tiny drawings that could only have been realized
by divine hands. And while I was plunged into exotic reveries,
admiring these glimpses of a marvelously enigmatic world where
I imagined that the claw-foot table would transform into a real
lion and devour us whole, us and our cakes, my father, who sat
beside me, saw a completely different story in this whole fiefdom
of furniture and porcelain.

✿   ✿   ✿

Volker started to see the dining room in a new light once he discovered photos of the apartment as it was before the war. There,
he observed the much more rustic furnishings that had come from
Lydia's dowry. Another room also underwent a major redecoration
during the war—the *Herrenzimmer*, the living room reserved
for men, where a handsome set of Art Deco pieces (a bookcase,
a big desk, and a table) suddenly appeared. "This furniture, in
particular the pieces in the dining room, which radiated an aura
of grand bourgeoisie, didn't correspond to the social status of my
parents," my father says, "and since these rooms were already
furnished, and it wasn't a question of need, these purchases must
have been motivated by bargain prices. What else besides Jewish
possessions were sold for almost nothing during the war?" These
new additions included rugs, a piano where my father and his sister
learned music after the war, and probably a few of Oma's delicious
china teacups. My father never mentioned his suspicions to his
parents. "What good would it do? Already, whenever I spoke the
name Löbmann, my father's face would turn completely red, he
would get up, close the window for the benefit of the neighbors,
then start yelling so loudly that people actually heard him down
at the end of the street."

The pillage, persecution, and deportation of Jews was the aspect of
the Third Reich that posed the greatest problems for the German
people, since it was easy to find excuses for having succumbed to
the so-called magnetism of Hitler and having hailed his social and
economic reforms, which brought, in the short term, a welcome
relief after the years of scarcity. It was much harder to justify the
millions of citizens who were passively complicit with the removal,
in broad daylight, sometimes under their noses, of 130,000 German

Jews. In Germany, though the work of coming to terms with the past, the *Vergangenheitsbewältigung*, had progressed since the years of amnesia in the 1950s, the genocide of the Jews was still a taboo subject until the end of the seventies. Of course, people already knew about Auschwitz and the fact that the SS had committed atrocities on the edges of the Eastern Front, but these examples were not perceived as being part of the same whole, of a monstrous project whose dimensions still escaped the collective conscience. "There was little empathy when it came to the Jews, it was shocking," says my father. "You would sometimes hear, 'It was the English who invented concentration camps, in South Africa,' or even, 'We suffered too!' But most of the time, they dodged the question."

The omerta, this code of silence, was facilitated by Jewish discretion. There were so few of them. The community numbered 15,000, compared to more than 500,000 when National Socialism came to power. They founded a Central Council of German Jews, rebuilt synagogues and community centers with the help of the state, but they suffered from the scorn of Jewish communities in Israel and the United States, where people didn't understand why the German Jews remained in the country of their executioners. They were too worn down, too hollowed by fear, to protest when the Germans, mainly to avoid confronting the reality of their part in the genocide, drowned the memory of what happened to the Jews among the stories of all the victims of Nazism and the war. However, some Jewish survivors had the courage to break the silence. In 1947, the Italian scientist Primo Levi published *If This Is a Man*, an account of his experience of the dehumanization process in Auschwitz, which took fifteen years to garner international resonance. In 1958, the Romanian-born American writer Elie Wiesel delivered his account of his nightmare in Auschwitz and Buchenwald where he was detained with his father. The novelist François Mauriac helped him find a French publisher and wrote an introduction. *Night* was published in 1960 in the United States.

Another pillar of holocaust literature is *The Diary of Anne Frank*, kept by Anne Frank while she was in hiding with her family during the Nazi occupation of the Netherlands, before being deported to the Bergen-Belsen concentration camp where she died. *The Diary* was first published in 1947.

Many historians wrote about the Shoah only as a marginal event. The Austro-American Raul Hilberg was one of the few to take it on directly, writing *The Destruction of the European Jews*, a masterful book that describes, in a thousand pages, how one of the most modern and industrialized societies in the world had mobilized all its resources to kill a whole people by rationalizing the economic and technical means. Raul Hilberg had enormous difficulty finding a publisher, including in the United States, where the book was rejected by three publishers before finally coming out in 1961 with Quadrangle in Chicago after a long odyssey. Even the political theorist Hannah Arendt advised the editor at Princeton University Press to reject the book, because, among other reasons, she did not agree with his argument that the Jews had learned from antiquity onward to avoid resistance in order to become better integrated into society, which explained, according to Hilberg, why they had agreed to collaborate with the Nazis on the *Judenräte*, the Nazi-established committees of Jewish leaders. The Israeli memorial for the Shoah, Yad Vashem, also rejected the manuscript because Hilberg refused to cut the passages on the *Judenräte*. In Germany, the publication of *The Destruction of the European Jews* did not occur until 1982, after twenty years of denial about this book whose surgically precise, step-by-step descriptions of the functioning of the Final Solution implicated many sectors of German society.

One manifestation of the force of denial in the postwar period was the incapacity of the Nazi leaders who had been tried to admit, even after their release, that they had been aware of the Final Solution. This was how Albert Speer, the former architect and minister of armaments and war production for Adolf Hitler who was condemned to twenty years in prison after the war, managed to convince many Germans that he had not known. At the Nuremberg Trials, he was the only Reich commander of his rank to be spared the death penalty because he had been one of the few to admit an official shared responsibility, without admitting he had been aware of the Holocaust. He had written, "The trial is necessary, there is overall responsibility, even in an authoritarian system." This partial confession was strategically motivated to save his skin, and it worked. In prison, he created his own myth, that of a "decent Nazi," expertly minimizing his role and expressing remorse to bolster his credibility, qualifying Hitler as a criminal and collaborating with historians and journalists. In truth, Albert Speer had millions of lives on his conscience. The Führer was wild about this handsome young architect, so refined and charming. Speer went on to draw monumental structures to satisfy his commander's taste, structures inspired by Greco-Roman architecture, but more massive and cold, designed to provoke admiration and fear. Later, Speer said, "For a large building project, I would have, like Faust, sold my soul. And I found my Mephistopheles." Together they came up with Germania, a megalomaniacal project that would convert Berlin into a "World Capital," harboring the largest assembly hall in the world, with an 180,000-person capacity, and a palace for the Führer where a visitor would have the impression he was entering the home of the "Lord of the World." To make room, Speer, who had been named general building inspector, started tearing down buildings, chasing Jews out of their apartments, and giving deportation lists to the Gestapo, while at the same time relying on forced laborers to deliver stone for his constructions. What's more, he authorized the expansion of Auschwitz and diverted a budget of 13.7 million Reichsmarks for the project.

The SS construction management documents submitted to him could not have been clearer: they specified the type of material needed to construct "fumigation facilities for special treatment," i.e., gas chambers, and "mortuaries with incinerators." In January 1942, the Führer promoted his protégé to minister of armaments and war production. Albert Speer's power continued to grow, and he was granted great leeway in the allocation of forced laborers, who numbered up to 8 million in 1944: slaves at his disposition, disposable once utilized. Under his direction, arms production attained levels that were unthinkable in the midst of war, under very difficult conditions, which brought him the admiration of the Führer. Without Speer, the war would have ended sooner, and millions of lives would have been spared. In a remarkable documentary by Marcel Ophuls titled *Memory of Justice* that came out in 1976, and which has unfortunately been somewhat forgotten, the director interviews Speer after his release from prison, and finally asks him the question burning on his lips: "Herr Speer, what did you know?" The former minister answers: "Though he [Hitler] never spoke directly about what happened to the Jews after 1942, the evidence was clear enough that one could have understood if one would have understood, and I should have understood if I had wanted to understand." In lying about the extent of his knowledge and sloughing off his own responsibility, Speer encouraged a whole nation to forget its guilt. If Hitler's closest friend, one of the most powerful ministers of the Reich, didn't know, how could other Germans have known?

Raul Hilberg estimates that hundreds of thousands of people were knowingly implicated in the logistical organization and execution of the Shoah: the highest-ranking leaders of the Reich, bureaucrats in almost every ministry, the staff of the extermination camps, the death squads or *Einsatzgruppen*, some parts of the Wehrmacht, the railway workers, the doctors, the experts from IG Farben, German businesses that exploited forced labor from the camps . . . As for the number of those who, without knowing the ends of their criminal participation, paved the way for the Final Solution, it is crushing, particularly in the heart of the administration and bureaucracy. "Whether in work, health, foreign affairs, justice, nutrition, economics, or education," writes the historian Dietmar Süss, "these ordinary civil servants were involved in the expropriation of Jews, exploitation of occupied territories, or in the anti-Semitic tax legislation," and through their participation contributed in "setting the extermination machinery in motion with German thoroughness."

Most other Germans could not have known that the Jews were gassed like insects after their "relocation." Even Karl Jaspers, a determined opponent of Nazism, has confirmed that he never heard anything about gas chambers before 1945. Even the Jews detained in concentration camps, who saw their comrades taken away on trains to the east and heard terrible rumors circulating among the prisoners, didn't believe what they were told. Survivors, both victims and executioners, have testified that the Jews did not know what was waiting for them as soon as the doors of those cattle cars opened onto a ramp where ferocious guards with whips drove them in the direction of barracks, shouting, "Quick! Double time!" In *Shoah*, Claude Lanzmann's immense documentary, a witness who was a hairdresser remembers how, when he was assigned to cut the hair of women who hadn't been gassed, he recognized some from the Polish village where he was born. "When they saw me they started asking me: 'Abe this and Abe that, what are you doing here, what's going to happen to us?' What could you tell them? What could you tell? A friend of mine, he worked as a barber—he was a good barber in my hometown—when his wife and his sister . . . came into the gas chamber." The hairdresser stops for a long moment, overcome with emotion. "It is too hard," he admits, before going on with the director's encouragement. "They could not tell . . . because behind them was the German Nazis, the SS men, they knew the minute they will say a word, not only the wife and the women, which are dead already, but also they will share the same part with them. But in a way, they tried to do the best for them, to stay with them a second longer, a minute longer, just to hug them, just to kiss them, because they knew they will never see them again." Not divulging the secret was the unspoken condition of the smooth functioning of the Final Solution. Another victim explains in the film, "The new arrivals were supposed to be kept orderly and without panic marching into the gas chambers. Especially the panic was dangerous for women with small children. So it was important for the Nazis that none of us give some sort of message which could cause a panic, even in the last moment. And anybody who tried to get in touch with the newcomers was either clubbed to death or taken behind the wagon and shot. Because if a panic would have broken out, a massacre would have taken place on the spot, on the ramp. It would already be a hitch in the machinery. You can't bring in the next transport with dead bodies and blood around."

This lack of knowledge about the precise objective of the Jewish deportations doesn't absolve the majority of the German people of their guilt in letting their neighbors, their colleagues, and the business owners on their street be persecuted and pillaged, in sometimes participating, and in witnessing the deportations without protest. "For while the German people were not informed of all Nazi crimes and were even deliberately kept ignorant of their exact nature, the Nazis had seen to it that every German knew some horrible story to be true," wrote Hannah Arendt, "and he did not need a detailed knowledge of all the horrors committed in his name to realize that he had been made accomplice to unspeakable crimes." Anyone who was even moderately attentive to Hitler's declarations must have wondered how far he would go where the Jews were concerned. On January 30, 1939, during a speech on the anniversary of his seizure of power, he pronounced this dark sentence: "Today I want to be a prophet again: If international financial Jewry inside and outside of Europe succeeds in once again overthrowing the people in a world war, the result will not be the Bolshevization of the earth and thus the victory of Judaism, but the annihilation of the Jewish race in Europe."

If conceiving of Auschwitz was difficult, it was still impossible to have "seen nothing, heard nothing," and for some, "done nothing," as my grandparents' generation claimed until their deaths.

My father recently toured the area around his parents' apartment building in Mannheim, and discovered a single *Solperstein*, those little brass squares inscribed with the names of Nazi victims that have been pressed into the sidewalks in front of their former homes in Germany and elsewhere in Europe. Apparently, very few Jews lived in Lydia and Karl Schwarz's neighborhood, but the community in Mannheim was one of the largest in the region, and it wasn't isolated in a ghetto, but assimilated and dispersed throughout the city like any other group of citizens. All they had to do was cross the nearby Neckar River to reach the vast pedestrian zone bordered with shops at the city center, and they would have seen the front windows of Jewish stores decorated with Stars of David. My grandparents must have been aware of the ever-present anti-Semitic propaganda. How could they not have heard about this or that doctor, lawyer, or civil servant, thrown out on the street after years of loyal service? Or how a mother had suddenly watched her child's school toss out an entire segment of the student body, excluded for being Jewish?

❀   ❀   ❀

Ingrid remembers that one day when she was with her mother, they ran into a man with a yellow star on his clothing, a measure inspired by the Middle Ages that the Third Reich instated after September 1941 to distinguish and humiliate the Jews. "I asked her, 'Mom, what sign is that man wearing?' I asked her the question several times, and she finally said, 'It's not important.' But what else could she have said to a little girl?" As for Karl Schwarz, he was more informed about the persecutions, as he had made several trips with Julius Löbmann just at the moment when the Jews faced a rapidly deteriorating situation. He had to have seen the aftermath of *Kristallnacht*, and neither Oma nor anyone else could have missed the remains of the torched synagogue in the middle of the city center, near the main market.

On October 22, 1940, the population should have had a surge of empathy, compassion, and revolt when approximately two thousand Jews from Mannheim were torn from their homes, assembled in various rallying points in the city, and transferred on foot and by bus to the station to be deported. Some crossed the city center in a cortege under the watching eyes of the inhabitants, who, at the sight of these families, including many elderly, maintaining a remarkable dignity while being chased out of their own municipality, should have intervened, should have asked the police: by what right are you taking away our comrade, with whom we fought in the First World War? Our brother in the eyes of God? Our hairdresser, to whom we confessed all our troubles, our friend from university, our neighbors whose children played with our kids, or our tailor who fashioned our outfits for three generations? But nothing like that happened. According to Jewish witnesses: "Some people applauded, others looked on, and a few turned away, visibly ashamed."

To prepare the general population beforehand, the anti-Semitic propaganda film *Jud Süss* by Veit Harlan had been screened in movie theaters. The story follows a Jew who insidiously makes himself head of state thanks to a predatory lending trap, succeeds in imposing the domination of Jews over Christians, and rapes a young Christian woman, who kills herself. This film certainly created a stir. But not enough to explain the total abdication of humanity before the deportation of Mannheim's Jews along with 4,500 other Jews from southwestern Germany—the first of its scale in the Reich—which served as a test to gauge the reaction of other citizens. If there had been numerous protestors, if the prominent citizens of the city or the clergy had spoken up, perhaps Adolf Hitler would have stepped back, as he did with the program for euthanizing disabled people. In his report, Reinhard Heydrich, the chief of the RSHA, the Main Security Office in the Reich, wrote that the operation had been handled "smoothly and without incident."

I found two photos in the archive of that black day for Mannheim. In one of them, you can see a group of some twenty Jews waiting in front of an empty bus, sitting on suitcases or standing with blankets folded over their arms, elegantly dressed, the men in three-piece suits, overcoats, and felt hats, the women in long dark coats with matching scarves, some wearing cloche hats. In another image, a portly policeman in front of a brick wall seems to be explaining the procedure to three men and three women standing in single file next to him, as if waiting their turn. The last man in line is hidden a bit behind the others, his eyes fixed on the lens with an alarmed look. His mouth seems poised to call upon the viewers of the photo for help. I tried to find Julius and Siegmund Löbmann in these photos, since they were also deported that day with their loved ones, but what's the point—I don't know what they look like. Aside from the portrait of the three sisters, Mathilde, Irma, and Sophie, and a snapshot of little Franz, one of the children of Izieu, I never found any photos of this vanished family's faces.

❋   ❋   ❋

I don't know if my grandparents saw the Jews being led to the rallying points, then to the station, but when Karl Schwarz went to work that morning, when he stepped out for lunch, and when Lydia went out to take her little four-year-old girl for a stroll, didn't they feel the tension in the air, that heaviness on the faces of passersby, who were more hurried than usual? In the evening, didn't they talk about the roundup over dinner or with their neighbors on Chamissostrasse? Didn't it come up the next morning, with colleagues, shopkeepers, or friends? This episode probably passed in silence, like a bad dream you forget moments after you wake. For a long time, I was stuck on that date, October 22, trying to understand if it had actually been possible to intervene, and if it wasn't unjust to judge my grandparents, since I myself hadn't lived through the dictatorship. Then I read an arresting passage in Christiane Fritsche's book, where I understood that the key date for measuring the guilt of Mannheim's *Mitläufer* wasn't October 22, but just after.

The Jews had barely been deported when their apartments were sealed. After the first raids on the city of Mannheim, on December 16, 1940, it was decided that these homes would be used to shelter those who had lost their housing during the bombing. The idea was to leave them the minimum—a few furnishings, mattresses, and linens—and to sell the rest at auction. Dishes, porcelain, rugs, books, silver, furniture—these sales were announced in the paper, and it was clear that they were goods from Jewish households. The announcement wouldn't hesitate to occasionally specify: "Household items from non-Aryan property." What made these auctions truly nauseating was that most of them took place in the original apartments, so that the buyers were acutely aware of the people who had once owned these belongings. Considering the massive size of their furnishings, my grandparents must have also acquired their pieces on the spot. Did they know the former owners? Probably not, but I imagine at least Opa, entering these vestibules like thieves, intruding into these homes that had been abandoned in the haste of a last-minute departure, where there might still have been laundry on the line, coffee cups on the kitchen table, and a few hairs in the shower drain. At the sight of a child's bedroom strewn with toys and little shoes waiting for the return of their young owner, or at the family photos still on the wall, existences that were savagely interrupted—how is it possible that these scenes didn't grab them by the throat and force them to refrain from buying anything? Greed and indulgence made them all ruthless. Observers described the mood across the country: a real gold rush atmosphere. Joseph Goebbels said that his compatriots plunged "like vultures on the warm crumbs of the Jews." Some asked the authorities to reserve this or that piece they had spotted, sometimes even before its owner had been deported.

This behavior seems crucially important to me, because in my opinion it discredits the principal excuse used by that generation—of not knowing anything about the eventual fate of the Jews. Those who bought valuables in this medieval atmosphere of redistributing the fruits of pillage—weren't they sure that the owners would either never return, or would never be in a position to reclaim them, because they were dead or near death?

On the train that left Mannheim on October 22, 1940, there was profound anxiety among the Jews who didn't know where they were being deported. A witness described the great relief the passengers felt when they realized the convoy was headed west and not toward the east, a destination that portended nothing good. They didn't know that Vichy France had, in turn, succumbed to the hysteria of anti-Semitic laws. After a three-day journey, the deported people reached the foot of the Pyrenees, arriving at the

Gurs internment camp. Like many internment camps in France, Gurs was originally set up for refugees from the Spanish Civil War, then, at the start of the Second World War, indiscriminately filled with German anti-Nazis or pro-Nazis living in France, along with prisoners of war. Following the French-German armistice, these camps were filled with Jews, first coming from abroad, then also from France. Certainly, in many cases, the Germans forced the French to make space in these camps for Jews, despite the fact that most of them were located in the free zone where they didn't have jurisdiction. But in the end Vichy cooperated entirely, administering many of them, including Gurs, one of the largest internment camps where 20,000 European Jews were detained under catastrophic conditions that would lead to the death of at least a thousand prisoners.

The persecution of Jews and their deportation to death camps is Vichy's greatest shame. No other facets of the occupation have unleashed as much passion, questioning, wounds, debates, and attempts to relativize as this one. Nothing is more unbearable than what Robert Paxton revealed: that the immense majority of the 76,000 deported Jews were arrested by the French military and civilian police, and that in many cases, the French authorities delivered more Jews, and especially more Jewish children, than the Germans had asked for.

My grandfather Lucien is no longer here to give his account. Besides the story of hiding weapons under the noses of the Germans, nothing else filtered through the two generations between us. Of course, he was nothing but a minuscule pawn of the regime, posted in a forgotten hole in the south of Burgundy. I still wanted to go see the little hilltop village of Mont-Saint-Vincent. It unveils itself slowly as you come around a series of hairpin turns, suddenly appearing and bowling you over with its charm—the stone houses where wildflowers sprout, the Romanesque church, and the medieval ramparts that offer a panoramic view of the surrounding valleys. The police station is still there, at least that's what the letters indicate in black paint on a large pale building near the parking lot. What was there for police to do in this isolated place during the occupation? The answer lies at the back of the hillside to the north of the village. That was where the line of demarcation passed between the free zone, where Mont-Saint-Vincent was located, and the occupied zone. That was where people in hiding, like Jews and members of the resistance, fled from the northern zone. Did my grandfather arrest them? Did he send them back the other way and deliver them to the Germans? Did he fire on the men who ran? I'll never know, but my mother and my uncle remember that after the war, their father would say that he looked the other way whenever he could. And from what I know of him, I'm inclined to believe it.

Lucien was born on an isolated farm in the Jura, where he walked two hours a day to go to school, and God knows the winters are harsh on those snowy, high plateaus where the wind tears at your face. When he got home, heavy chores awaited him, chopping wood, milking cows, breaking his back in the fields before going to bed after a meager supper, with an orange for dessert at Christmas. But early on, my grandfather had a dream, the USSR, that "land of plenty" he spoke to his children about, a country where comrades would not allow anyone to be at the bottom of the ladder, a sweet illusion that kept him going as he studied for his diploma at the end of strenuous days, so that he could become a police officer, the best fate a kid of his standing could hope for. Then he met Jeanne. She fell for this very tall, thin man with a haughty bearing who looked sharp in his uniform, and he was taken by this little woman, as tall as his chest, so elegant in the impeccable outfits that she created herself, her bag always matching her shoes. They were married a year after the armistice, relieved, like most French people, that the war was over, because otherwise my grandfather would probably have been drafted. Then Lucien was moved to Mont-Saint-Vincent, and Jeanne became pregnant with my mother in the summer of 1942.

My French grandparents, Jeanne and Lucien, in 1942,
at their wedding in Chazelles, near Lyon.

This happy event coincided with a sinister episode in the region. On July 13 and 14, about seven miles away at Montceau-les-Mines, the town closest to the village, thirty-four Jews (a third of the community) were arrested and deported. I found a priceless study, *La Tragédie des juifs montcelliens* (The Tragedy of the Jews of Montceau), written by Georges Legras and Roger Marchandeau, who questioned witnesses. Montceau-les-Mines is located on the other side of the line of demarcation, in the zone occupied by the Germans, but the testimonies are unambiguous: those who conducted the arrests were French police officers. The Jews must have been woefully surprised to receive such treatment from men they knew well. They had tailored their uniforms, given their wives advice in the hardware store, or dealt cards to them when they played together at the bistro. The group included a few German Jews who had fled Nazi persecution, but they were mainly Polish miners, some of whom had arrived in the twenties and thirties, and others at the end of the nineteenth century, chased out by poverty and pogroms in their country. The oldest among them had perhaps benefited from the 1927 naturalization law, which expanded the right to French nationality, a dream for many immigrants who hoped to become French. Sarah Pulvermacher, a survivor of the raids in Montceau-les-Mines who was born in France, confessed to the authors of the above study that her parents "would have been terribly proud to obtain their French citizenship" and described how they did everything to behave like French people. They didn't think to flee because they "didn't suspect anything." Many were infinitely grateful to France for welcoming them, and continued to perceive it as the country of the rights of man, which would never renege on its promise to protect them from discrimination. According to accounts, law enforcement acted in broad daylight, tearing sick women from their beds, arresting men at work in front of their colleagues, handcuffing anyone who was reluctant as if they were criminals, and abandoning children in distress, leaving them without their parents. At the station, a train awaited the victims, cattle cars with straw on the floor and little windows fortified with bars. Agents from the local police escorted the convoy as far as the transit camp in Pithiviers, and from there they were deported directly to Auschwitz on convoy number 6, which departed on July 17, at 6:15 in the morning, with 928 detainees on board, mainly from Poland and Russia. The convoy, which was the first to transport so many women and children, was escorted to the border by French gendarmes who must have heard the cries of the passengers, deprived of water and food. When they slid the wagon doors shut for their departure, the last image they had was of the faces of Jewish men, women, and children consumed with fear, wearing the yellow star, their bodies compressed in a tight space like livestock, work uniforms in their bags so that they could officially become slaves of the Reich, far away in the east where the British media had already been reporting that the Germans were shooting Jews by the tens of thousands. That sight and this information should have been enough to quickly put an end to any French collaboration.

But the raids multiplied. Moïse and Jacqueline, friends of my parents of Polish origin but raised in France, lived through this nightmare. On the night of July 15 and 16, 1942, a neighbor who was a police officer came to warn Moïse's family in Paris. "He told us to get out of there, tomorrow we're arresting all the Jews," Moïse remembers. "My mother answered him, 'You're joking, there's a curfew, if we go out the Germans will fire on us!'" It was the night before the largest roundup of Jews in France, a raid named for the Vélodrome d'Hiver, or Vel d'Hiv, where the detainees were held. On July 16, at noon, the French police knocked on the door. "I was with my little brother, my mother, and my grandmother. Of course, we didn't answer the door. I heard them say, 'No big deal, we'll come back to get them in a couple hours, first we'll go have a bite to eat.' The lunch hour is sacred in France! It saved us." Moïse and his family took refuge in the home of a neighbor who had gone to live with her daughter and had left them a key. "We couldn't make any noise, or flush the toilet, since the apartment was supposed to be empty. The cops came back, they went to our house and broke down the doors, we could hear them. I remember, it was a Thursday, it was very hot." For two days, they didn't

move. "We waited until Saturday, the day when the concierge went
to the market. The cops had promised her five hundred francs a
head, so you can bet she'd have denounced us. Especially since she
was a notorious anti-Semite." Thanks to the help of a Communist,
the family managed to sneak out of the apartment building. That
same night, Moïse and his brother were on a train to Normandy.
"My mother couldn't go, the stations were under surveillance, but
for the children, it was less risky. We didn't know if someday we
would see her again." During the trip, German officials checked
the passports of the passengers twice, but they weren't interested
in the two brothers. "It was Vichy that wanted to deport kids, the
Reich couldn't have cared less about it at the time." For a month
after the raid, Moïse began to wet the bed again, at the age of
eleven. "You can't master it, that kind of fear. You have to realize,
I was an innocent, timid little boy, and the world collapsed that
day." His wife Jacqueline's story is miraculous. Only a few days
before the Vel d'Hiv roundup, she left in a truck with her little
sister and her mother to join her father, who had taken refuge in
Lyon. "We hid with two other guys down inside the vehicle at the
level of the batteries, in a sort of case with some straw. At the line
of demarcation, they searched the truck with dogs who sniffed
everything. We were in our hiding place, but they didn't find us
because the sulfuric acid in the batteries threw them off the scent.
Once they left with their dogs, I started throwing up. There were
smugglers who betrayed the guys. You know things like this . . .
they change your life. I was nine years old."

During the Vel d'Hiv roundup, more than 13,000 Jews, a third
of whom were children, were arrested in Paris and the surrounding
areas with the involvement of 6,000 agents of the French police.
Eight thousand detainees were held under French surveillance at
the Vélodrome d'Hiver for five days in horrible heat and stench
with a single source of water. Adolf Eichmann had demanded an
initial contingent of 40,000 Jews from France, but the Reich didn't

have enough personnel in the country and got Vichy to make the arrests using the French police. The Paris Prefecture turned over 27,000 registered addresses of "stateless Jews" living in the region. Entire families were deported to transit camps, though the Germans hadn't asked for children younger than sixteen. It was Pierre Laval, Vichy's second in command, who wanted to get rid of them, because he didn't want to burden France with future orphans. The pastor Marc Boegner intervened, asking him to let French families adopt the children, but to no avail. Terrible scenes took place in the camps as they tore children from their parents, deporting the adults first, while they waited for Eichmann's response. Three thousand children remained without their parents, plunged into terrible mental and material distress, before being deported as soon as Berlin gave the green light. None survived.

The Vichy chief of police, René Bousquet, had negotiated with the Germans to limit the arrests of French Jews and had proposed to deliver 10,000 foreign Jews from the free zone in compensation. This so-called protection of French Jews is an excuse some French people still brandish in defense of Vichy. But what difference does it make? To make that argument is to claim that human lives do not matter, or that some are worth more than others. It also avoids the essential point: without the massive mobilization of French police and corresponding access to administrative documents, the Germans would never have been able to deport 76,000 Jews so quickly. The argument that French Jews were protected is even more truncated because, in truth, Vichy delivered children born in *France* to foreign parents as well as *French* people whom they'd taken care to denaturalize beforehand. Moïse's family experienced this humiliation. In May 1940, as the Germans swooped down on France, a French policeman knocked on the door of Moïse's home with a naturalization certificate in one hand and his father's draft papers in the other. "My mother said to the man, 'What do you mean by this, he didn't wait for naturalization to go to war, he volunteered.'" He was bitterly rewarded: on July 20, 1942, the Vichy regime denaturalized Moïse's whole family, along with many other Jews who soon became "stateless" so that they could be deported more easily than Jews who were "French." What a blow for these naturalized citizens. The minister of justice, Raphaël Alibert, justified it this way: "Foreigners must not forget that the quality of Frenchness has to be earned." In spring 1941, like many "stateless" Jews, Moïse's father received an order asking him to present himself at the nearby police station, to "normalize" his situation. "I remember all the men in the family had a meeting. Some said, 'Don't go, it's a fool's errand.' Other's said, 'But no, look, it's the French government that's calling us in, not the Germans.' But Vichy had already discredited itself with a whole series of anti-Semitic measures. My father didn't go, and entered the resistance instead." The family no longer saw him at home, until one day, when he came undercover to hug them. Someone must have seen him and denounced him. Once the police realized that he was a Jew in addition to being a member of the resistance, they sent him to Auschwitz.

Jacqueline's father received the same notice, but he did present himself, trusting the French authorities. "My sister and I were little, so my mother brought us to the police station while Papa went in. They said, 'Please, Mesdames, go prepare a little suitcase for your men with toiletries and a change of clothes.' We went home to pack a small suitcase and bring it to him." The next day, her father was interned at the Beaune-la-Rolande camp. One day, while he was working in the camp administration, he saw lists handed out announcing the start of deportations to Auschwitz. With a friend in the resistance, he convinced a farmer who cleaned the camp to get them out in his vehicle, where they hid under a pile of garbage. They managed to get to Lyon, where they joined the armed resistance, participating in attacks against the Germans.

For a while, the French population seemed indifferent to the raids that began in 1940. But the Vel d'Hiv roundup moved public opinion because it was so large and because it threatened French Jews and foreigners alike. A police report states: "Though the French population, as a whole and in general, is relatively anti-Semitic, it has not judged these measures less harshly, and calls them inhumane." But no one intervened when the buses full of Jews wearing their yellow stars crossed Paris in broad daylight to reach the Vélodrome. At Pithiviers and at Beaune-la-Rolande, where the transit camps were located, the prefect noted, "for the most part, the inhabitants watch with indifference as the detainee convoys pass." Nonetheless, many representatives of the Church openly expressed their indignation, including during mass. The episcopacy protested officially, and religious and charitable institutions came together to protect Jews and support Jewish organizations. The resistance, which included Jews, but also a certain number of brave citizens, organized to hide and help the fugitives. And so Moïse and his brother were able to survive in a village in Normandy for two years, thanks to a nurturing mother who took care of orphans and let the brothers pass for her usual boarders. The local police also supported her and would warn the orphanage when the authorities announced an inspection. "Agents would come and tell the woman, 'You know, tomorrow it would be better if the little new arrivals went to gather wood in the forest so that no one sees them . . .'" Moïse's wife, Jacqueline, who was the only one in her class to wear the yellow star, remembers that her teacher was very kind to her and even offered to let her stay with her sister in the teacher's studio. "They weren't all bastards," they say. There were even heroes. Like Édouard Vigneron, head of the immigration authorities at the Nancy police station, who, with his men, organized the escape of 350 Jews by train, giving them passes to reach the free zone. Édouard Vigneron was imprisoned for several months, released, and then removed from his post.

❖   ❖   ❖

On October 9, 1942, a new wave of arrests carried off seventeen
Jews from Montceau-les-Mines. This time they were also looking
for children, even going into the school if necessary. And they did
this knowing something of the fate that awaited the Jews, since the
police who had escorted the July convoy to the transit camp must
have described what they saw and heard. After being transferred
to Drancy, the new victims left for Auschwitz on November 6
with convoy number 42. Other members of the community had
succeeded in hiding or escaping, but ten of them were ultimately
arrested. Of the deported, only four returned from the camps alive.
To escape the raid, the Jews of Montceau-les-Mines tried to flee
the occupied zone by sneaking across the line of demarcation, at
the precise spot where my grandfather was stationed. Did Lucien
help them or arrest them? He must have known that if he sent
them back, they would go directly to a transit camp with unenviable
living conditions, before being deported toward dark prospects in
the east. I couldn't find any trace of raids in Mont-Saint-Vincent,
probably because there were no Jews in that little village, with the
exception of one fugitive, Georges Levy, the proprietor of the big
hardware store on the rue Carnot in Montceau-les-Mines, who took
refuge in the free zone, in Mont-Saint-Vincent, where he owned
a house. He was deported to Auschwitz on March 7, 1944, after
being arrested at his home. By whom? By the local police? The
Germans? And why so late? The whole village, including the police
force, must have known that Georges Levy was a Jew, and they had
probably protected him. But there must have been a traitor among
them. The archives specify that Georges Levy was "denounced."

If Moïse and Jacqueline were rescued, it was mainly because both
of their fathers were in the resistance and could benefit from their
impressive clandestine networks. And even if, outside of those
circles, many French people demonstrated a brave solidarity with

the Jews, there were not enough of them. The sudden momentum that had allowed Bulgarian citizens to blockade the deportation of Jews from their country, or that had caused Italian bureaucrats to categorically refuse to deliver the Jews from their zone, was missing. What would a French officer risk by disobeying anti-Semitic orders? This telegram sent out before the raids by a regional prefect gives an idea: "negligence in completing" the roundups "will result in immediate suspension." There was no question of being executed, or going to prison, or being fined. But you could lose your job or your chances at a career. There were also more severe directives, like those from René Bousquet, who planned the administrative internment of "people whose acts or attitudes hinder the execution of my orders for consolidating Israelites." He also asked people to "indicate the bureaucrats whose indiscretion, passiveness, or bad intentions would have complicated your task." But these orders were rarely followed to the letter.

Perhaps if the French population had reacted as soon as the persecutions against Jews began, Vichy would not have resorted to murder. But it remained stony for too long, not only in the face of the raids on foreign Jews, but also regarding a whole series of anti-Semitic laws that concerned French Jews, laws Vichy initiated on its own. There was the introduction of numerous clauses to limit the presence of Jews in multiple fields; the banning of Jews from elected positions, from occupying leadership roles in civil service, the justice system, and the army, and from practicing activities that influenced cultural life. Neither did anyone protest when Vichy began the process of Aryanizing Jewish assets; the state had no problem with stealing valuables, cash, precious metals, jewels, and works of art from Jews during their arrest. Other profiteers included buyers who drove the prices down, competitors who got rid of their rivals, not to mention the lawyers, auctioneers, gallerists, collectors, and museums implicated in this pillage. And there are also accounts of neighbors who came into the apartments of the deported to rifle through the cabinets once they had gone.

These anti-Jewish measures didn't only arouse indifference; they were sometimes accepted as necessary for the good of society. Robert Paxton estimates that in French society, like elsewhere in Europe, the dominant idea before the war was that a Jewish "question" existed that needed to be solved, and this was well before the rise of the Third Reich. In the last decades of the nineteenth century, French media and publishing were among the most virulently anti-Jewish in Europe. French anti-Semitism culminated in the Dreyfus affair, named after a Jewish captain from the French army who was thrown in jail for supposedly having turned over documents to the Germans, though the evidence pointed to another man. The affair caused a scandal, and numerous prominent people joined the power struggle between Dreyfusards and anti-Dreyfusards. The first camp included the writers Marcel Proust and Emile Zola, and the second camp included nationalist men of letters like Maurice Barrès and, above all, Charles Maurras, the future figurehead of the extreme-right group Action Française.

Unlike the Nazis, Vichy didn't plan to murder Jews as a solution and was reluctant to deport them. Pétain successfully blocked the establishment of the yellow star in the free zone, and until summer 1943, Pierre Laval stubbornly resisted German pressure to rescind the French citizenship of all Jews who had obtained it since 1933, to facilitate their deportation. But the regime was no less anti-Semitic, and by clinging to the image of French independence from the Germans, they ended up organizing a large part of the occupier's sinister agenda themselves.

Thanks to the resistance's help, Moïse's mother moved from one safe house to another and managed to escape deportation. His father was not so lucky. Though he managed to survive working like a beast for a cement-making business at Auschwitz, he was sent on a death march in January 1945 as the Allies approached. He died on the chaotic roads at the end of the war, while the SS themselves were fleeing. "I think he was free when he died," Moïse says. At the liberation, his mother went to the prefecture. "She said: 'I want my French nationality reinstated.' The boys told her: 'Oh, that's going to take a while, it's better to apply as a new citizen; with your record of serving in the resistance, that should be easy.' She said, 'No, I want to be reinstated, so that they recognize the error, the mistake . . .' All of a sudden the functionaries started dragging their feet." Officially, Moïse and his mother have been French only since 1947. They have not received any pension or compensation from the French government, since they were considered "stateless" when the events took place. They had to wait for reparations from the Germans, who compensated the stateless Jews in France.

After the war, there were very few Jewish survivors to bear witness, since only 2,500 people, or 3 percent of the deported, had returned from the camps. The stories of the political prisoners—out of 85,000 deported, 60 percent of them had survived—eclipsed the Jews, and people listened more willingly to heroic tales that confirmed their idea of a resistant France than to accounts from victims of racial persecution. Yet the experience was completely different, since in general, political prisoners had been through the ordeal of detention camps, but they had not lived through the horrors Jews had endured in the extermination camps. The survivors of hell, phantoms emptied of everything, preferred to keep silent so as not to be marginalized in a society that, by the look of things, had chosen to move on. Even the very celebrated documentary by Alain Resnais, *Night and Fog*, about the Nazi camps manages to mention only once the word *Jew*, lost in a long list of victims.

This amnesia was shared by the entire international community. The British and American attitude toward the distress of Europe's Jews during the war didn't encourage them to refresh their memories. Once they were informed of the genocide, they refrained from making it a reason to justify their war against Hitler. After all, their societies were not exempt from anti-Semitism. In May 1944, Jewish representatives had asked them to bomb the railways linking Budapest to Auschwitz to stop the deportations of Hungarian Jews and to destroy the gas chambers and crematoriums at Auschwitz. The Allies, who had precise photos of the camp, replied that their planes were all mobilized for priority war efforts. One argument was that they were afraid of killing detainees. But for the American historian Walter Laqueur, the opposite is true: "hundreds of thousands of lives could have been saved." Neither did the Soviets intervene to help the Jews or the resistance. During the insurrection by the Polish resistance in Warsaw in August 1944, which also included Jews, the Red Army was at the gates of the city, but it did nothing to aid the rebels.

As astonishing as it seems, what opened repression's floodgates in Europe and the United States was an American television series called *Holocaust*, by Marvin J. Chomsky and Gerald Green, which aired in 1978 in America. It's the story of a Jewish family, the Weisses, who fall victim to the crimes of the Third Reich one after another, and of a Nazi couple, the Dorfs. The husband, Erik Dorf, is initially reluctant to participate in National Socialism, but he is pushed by his wife, who eagerly wants to climb the social ladder. He joins the SS, where he soon excels at his new duties. Like the Weisses, Erik Dorf ends up at Auschwitz, but on the side of the executioners.

The history of these individual dramas suddenly made the unimaginable imaginable for the general public, and unleashed an international upheaval of collective conscience. In the United States, where one in every two Americans watched the series, plans were announced for a vast memorial museum in Washington, D.C., with a research center, and money flowed in from every quarter to finance the construction. Conferences and exhibitions proliferated on the topic.

In 1979, the *Holocaust* series was released in Europe. In West Germany, where one third of the population, or 20 million people, watched it, the citizens were shocked and angry, accusing the powers that be of not fulfilling their task of commemoration. This ire was combined with a certain shame, the shame of neglecting a monstrous crime though its memory had always been within reach. After each episode of *Holocaust* aired, thousands upon thousands of people called the television station, where a panel of historians would lend their expertise and respond to questions from viewers. The switchboards were overwhelmed by urgent questions from dumbfounded, incredulous citizens, some in tears and others indignant: "How could people have let such things happen?" After a poll, 65 percent said they were "shocked," 45 percent "ashamed," and 81 percent confirmed that the broadcast had provoked discussions with the people around them. *Holocaust* was selected as the "German word of the year" by the German Language Society. Three months after the series came out, the Bundestag decided to make murder and the crime of genocide subject to no statute of limitations. A short time later, in 1982, Raul Hilberg's monumental book *The Destruction of the European Jews* finally came out in Germany. It was translated into French in 1988, into Italian in 1999, and into Spanish in 2005. It became an essential reference.

In France, which harbors the largest Jewish community in Europe, it was mainly a documentary film released in 1985 that rattled consciences in addition to the series *Holocaust*. *Shoah*, a monumental, ten-hour-long film by Claude Lanzmann, was the culmination of twelve years of work. Lanzmann went to the ends of the earth to research the last survivors, who had been silent for so long and had finally begun to speak. Through their stories, he reconstituted the Final Solution, step by step.

I have seen *Shoah* twice, but always in small pieces, such is the excruciating intensity of the accounts. I will never forget the melodious voice of the man who sings in front of the camera, as the Nazis asked him to as a child, to entertain them while his family, and his entire village, were dying nearby in trucks filled with gas. Nor the story of the detainee from Treblinka who describes how, while he unearthed from common graves naked corpses that the Nazis wanted to burn on enormous pyres, he recognized his loved ones amid the mass of decomposing bodies. One of the greatest distinctions of the film is that thanks to descriptions cross-referenced with places, people, methods, dates, and procedures, it was able to prove, in the face of Holocaust deniers, that the industrial organization for the massive extermination of Europe's Jews in gas chambers and trucks had truly existed. In that regard, one of the key witnesses in *Shoah* is SS Sergeant Franz Suchomel, who was formerly stationed at Treblinka and is one of the rare members of the SS to have voluntarily described the functioning of the camp with extreme precision, using a large map on the wall. When he arrived in August 1942, the gas chambers at Treblinka were running at the height of efficiency: "In two hours, in two and a half hours, everything was over from arriving to dying, a whole train," he explains. "The train cars came all at once, and more and more people kept arriving, you understand? There were already people, Jews, waiting for two days, because the small gas chambers could not yet process them, they were in operation day and night." The men came first, the women had to wait, naked, in summer and in winter, at minus 15 degrees. "They heard the engines of the gas chambers, maybe they also heard the people in the gas chambers screaming and praying, and when they stood there, the fear of death came over them."

X

The Pact

I never knew Opa. He collapsed on September 20, 1970, while he was walking in the center of Mannheim, felled by a heart attack at the age of sixty-seven. "My father knew that at the end of the year, he would have to give up the land that his business occupied, since it belonged to the city," my aunt Ingrid says. "Everything was going to be destroyed to revitalize the neighborhood. My mother said to him, 'It's not so bad, at your age, you've already worked long enough!' But I think it weighed on his soul to see that business disappear when he'd worked himself to death for it: the thought ended up killing him." In December 1970, the buildings that made up Schwarz & Co. were demolished, and its history of misfortune vanished beneath the asphalt of a brand-new road, until I undertook the process of reassembling the debris of its story with the story of my grandfather. For a long time, all I had known of him was from the portraits that hung on the apartment wall in Mannheim where he appears at age 60, his hair turned completely white, with thick, black, rectangular glasses that give him a harsh air.

Today, I have the impression of knowing him better. My aunt Ingrid always defended him when I interviewed her, excusing his actions and exaggerating his worries, as if she feared that I would tarnish his memory. As for my father, he has a very different image of Karl Schwarz: "On a material level, he made sure that we didn't want for anything, but nonetheless, he wasn't a role model for me," he confesses. "He didn't try to be close to me. Everything I learned, I learned without him. He didn't try to teach me about life." My aunt says that in truth, her father was proud of his son, proud that he had earned his university degree.

If I asked her about her parents' Nazi past, Ingrid would say: "We can't put ourselves in the shoes of people who lived in an era we didn't experience, when everything was so different." She didn't confront her parents, probably held back by her empathy for them in the difficult postwar context, and the blind respect that young people once had for parental authority. When my father, who was seven years younger than Ingrid, entered the heyday of his adolescence, the family's financial situation had eased, giving him free rein for other ideas. His schooling at the Gymnasium, his reading, and his character all created favorable conditions for the emergence of a critical spirit, allowing him to consider his parents' position from another angle. "I said to them, 'What bothers me isn't that you gave the salute, because who knows, perhaps I would have done the same, out of enthusiasm or cowardice. What bothers me is that even after the revelation that this regime committed the worst crimes imaginable, you still won't condemn it clearly.'"

The divergence between brother and sister might also be due to the fact that, unlike Volker, my aunt was born in 1936 and has a clear memory of the terror of the bombardments in Mannheim, the family's flight to the countryside, and their traumatic return to a devastated city peopled by wandering ghosts. Much more than her brother, who was only a child, she was marked by the long conflict between her father and Julius Löbmann, which she perceived, through the filter of daughterly love, as an injustice to her family.

* * *

As I researched this book, it reinforced my idea that without the more or less active support of the *Mitläufer*, Nazi Germany could not have descended so far into chaos and crime. A complex question kept nagging at me. In what sense was it possible for ordinary men and women like my grandparents to refuse to be Nazis under the Third Reich? To say no without being the stuff of legends and heroes? Without risking their lives or being sent to a camp?

The Nazi regime was two-pronged—on the one side, it deployed a seduction arsenal to solicit public admiration and undying loyalty, and on the other it used a formidable system of repression to create fear and discourage all dissidence. I imagine that it was easy to be intimidated by the SA's violence, or by the specter of the Communists and social democrats who were murdered and sent to concentration camps. During the war, as the Reich began to show signs of weakness, the sanctions became much harsher. The special courts and local hearings became antechambers to death, where capital punishment was issued with a word, in a terrified atmosphere of paranoia and denunciation. For those who had the misfortune to be tried before a fanatical judge, a defeatist remark, even spoken in a small circle, could warrant the death penalty, as could stealing a few sickly chickens, if it was defined as "sabotage." Between 1940 and the surrender, 16,000 German citizens were condemned to death.

But before the war, the population had more room to maneuver. Belonging to a Nazi organization was preferable if you wanted to speed up your career, but not obligatory. Preferring to say "good morning" over the Hitler salute, the daily symbol of loyalty to the Führer that the Nazi Party tried to impose, or even criticizing the regime, generally had few consequences unless you were a public figure. There's a photo taken in 1936 at the christening of a boat in Hamburg, with Adolf Hitler present, where, in the middle of a crowd of people with raised hands, you can see a man conspicuously crossing his arms. This brave gesture was not reprimanded.

(But in 1938 the same man was condemned to three years in a prison camp for another reason, after being found guilty of "polluting the race" because he was in a relationship with a Jewish woman, the mother of his two children.)

If the majority of Germans conformed to the Nazi mold, it was also because many were not exactly opposed to the violence. Some eventually habituated themselves to it, letting themselves be convinced that violence was necessary to create a new order opposed to the so-called Bolshevik threat and to prevent the return of a hated republic along Weimarian lines. Others were seduced by what they saw as a celebration of virile force and German superiority, or the chance at a professional or material boost. Lawyers hurried to give the violence legal legitimacy, making it that much easier to tolerate. Tolerating crime was only one step away from participating in it, though it was nonetheless possible to avoid crossing that line. It was easy to refuse to take over the job of a colleague who had been fired for being Jewish and to avoid taking part in Aryanization. For a while, it was also possible to keep buying from Jewish business and shop owners, in the absence of a law against it.

As for saving Jews during the war, it was riskier, but not impossible. Some 10,000 German citizens participated in the effort, out of empathy and sometimes to line their pockets. If they were denounced, their fates differed: they might either be sent to a camp or spared, but the death penalty remained rare in Germany and in German-controlled territory, except for Poland, where the Reich regularly applied it to those who had rescued Jews. At the front, if a soldier in the Wehrmacht or the SS deserted, he could be put to death. If he recoiled from killing a Jew, a civilian, or a Soviet prisoner, he might lose face with his comrades, receive a warning from higher up, or be transferred. But as far as I know, there are no cases where a soldier paid for such a refusal with his life.

✿   ✿   ✿

"My parents lived under a dictatorship," my aunt says. "To resist the demands of the party or protect Jews, you had to be a hero. The people who did that put their lives in danger, they had to have a rare kind of courage few people possess." Volker is less forgiving. "My father played the game without being forced into it. He got a party card and he bought a business from Jews when he knew they had knives at their throats." Of course, they weren't aware, at the time, of everything we now know, and as a result, it wasn't always easy to gauge the risks. But in some situations, it was clearly possible, and even preferable, to say no. And as my father says, "If, from the beginning, people had refused to play along with each stage of the regime, the Nazis probably wouldn't have gone so far." I often ask myself what I would have done. I'll never know. But I understood what matters when I read, in Norbert Frei, that if we cannot know what we would have done, it "does not mean that we do not know how we should have behaved." And should behave, if it ever happens again.

Volker and Ingrid also disagree on another subject: how important it is to transmit the memory of the Nazi past. A book on the Third Reich is always lying on my father's bedside table or on the floor beside the bathtub. Recently, he was reading the umpteenth biography of Joseph Goebbels, a habit that doesn't prevent my father from being fun and full of life. As for his sister, she prefers "to live in the present and dispense with those stories," yet she still spends her time telling these tales, on a smaller scale, focused on people rather than major events, with which she identifies less.

Ingrid straddles two generations: my father's, born during or after the war, the generation that rose up in the sixties against the amnesia of German society, and the earlier generation of people born at the beginning of the thirties, who spent their childhood and adolescence under the Third Reich in the Hitler Youth and the Flackhelfer, the military reserves made up of young people. The people who belonged to that last generation had a particular relationship with National Socialism. They were both victims of the system and actors in it, certainly innocent, for the most part, but inevitably marked. They were the ones who, though they were too young to have responsibilities under the Third Reich, had to confront the heavy inheritance of "German Guilt" after the war. Decades after the end of the war, some couldn't bear the burden anymore and wanted to turn over a new leaf. When, after thirteen years with a social democrat in power, the Christian Democrat Helmut Kohl rose to be chancellor, they saluted his intention to inaugurate a "moral turning point" to reinforce the Germans' self-confidence by liberating them from the past. In 1984, Kohl declared before the Israeli Knesset: "I speak before you as one who could not be guilty of Nazism because I had the mercy of a late birth and the luck to grow up in a special household." The chancellor was accused of using that alibi to renege on his country's historical responsibility to Israel. A historian by training, he was also criticized for trying to shrink the Third Reich to a mere episode of German history. Along these lines, he pulled another memory—of the Great War—from the shadows where it had been crushed by the ever-present Second World War. To this day I still tremble at that scene filmed on September 22, 1984, at Verdun, where, in ten months, more than 310,000 French and German soldiers were killed. The French president, François Mitterrand, and Helmut Kohl stand frozen in solemn dignity at the foot of the ossuary. The German hymn ends. They lift their hands almost simultaneously, join them, and remain that way while the "Marseillaise" rings. The colossus and the little man linked by this gesture of enormous humility as they ask the dead to bear witness, to say *never again*.

In his hopes for a clean break, Helmut Kohl had the support of part of the population, but many others, still shocked by the airing of the *Holocaust* series and the proliferation of eyewitness accounts of the Shoah, had an urgent need for the truth.

The confrontation between the two camps intensified in 1985 when, on the occasion of a visit from President Ronald Reagan, Helmut Kohl invited his guest to pay his respects to the soldiers of the Reich at the German military cemetery in Bitburg, where members of the Waffen-SS are also buried. The visit, which was perceived as an attempt to downplay Nazi crimes and was announced beforehand by the White House, sparked a sharp polemic. Elie Wiesel, chairman of the United States Holocaust Memorial Council, had implored Reagan to cancel the planned visit at an unrelated White House ceremony a few weeks before, saying "That place, Mr. President, is not your place. Your place is with the victims of the SS." Fifty-three senators signed a letter asking the president to cancel and 257 representatives signed a letter urging Chancellor Kohl to withdraw the invitation. In vain. They carried out the visit. *Time* magazine called for Ronald Reagan to abstain, from then on, from visiting any German military cemeteries. Günter Grass accused Kohl of hiding behind innocence through ignorance. Through this maneuver, the chancellor wanted to create an equal relationship with the former victors of the war, especially since they still had troops in Germany. But his gesture managed to awaken old fears internationally and to provide fodder for German revisionists. Historians such as Hans Mommsen observed a worrisome "backward revision of the historical picture" among the ranks of the CDU/CSU and their supporters.

Three days after the visit to the cemetery, on the anniversary of the Allied victory over Nazi Germany, the Christian Democrat German president, Richard von Weizsäcker, would, in a legendary speech, decisively put a stop to this policy. I watched the forty-five-minute video of his speech, and if there could be only one thing to show the younger generations to make them reflect on the memory of National Socialism, this is it. That day, Weizsäcker, who was himself the son of a state secretary in the Reich Foreign Office, would form the basis of a national memorial consensus, transcending the divisions between right and left.

"The eighth of May was a day of liberation," he began, a modest figure behind a podium, facing the Bundestag. "It liberated all of us from the inhumanity and tyranny of the National Socialist regime." This declaration seems obvious today, but wasn't in 1985, when many people still had trouble hearing certain historical truths and saw the end of the war as a defeat, not a liberation. "We need and we have the strength to look the truth straight in the eye—without embellishment and without distortion," he insisted. While paying his respects to the suffering of Germans during the dictatorship, the war, and the postwar period, Weizsäcker firmly reminded people that their struggles were the fault of the Third Reich and not the Allies. "But we must not regard the end of the war as the cause of flight, expulsion, and deprivation of freedom. The cause goes back to the start of the tyranny that brought about war." In the same vein, he emphasized that "without the war started by Hitler," the division of Europe into two political systems "would not have happened at all." Richard von Weizsäcker, who had fought on the Eastern and Western Fronts and had been wounded twice, enumerated with great seriousness the long list of victims of Nazi barbarity and had the courage, unprecedented for a politician of that stature, to critique, head-on, the attitude of the German people under Nazism: "Who could remain unsuspecting after the burning of the synagogues, the plundering, the stigmatization of the Star of David, the deprivation of rights, the ceaseless violation of human dignity? Whoever opened his eyes and ears and sought information could not fail to notice that Jews were being deported. . . . There were many ways of not burdening one's conscience, of shunning responsibility, looking away, keeping mum. When the unspeakable truth of the Holocaust then became known at the end of the war, all too many of us claimed that they had not known anything about it or even suspected anything." The German president closed his speech with a warning. "From our own history we learn what man is capable of. For that reason we must not imagine that we are now quite different and have become better." Therefore, he reasoned, Germans should "use the memory of our own history as a guideline for our behavior now and in tackling the unresolved problems that lie ahead."

His speech was acclaimed across the world, translated into at least thirteen languages, and had a print run of 2 million copies. It allowed an international trust in Germany to be restored after Helmut Kohl had put it at risk. *The New York Times* reprinted the whole of the speech in its pages, and more than 60,000 citizens wrote to the president. Richard von Weizsäcker had made a pact between Germany's politics and the moral of its history.

Nonetheless, among German historians and intellectuals, not everyone was on board with this political consensus. Most experts agreed that the research on Nazi crimes was still very incomplete. But while some thought it was urgent to put genocide at the heart of German memory work, and to raise public awareness by creating museums, monuments, and commemorations, others were opposed to this evolution, and contested the uniqueness of the Holocaust, claiming the right to compare Nazi crimes with those committed by the Bolsheviks. How many witnesses have recounted the daily experience of forced labor in the gulag, where 18 million people were imprisoned; having to break ice to search for minerals while battling slicing winds, sleeping on concrete floors while contorted with cold and dying of hunger. Deaths in the gulag numbered in the millions, in addition to the 10 million victims of the famines caused by Soviet politics, the 6 million people who were deported, and the innumerable lives broken by Stalin's merciless regime.

In 1985, the German historian Martin Broszat argued, in an essay called "A Plea For the Historicization of National Socialism," that Nazi Germany should be treated as a "normal" period in history and called for historians to get rid of the moral filter, focus on a scientific approach, and allow shades of gray, especially by distinguishing between everyday life and the murderous regime. This argument provoked a rich debate with historians, especially with the Franco-Israeli Saul Friedländer, one of the most important experts on the Third Reich. Through a series of letters, Friedländer argued, among other things, that aspects of normality and criminality very much overlapped in the everyday life of Nazi Germany, and that the vague definition of "historicization" could open the door to apologetic arguments about National Socialism.

In 1986, the historiographic disagreements culminated with the "*Historikerstreit*," or "historians' dispute," after the publication in the *Frankfurter Allgemeine Zeitung* of a piece by the German historian Ernst Nolte titled "The Past That Will Not Go Away." According to Nolte we must "be allowed to ask an unavoidable question . . . Didn't the gulag archipelago come before Auschwitz? Was Bolshevik class murder not the logical and factual *prius* of the 'racial murder' of National Socialism?" In raising these questions rhetorically, the historian put forward the argument that the "class murder" perpetrated by the Bolsheviks was at once the model and the specter that pushed Hitler to murder the Jews.

Retaliation was swift, led by Jürgen Habermas. In an article titled "A Kind of Damage Control" that came out in the weekly *Die Zeit*, the philosopher writes that Nolte "kills two birds with one stone: Nazi crimes lose their singularity in that they are at least made comprehensible as an answer to the (still ongoing)

Bolshevist threats of annihilation." In this context of horror, he continues, "the extermination of the Jews appears as a regrettable, but perfectly understandable result, of what Hitler saw as the threat of annihilation."

Several historians counterattacked, accusing the philosopher of imposing a moral censorship on their work. Without agreeing with all the philosopher's accusations, many intellectuals took his side. Eberhard Jäckel made the point that the problem wasn't in comparing Bolshevik and Nazi crimes, but the cause-and-effect relationship Nolte traces between the gulag and the Holocaust, which suggests a "thesis of preventive murder" that is historically false. "The Aryans were not afraid of Slavic and Jewish subhumans," wrote Jäckel in *Die Zeit*, but Hitler had absolutely "understood how to mobilize the bourgeoisie's anti-Bolshevik fears for his own ends." Far from being a scientific debate, the historian Hans Mommsen argues, this conflict revealed the tendency among West German historiographers to make older authoritarian models "bearable once again through the historical relativizing of National Socialism." These attempts backfired and actually contributed to reinforcing the idea of the Holocaust as a defining element in the historical identity of Germany.

In November 1989, the collapse of the Berlin Wall made remembering National Socialism even more imperative. From then on, the way was clear for remembering Nazi crimes without worrying that they would be weaponized by the GDR. During the fifty-year anniversary of the end of the war, in 1995, a real "commemorative marathon" celebrated, without hesitation, the "liberation" of the German people. The historical and political culture of Germany seemed to have reached maturity. "The Past, Mastered," proclaimed the headline in *Der Spiegel*. A year later, the German president, Roman Herzog, made January 27, the date of the liberation of Auschwitz, a day of remembrance for the victims of National Socialism.

When the wall came down, it nullified the last myths the FRG had managed to preserve about the Nazi past, like the untainted, untouchable Wehrmacht that had miraculously resisted all the battles over memory. The legend had begun to form during the Nuremberg Trials, when the tribunal had decided not to include the Wehrmacht on the list of "criminal organizations." This decision passed for an acquittal in the eyes of many Germans. This impression was strengthened when the condemned members of the Wehrmacht were amnestied one after another, under pressure from the very powerful soldiers' lobby. Then the proliferation of autobiographies, eyewitness accounts, films, and books dedicated to ameliorating the Wehrmacht succeeded in anchoring, in the public opinion, the image of the "upstanding soldier" and an army spared from Nazi ideology, an army that did not massacre civilians and Jews.

In 1995, an exhibition organized by the Hamburg Institute for Social Research entitled *War of Extermination: Wehrmacht Crimes, 1941–1944* finally dismantled this myth. Thanks to the help of historians, the exhibition proved that if, at the start, the Wehrmacht had disapproved of the SS actions, it had ended up giving way to them, actively collaborating, and even voluntarily giving out innumerable criminal orders against Jews, civilians, and prisoners of war. It was also consumed from within by anti-Semitism and racism toward the *Untermensch*, the subhuman. The exhibition was controversial enough that in quite a few cities opposing camps formed over whether or not it should be shown. Demonstrations took place. The Bundestag devoted a much-talked-about debate to the issue. The exhibition had a runaway success with viewers of all ages, social classes, and professions, with nearly a million people waiting in long lines to see it.

❖   ❖   ❖

Another major forgotten accessory to Nazi crimes returned to the surface: the economic sector. Aside from the Aryanization of Jewish property and business dealings with the Nazi regime, companies had profited hugely from the 10 million forced laborers in the Reich. After the war, both state and private businesses benefited from the fact that most of the victims lived behind the Iron Curtain, and therefore couldn't be reimbursed. The collapse of the Berlin Wall opened the way for reparation agreements between the German state, certain former Eastern countries, and Russia, following the model of those made with Western countries after the war, but the negotiations dragged on when it came to repaying former forced laborers. No matter that the people concerned were either already dead or very old, and urgently needed money in the poverty-stricken East, certain businesses slowed down the legal process as much as they could. In 2000, the Foundation Remembrance, Responsibility, and Future saw the light, allocating 10 billion DM from both the federal government and more than 6,000 private businesses to compensate former forced laborers.

Furthermore, under pressure from public opinion, big businesses and banks slowly opened their archives to historians and independent commissions charged with unveiling their activities and their enormous reliance on forced labor during the war. Some were more reluctant, like Quandt, Flick, and Oetker, though they eventually succumbed to media pressure. Others still continue to drag their feet, like Siemens and Bayer, or persist in doing nothing at all, like Henkel, Roechling, and Wella. Nonetheless, these examples are exceptions, and in general, the majority of German big business has ended up belatedly playing the transparency card.

This was the context in which I moved to Berlin in 2000 to work as a correspondent for a French news agency. I immediately felt comfortable in this city—disfigured by wars and dictatorships, but energized by a thirst for life and an infectious sense of freedom. In Berlin, the memory of the twentieth century is unavoidable; it cohabits with the present, inscribing itself on walls and in the actions of citizens. Germany is made in its image, and it is impossible to decipher its political actions and public opinions without seeing them in a historical perspective. My move to Berlin was probably a logical outcome of my interest in twentieth-century history, which I had been studying during my previous years in Paris. But I never thought the move would be permanent. So this choice—the opposite of my father's, who at almost the same age, said his goodbyes to Germany to move to France with my mother, a French woman—what does it tell us? That memory, when it is deliberately cultivated, can heal many wounds.

My arrival in Berlin coincided with the beginning of a new relationship between Germany and its history, sparked by the Green Party/Social Democratic coalition government that had been in power since 1998. Perhaps because these parties were rarely suspected of revisionism, they succeeded where Helmut Kohl had failed: in imposing a certain normalcy on the country's international status. In 1999, Germany participated for the first time in a NATO military intervention, in Kosovo. In spite of the deep pacifism embedded in the society, the government had pulled off this tour de force by raising the menace of genocide in ex-Yugoslavia. "Never another war" had been supplanted by "never another Auschwitz." A line had been crossed in Germany's return to the global scene, which would be confirmed when Chancellor Gerhard Schröder refused outright to follow Germany's long-standing ally, the United States, into Iraq during the military invasion in 2003, and when he undertook a campaign to get Germany a permanent seat on the UN Security Council.

One of the strongest symbols of this "normalization" was the first participation, in June 2004, by a German chancellor in the annual festivities surrounding the Allied landing in Normandy. Gerhard

Schröder had agreed to commemorate the "liberation," completing the gesture Richard von Weizsäcker had begun twenty years earlier. I was sent to Normandy to cover this sixtieth-anniversary celebration, where they were expecting twenty-two heads of state and tens of thousands of people.

In this tumult, I met a group of elderly Germans who had come specifically from Nuremberg to gather at the graves of their loved ones, who had died in combat during the Battle of Normandy. These three sisters had lost their brother Hans, whose photo they showed me: a face that had barely emerged from adolescence, with two candid, big brown eyes and a rather timid smile, sharp in his dark uniform with polished metal buttons, with the insignia of the Waffen-SS on his collar, the double S shaped like lightning bolts. Their bus was about to take them to the large German cemetery at La Cambe, and I offered to meet them there. I found a magnificent cemetery, resembling a golf course, carpeted with an impeccable lawn, cropped close, glossy, almost glowing, where thousands of funerary slabs were lined up as far as the eye could see; here and there, little granite crosses poked up in series of five, sticking together as if holding hands, a last homage to camaraderie in the face of death's solitude; and 1,200 maples fanned the sanctuary with their large branches, a symbol of peace. I strolled down the paths and found my group in front of slabs that were more decorated than the others, the tomb of the fearsome SS member Michael Wittmann, head of the armored tank corps and the most decorated soldier in Germany, a hero of Nazi propaganda who pulverized no fewer than 138 tanks before dying in his Tigre 007, blasted to bits in Normandy. In a flower pot placed close to his funerary slab, a small black flag waved and on it you could make out the insignia of a white key, the sign of the Leibstandarte-SS-Adolf Hitler, the armored division of the Führer's SS corps. As I was readying myself to ask these senior citizens why they had chosen that exact tomb, they intoned, as a chorus, a German war song. I wondered if my reporting was beginning to take a bad turn, and I was admittedly relieved when they didn't hold out their arms in a horizontal salute. Once the song ended, I decided to ask the three sisters who dried their damp eyes with a tissue if they knew they were standing before an SS grave. "But our brother, too, he was in the Waffen-SS, what difference does that make, they were also brave soldiers," they replied. In the eyes of the sisters, and for many other Germans of their generation, the end of the war was far from being a day of liberation.

The next day, I found myself surrounded by other journalists at the Anglo-Canadian cemetery in Ranville, where Gerhard Schröder was to place two wreaths, one for the Allied dead, and the other in a small patch reserved for German soldiers. Everyone held their breath during this delicate choreography—a German chancellor walking through an ocean of crosses, knowing that each of his movements, each of his expressions would be scrutinized, compared, interpreted. But Schröder handled the moment perfectly—neither too solemn nor making light of it, he conveyed the image of a Germany that could no longer be asked to feel guilty, but which had made the work of memory an unavoidable foundation of its identity.

In this climate of appeasement, people began to allow themselves to break new taboos in Germany. As a journalist, I followed the passionate debate surrounding the publication in 2002 of a novel by Günter Grass where the author treads on very unusual ground—the suffering of Germans during the war. Mixing reality and fiction, past and present, *Crabwalk* tells the story of the drama of the *Wilhelm Gustloff*, a German ship sent to a port in the Baltic Sea to rescue columns of East Prussian refugees from the clutches of the Red Army. Grass describes their fight to get a spot on the

Gustloff, their only chance at survival, since remaining on land would trap them with the Red Army. The rumor was that they killed the men, raped the women, and slit the babies' throats in front of their mothers, partly in retaliation for the scorched earth practices of the Wehrmacht during its retreat from Russia. But the fate of those who embarked on the *Gustloff* was no better—though the authorities knew it was carrying mainly civilians, the *Gustloff* was torpedoed by a Soviet submarine and shipwrecked in the icy waters of the Baltic with more than 10,500 refugees on board, very few of whom survived. The torpedoes were named "For Leningrad," "For the Soviet people," "For Stalin." It was the same ship my grandmother had taken in 1938 to visit the fjords of Norway, amid the general euphoria that characterized Nazi Germany in those years.

Almost at the exact same moment Grass's book came out, *Der Spiegel* published a long series entitled "The Escape," on the exile of Germans from Eastern Europe, along with an analysis of "The Germans as Victims." The debate nourished a new interest in the crimes of the Red Army. In 2003, the reissue of an autobiographical book by Martha Hillers called *A Woman in Berlin* related the daily life of a woman relegated to the status of sexual prey in Soviet-occupied Berlin, reminding people of the infamous rape of more than 1.4 million German women by Russian soldiers.

I met two victims of these rapes in Berlin: Elizabeth and Martha, originally from Silesia, a now-Polish province that they were forced to flee in winter 1945, before the advance of the Red Army. They received me in their little apartment in Berlin, where they had moved in together after their husbands had died. "We've lived through so much together," Martha said with an uncertain smile, and their very sweet way of looking at each other, their kind welcome, their table set with such care to serve me tea and little cakes—all of it made me tear up before the interview had even begun.

They were fifteen and sixteen years old, when, after losing track of their family in the chaos of their flight, they jumped on a cart in the middle of an interminable column of refugees, already packed to the hilt with everything the people could quickly carry from their meager homes. But the draft horses were not hardy enough to run the 375 miles to Berlin in the sharp cold of winter, and the roads were bad because you had to take little paths to avoid encountering the Russians, whose very name petrified Elizabeth and Martha. They jumped each time they saw human figures in the distance, but one day it really was the Russians who burst out and surrounded them. The young girls were immediately pulled to the ground and pushed a little way into the forest, where the soldiers ripped off their pants and raped these bodies already scarred by hunger, fear, and cold, who knows how many times on the frozen ground. "I remember that I had one idea fixed in my head: that I had my period and that there would be blood all over my clothes," says Elizabeth, who bursts into sobs. Martha also begins to cry but manages to say, "In those moments, the survival instinct forces you to think of something else, to turn yourself away from the horror you're undergoing."

Once they had gotten what they wanted, the soldiers turned their interest to the contents of the cart, and, while they rifled through everything, drinking and terrorizing the peasant family, the two girls, abandoned on the ground, took their inattention as a chance to flee. On their way, they ran into a group of fleeing Germans who welcomed them. Once again, the Red Army stopped them, and once again the sisters were raped and brutalized. In Germany, Martha and Elizabeth found their family in the American Zone and put their lives back together, but for a long time, they lied about their origins, to colleagues, boyfriends, neighbors.

"Everyone knew that if you were a woman who came from the East, that meant you had been raped by the Russians. We were ashamed."

During those years in Berlin, I interviewed many witnesses. They were the last survivors. Who—or what—would take up the succession of memory?

Monuments, first of all. The Memorial to the Murdered Jews of Europe was inaugurated in 2005 near Brandenburger Tor, 2,711 steles of anthracite-colored concrete extending as far as the eye can see, a labyrinth of slabs whose varying heights are dizzying, representing the tombs that were not granted to those who died in the Shoah. Several intellectuals denounced this construction in the center of Berlin. The writer Martin Walser protested the "manipulation of the Holocaust," claiming the right to "look away." Other monuments followed, recognizing the victims of National Socialism who have remained in the shadows. In the middle of a clearing in the Tiergarten, a central park in Berlin, a black circular basin filled with water symbolizes the tears of the Roma and Sinti peoples. Not far away, under the trees, a block of concrete is pierced with a window where you can see a film projected on the inside, in commemoration of persecuted homosexuals. On the edge of the park, a long, transparent wall of blue glass has been placed in the ruins of the villa where the Aktion T4 program was developed, in remembrance of the euthanized martyrs. The forced laborers have a memorial in Leipzig.

Archives are also a bulwark against forgetting. From 2005 onward, ministries and public institutions demanded one by one that commissions of independent historians examine their role under National Socialism and during the first postwar decades, which were marked by ideological and personal continuities between the Third Reich and the FRG. Even the West German

Secret Service opened its archives up to 1970. This measure was completely unprecedented in Europe, where intelligence still cultivates a questionable secrecy over the remote past, preventing historians from shedding light on episodes as important as the Algerian War in France or the end of the British Empire.

Now that the eyewitnesses are dead, victims and executioners alike, all that's left is the memory of their words, the memorials, and the history books, to remind the living what Germany no longer wants to be. And family memory also remains. I wanted to weave together the threads of major and minor history, to arrange these traces so that they connect in my imaginary fabric, crossing them over and under one another, until a vivid scene emerges, a world of yesterday with its décor, its spirit, its lives, in all their shadows and light. My father and my aunt knew them, these past existences. Emotion filters their memory, the anger of a troubled childhood, the remembered feeling of injustice, the hurt of deception, the sadness of no longer being able to communicate with those who have gone forever, and love as well, loyalty in spite of everything. My grandparents are ghosts to me. Opa died before I was born and Oma died six years later. I can reflect on them with a clear head, putting the search for truth above emotion. But the facts alone won't open the door to what's real; I have to use the forces of representation, intuition, and psychology. And I must not lose my empathy for these lives crushed by megalomania, for Lydia and Karl, who had the misfortune to be born at the dawn of a cursed century.

One day, no one knows exactly which, bouts of anxiety began to consume Oma, who was convinced that she would run out of money and fall into poverty, that at her age she would have to humiliate herself by having to ask others for financial help. After her husband died, she continued to live alone in the family home. Her children and friends certainly tried to tell her that she had nothing to worry about, considering the revenue from the apartments in the building she had inherited from her father, but it did no good. "She said to me, 'Without money, what's there to live for?'" remembers my aunt Ingrid, who remained close to her until the end. But who can understand the traumas of a German woman born in 1901, who knew only wars and postwar periods, for whom the next day could only be worse than the present. After living through a half century as if she were racing across hot coals, she had devoted her remaining energy to watching over her daughter until she got married, and fighting for her son to study, against her husband's wishes, as only a mother could. Then she waited impatiently for her son to give her grandchildren, so that she could coddle and adore them.

As soon as Oma could finally rest, she suddenly understood that it wasn't possible. The spiny past she had carted around for the whole of her existence, like a suitcase that she never had time to set down, suddenly unfastened with alarming speed, ceaselessly unspooling the poison of memory. The bouts only got worse, and the irrational anxiety of ending up poor plunged my grandmother into a spiral where no medicine or reassurance could reach her. She suffered deeply, repeating over and over this prayer to God: "If only He would come to get me." And so, one evening, despite her Protestant faith, which forbade her from deciding the day of her death, she chose to stop waiting for God. A friend who lived close by had come to watch television with her. Around 11 p.m., she left, saying, "You're scaring me tonight, Lydia, why don't you go to bed." Oma reassured her and closed the door, then she went back out to the landing and climbed up to the last window in the stairwell. When she opened the double window, Oma swept her eyes over the homes full of light and life, breaking through the shadows from afar, and waved to the dark silhouette of the tall oak in the courtyard that had watched her grow up. Then she jumped.

My German grandparents, Lydia and Karl Schwarz, on their wedding day, 1927.

XI

Memoirs of a Franco-German

Until adulthood, I spent every Christmas of my childhood in Mannheim, in the apartment building inherited from my grandparents. This fixed ritual was part of a double Franco-German education that my parents rigorously oversaw. Since we lived in France, it was understood that for the sake of balance, almost all my school vacations would be devoted to immersion in German society. When I spent my first Christmas in France at age twenty with a French family, I was disconcerted by the way they had turned the grave and solemn event of Jesus's birth into a party bordering on pagan bacchanalia. And they were certainly not the only ones in France, a country where secularism had been a treasured principle since 1905, when the sacrosanct law separating church and state came into effect. No fewer than eight or ten courses, oysters, foie gras, stuffed capon, smoked salmon, scallops, duck à l'orange, and bûche de noël unfurled across the table, drowned in gallons of champagne, wines, and cordials, amid a whirlwind of blinking multicolored lights and a pine that was lost under an avalanche of decorations. The next day, the Christmas conversation centered on the quality of the cuisine from the night before, which had already been largely discussed the previous night, but merited a new examination in the light of day.

In Mannheim, we used to celebrate Christmas Eve in a Protestant church lit only by candles—a building faithful to the sober, severe Lutheran tradition, but with the flickering of candle flames in the darkness and the clear, vivid music by Bach and Handel, it became sublime for a night. This religious ceremony was an indispensable ingredient in the magic of Christmas, and my sister and I never gave up that ardent induction into the mystery of Christianity, which we renew every year. With the exception of the sermon, the ceremony was all powerful music, pouring out of the organ pipes, accompanied by the voices of the choir.

This Christmas celebration, so different from its French equivalent, contains a search for purity and essence that I like to associate with the German soul. Lest I be accused of giving in to clichés, I should say that I experience this sense from outside, as a French person, and that I feel it from the inside, as a German: a distaste for lightness, an inclination toward the absolute, be it evil or goodness. In love, too, seriousness prevails. The German romantics have left an indelible legacy—the vision of love as mystical and predestined, unique, tortured, and irrational, an absolute value surpassing reciprocity which can lead to despair and even to death, as in Goethe's epistolary novel *The Sorrows of Young Werther* (1774), whose hero commits suicide. What a contrast with the "art of loving" as it was described in the libertine writings of the French eighteenth century! In the epistolary novel *Les Liaisons Dangereuses* by Pierre Choderlos de Laclos, seduction is elevated to a psychological art, a strategy designed to fulfill the pride, sensuality, and pleasure of the game. Then, in the nineteenth century, love as defined by Stendhal, Flaubert, and Balzac became much less cynical but still a "cerebral love" where thinking came before feeling. In Stendhal's *On Love*, he proposes the concept of "crystallization," love like an illusion: "it is enough to have an idea of perfection in order to discern it in the person we love."

After the religious Christmas service, we would go back to the family apartment, where my father, who always arranged to leave church early, would have transformed the living room with magical decorations, a metamorphosis that my sister and I would pretend was the result of a visit from the *Christkind*, who each year would make use of our absence to drop off presents and treats, light candles, and put on solemn music. I remember that since we weren't allowed to enter the living room until my aunt Ingrid and my uncle arrived, we waited, pawing the floor with impatience in front of the door, whose glass mosaic panel reflected the light of candles into a galaxy of stars. Once the crystal notes of a little bell rang out, signaling the beginning of the festivities, we would hurry inside, seized with wonder before a cave like Ali Baba's, overwhelming in its red, green, and gold, where a large pine reigned, haloed with candles and red figurines, its resin perfume mixing with the smell of homemade cinnamon, almond, and citrus cookies, cut into little moon, star, and heart shapes. This enchantment of lights and smells was accompanied, as our tradition required, by the galvanizing sound of a Christmas oratorio. Only my mother's clear singing voice wasn't a cacophonous insult to this sublime music, and I remember being moved by this intimate connection with the sacred—a rare moment for us, since we weren't very religious. For all that, our celebration was no less consumerist, and while my music-loving uncle sat in his favorite spot in the back of the room—immersing himself in the music, his eyes half closed, his fingers drumming secretively on the armrests of the chair—my sister, Nathalie, and I unwrapped presents. My father took great pleasure in watching us discover the surprises he'd affectionately chosen for us. As soon as we were old enough to read, he made sure to include books that, beyond their literary value, would allow us to deepen our understanding of Nazi trauma.

He had an embarrassment of choices, so numerous were the Germanophone authors who had written, almost obsessively, about this black page in German history. Immediately after the war, a literary movement called *Trümmerliteratur* (Literature of the Ruins) had emerged, characterized by a complete rupture with the vocabulary, the values, and the sentimentality of "Old Germany," in favor of realist, nonpsychological writing that aimed to capture the truth, such as it is. One of the figures in this movement was Heinrich Böll, who after serving reluctantly in the Wehrmacht returned to his native city of Cologne, where an apocalyptic spectacle awaited him that would haunt him all his life. When I read, at age twelve, his short story "Stranger, Bear Word to the Spartans We . . . ," I recognized the absurd cruelty of the war for the first time, through the eyes of a teenager, the same age as my older sister, Nathalie. Just a few decades earlier, on the same ground where I was living my innocent childhood, he had taken up arms, killed, and watched a part of himself die along with his comrades. I was moved by the interior monologue of this gravely wounded and very young soldier. Brought into a school that has been transformed into a makeshift hospital, he realizes that he is in his former classroom, which has become an operating room, and he recognizes his own handwriting on a desk. Forced to come to terms with reality, in the same moment he understands that his arms are gone, and that he has only one leg. What had he written on the table just before being sent to the front? "Stranger, Bear Word to the Spartans We . . . ," the start of an epitaph from ancient Greece in memory of the Spartans who sacrificed themselves to the last man to defend the strategic passage of Thermopylae against the Persians. This story from antiquity was taught in classes under the Third Reich and served as a model for the Germans, so that they would develop, from childhood, a taste for the total sacrifice Hitler demanded.

In the wake of this Literature of the Ruins, which lasted until the early fifties, more and more German-speaking writers deepened their critique of heroic values and patriotic sacrifice, and they also reflected on the dangers of conformity. In 1947, some of them founded Group 47, which began as a simple platform for discussions and informal lectures before becoming an essential literary institution in the second half of the twentieth century. A leading author in that group was Günter Grass, whom my father seemed to particularly appreciate, since he often included his work among the Christmas gifts. His best-seller *The Tin Drum*, which came out in 1959, sold millions of copies all over the world and was adapted into a film by the German director Volker Schlöndorff. It exuberantly tells the fantastical life story of Oskar Matzerath, born in the free city of Danzig in 1924, who refuses to grow up into the hypocritical adult world. Oskar watches as the inhabitants of his city collapse into Nazism, less out of blindness than conformity, and eventually winds up sinking into Nazi banality himself, out of ego and opportunism. Millions of Germans from every generation have read this uncompromising novel, whose portrait of daily life captures how the German petite bourgeoisie surrendered little by little, without trying to understand the consequences of such a succession of small capitulations. When Oskar, despite his clear understanding of the immorality of the regime, ends up "adapting," we're left to be haunted by the question "What would I have done in his place?"

In 2006, Grass revealed that in October 1944, at age seventeen, he had volunteered for the Waffen-SS. The fact that this guardian of German morality waited so long to make such a confession provoked indignation. But it also gave new depth to the edifying work of this intellectual who, like no other, has questioned collective and personal memories and described this tangle of guilt, denial, and confession that has characterized Germany since the Second World War.

❖   ❖   ❖

Until I was ten, I went to a French elementary school in the village where we lived on the outskirts of Paris. I remember not feeling truly integrated, and without being able to recollect the exact sources of this discomfort, which might have had multiple causes at that age, I was certain that one source must have been my dual culture. Some difference must have exposed my doubleness.

In the eighties, most of Germany wasn't fashionable in France, and the French held many negative stereotypes about it—culinary mediocrity, disgraceful fashions, the notorious sandals worn with white socks, the way German city centers lacked charm—clichés that, in truth, were not always devoid of a certain factual basis. The hawkers of these ideas were generally ignorant of the constellation of philosophers, composers, and other geniuses that German civilization had produced. But this mockery was pretty inoffensive compared with the quite widespread suspicion in France that behind every German hid a potential Nazi, or at least a sort of robot, mechanically obeying orders and exempt from feelings, a suspicion that had the advantage of explaining the success of the German economy, a success that secretly made people jealous.

My particular family has not been the subject of Germanophobia, but I remember when, after showing us a film on the First World War, my elementary school teacher exclaimed: "Hurrah! We beat those dirty Krauts!" while making the V sign for victory. My classmates took up his hurrah with heart, leaving me stunned, all alone. Then there was the World Cup soccer match between France and Germany in 1982, which my sister and I watched with two cousins, supporting the German side while they rooted for the French. It took a bad turn when the German goalie, Toni Schumacher, struck the French player Patrick Battiston with such violence that he lost three teeth and had to be rushed, unconscious, off the field. The German player was unmoved by Battiston's fate, and his shocking attitude was very bad publicity for Germany, since the French media was only too delighted to unload all their hatred of Germans. Once a monster, always a monster.

I don't think Toni Schumacher had anything to do with it, but shortly after he compromised Franco-German reconciliation, I stopped speaking German with my father. Paradoxically, it was my mother, whose approach to authority diverged from my father's, who forced nine-year-old me to study German, with workbooks on grammar, conjugations, and applied vocabulary, though her evenings were already very full. A fierce arm-wrestling match occurred between us each evening: my mother, who, with her training as an English teacher, was accustomed to subduing some thirty rowdy little tykes; and me, tough and already lacking much fear of authority thanks to my father's teachings, not giving in until she carried out her threats. This attitude, which had no strategic value, must have cost me a nice bundle of slaps and a whole lot of time. But it was thanks to my mother's generosity and perseverance with her stubborn, fractious daughter that I managed to learn enough to miraculously pass the entrance exams for sixth grade at the international school in Saint-Germain-en-Laye, a Parisian suburb. Despite the long commute by bus, I immediately connected with the liberal philosophy of this institution that welcomed children from binational or expatriate couples from the Western European countries and from the United States.

The German curriculum was generally modeled on that of schools across the Rhine, and my middle-aged German teachers initiated us in the work of memory, placing a large emphasis on the Nazi past and reflecting on it through both history and literature. We read Max Frisch's 1961 play *Andorra*, which describes, step by step, the mechanism of creating a scapegoat, and Friedrich Dürrenmatt's 1955 play *The Visit*, which tells the story of an old billionaire who decides, after a long absence, to return to her native town. She promises money to its inhabitants, on the condition that they kill one of their own, the man she loved as a young girl, who jilted her after getting her pregnant. After being initially shocked by this proposal, the townspeople change their minds little by little, and set off on an appalling manhunt. The nature of these works, which were the object of lively classroom debates, invited us to explore our own integrity and promoted an independent spirit. In German class, for the first time, I heard a teacher praise disobedience to authority, provided it was motivated by the internal conviction to confront an injustice.

In French class, following the classic program of French schools, I don't remember ever covering those themes. After the war, French novelists rarely covered the ambiguous role their society had played under the occupation. In the first decades after the liberation, the Second World War did not become the object of an abundant literature like the First World War had in the interwar period, when Louis-Ferdinand Céline, Blaise Cendrars, Roland Dorgelès, Jean Giono, and Pierre Drieu la Rochelle recounted the horrors of the trenches: death appearing at any moment, the terrible suffering of the wounded, limbs amputated without morphine, disfigured, deaf, blind men, condemned to reliving the apocalyptic fire of war each night. In total, during that first industrialized war, 1.4 million soldiers died wearing their French uniforms and 3.5 million were wounded. Approximately 36,000 monuments to the dead were erected in almost every town in France. From this point of view, the trauma was much deeper than that of the Second World War, which cost approximately half a million military and civilian lives in both France and the colonies.

In 1990, a year after the Wall fell, my class took a trip to Berlin and discovered a city of surprising lightness of spirit in contrast

with the ever-present wounds of the Second World War and the
Cold War. From there, we went to Weimar, the symbol of Johann
von Goethe's and Friedrich Schiller's poetry and the cradle of the
Bauhaus architectural revolution. After these highlights of German
civilization, it was a harsh shock to arrive at the nearby Buchenwald
camp, where many of us were stunned by images from the camp's
liberation. The lines of Paul Celan's poem "Death Fugue," that we
studied in class suddenly divulged their dark meaning:

> Death is a gang-boss *aus Deutschland* his eye is blue
> he shoots you with leaden bullets his aim is true
> there's a man in this house your golden hair Margareta
> he sets his dogs on our trail he gives us a grave in the sky
> he cultivates snakes and he dreams Death is a gang-boss
> > *aus Deutschland*
>
> your golden hair Margareta
> your ashen hair Shulamite

In April 1970, this ill-fated poet whose Jewish family perished
in the camps was found dead in the Seine.

After I graduated, I decided to search for my paternal roots by
spending a year in Mannheim, which I knew only through the
filter of vacations. My father helped me move into the family
apartment on Chamissostrasse and went with me to register at the
university where he himself had studied, visibly delighted at this
Germanophillia on the part of a daughter who had brutally repu-
diated his language during her preteen angst, something that—I
now realize—must have saddened him. He was already affected by
living in a language and a culture that were different from his own.
Volker was never truly "assimilated" and had always maintained

an immutable tie to Germany, through his faithfulness to German news and literature and his loyalty to his childhood friends. He succeeded in giving his family a persistently German imprint that could have easily been lost in France.

I had a good year in Mannheim, where despite a city center that was hastily reconstructed on a rather harsh grid, life was good thanks to the green banks of the Rhine, the Neckar, and the surrounding region, which was more charming than the city let on. The university, situated in a vast, baroque castle, surrounded by modern additions, offered courses where students were allowed to speak up, even in cases where we disagreed with the professors, who generally treated us as independent adults. I became friends with Tina, a girl a few years older than I was, who made an impression with her mane of frizzy blond curls and her glibness in political science classes. She took me under her wing and initiated me into the internal democratic workings of the university, where she was a member of the student-elected parliament, which had the notable mission of defending students against abuses of power, for example when an ideological conflict resulted in a mediocre grade.

I had been immersed in the German education system when I decided to pursue my studies in the history department of the Paris IV Sorbonne University, my first experience with French schooling since primary school. I had chosen to take a class on the sixteenth-century Spanish Golden Age. During the tutorials, I watched, flabbergasted, as the lecturer poured out his opinions on the treatment of native peoples by the conquistadors, which he considered *a necessary evil intrinsic to the conquests*. He even allowed himself a little digression to declare that sometimes torture is necessary, and that he was one of the people who defended its use by the French army during the Algerian War. The conquest of the Americas by the Europeans, particularly by the Spanish, caused the death of at least 50 million native people, not to mention the theft of gold, silver, and other minerals. I made sure to bring this up during a written exam, while describing Spain's flourishing during that era. I received a very mediocre 9/20, flanked by the following comment: "Marxist view of history."

Taken aback, but encouraged by the memory of my friend Tina's activism defending students in Mannheim, I searched for an authority that would hear complaints from students about discrimination and the ideological drift of classes. I found no such thing in this cradle of French education, this symbol of the Enlightenment and the rights of man. As a last resort, I went to see the supervisor in charge of tutorials, a specialist in modern military history, to tell him my grievances and my intention to complain. With a large desk standing between us, he heard me out without looking up from the dais, and when I finished my tale, he replied: "Who do you think you are? We could crush you at any moment." Behind this dubious remark, this infantilizing tone, this abuse of authority, was something I would encounter at several stages of my studies and in my professional career in France. In the meantime, another disappointment was waiting for me at the Paris IV Sorbonne.

I was registered for a class on geopolitics, a fascinating but delicate subject, since it can easily be exploited for ideological purposes. In truth, I went only once, and I have to give the professor credit for immediately setting the tone of his course, allowing me to unenroll that same day without wasting time. He posed a rhetorical question, wondering why Africa was "the only continent that did not produce a great civilization," since with the exception of the Sahara, its nature and soil were rich, while at the same time, from the Himalaya to the Andes, other peoples succeeded "despite very difficult climates and geographical conditions." "I'm only asking," he clarified maliciously, proud of what he probably thought was audacity: his indirect reference to the logic of racial theories from the nineteenth century that were developed to justify colonialism. Not a single student, myself included, made a peep or left the room in protest.

I had barely remembered this professor's name, when to my surprise, I found him in one of the grandest amphitheaters of the Sorbonne, where he was teaching a course on Vichy France from the dais. His argument was contrary to Robert Paxton's, and he was rephrasing an old idea that had been contradicted by the archives, the idea that Marshal Pétain and his entourage were working against the German occupiers in secret. Over the course of the semester, the lecture hall emptied of students, offended that they were being served up this gobbledygook from such a highly regarded institution. This didn't stop the university administration from renewing the class, without any consideration for the majority of the community of French historians, who disapproved of the work of this same professor.

This episode was even more surprising because it coincided with a period of important changes in France. President François Mitterrand of the Socialist Party—who, like all his predecessors, had prevented an honest exploration of the past by rejecting any responsibility on the part of France for Vichy's crimes, repeating, "Vichy, that's not France," all the while decorating Pétain's tomb on the Île d'Yeu every November 11 until 1992—concluded his final term, and a decisive step could be taken. In 1995, two months after his inauguration, the new conservative president, Jacques Chirac, decided to break with this politics of amnesia. During the commemorative ceremony for the Vel d'Hiv roundup, on July 16, he was the first French head of state to acknowledge that Vichy and its crimes were part of the history of France: "These dark hours forever sully our history and are an insult to our past and our traditions. Yes, the criminal folly of the occupiers was seconded by the French people, by the French state. . . . France, the homeland of the Enlightenment and of the rights of man, a land of welcome and asylum, on that day committed the irreparable. Breaking its word, it handed those who were under its protection over to their executioners." Jacques Chirac was responding to a pressing demand from French society, which since the eighties had come to understand the dimensions of the Holocaust and had begun to ask for justice against the French executors of that horrendous crime. The first to fall was Maurice Papon, secretary-general of the southwest region around Bordeaux under Vichy. In May 1981, the satirical weekly *Le Canard Enchaîné* published documents he had signed demonstrating his responsibility for the deportation of 1,690 Jews, including 130 children under thirteen, from Bordeaux to Drancy, the antechamber of Auschwitz. These revelations came at the worst possible moment: in 1981, Papon was minister of the budget in Valéry Giscard d'Estaing's administration. Two years later, he was convicted for crimes against humanity, a first for France. He must have been quite astonished himself, since he had never had to hide his past, and maintained a successful career in civil service after the war. After a long judicial odyssey, in 1998 he was condemned to ten years of criminal detention for "complicity in crimes against humanity." Faithful to tradition, the accused maintained until the end that he never knew about the Final Solution, which he claimed to condemn. What did Maurice Papon and all his acolytes in public service think was happening when the Germans demanded that they turn over Jews? What possible interest could the Nazis have had in France being *judenrein*, if not to serve sheer genocidal folly? In his arguments for the prosecution, the lawyer Arno Klarsfeld, son of the Nazi hunters Serge and Beate, summarized the mechanism that progressively turned this dyed-in-the-wool republican into a criminal, "by believing that yielding in small ways is of no consequence. Everything finally accumulates, twig after twig, compromise after compromise. You find yourself at the crossroads between good and evil. You accept this, or that. You give in to yourself. You forget the man you were, the man you should be. You call yourself a spectator, but you are already a protagonist. And in the most natural way, you accept the irreparable."

In 1989, it was Paul Touvier's turn to be arrested. He was the former head of the Milice Lyonnaise, a paramilitary organization created by the Vichy regime to help the Gestapo track Jews and members of the resistance, using terror, torture, and execution. After the war, condemned to death twice in absentia, Touvier had gone on the run for forty years, passing from hideout to hideout thanks to the generosity of certain ecclesiastic circles in Catholicism that were moved by this man's faith, despite his bloody hands. In 1994, he was convicted of crimes against humanity.

Another man whose history caught up to him was René Bousquet, former general secretary of the Vichy police, who slipped through the nets of the purge after the liberation and began a career as an influencer among the French political elite, including François Mitterrand. In 1989, he was accused of crimes against humanity. Four years later, he was assassinated by someone who was mentally ill.

One of the most disturbing trials on French soil was held for a German, Klaus Barbie, the former director of the Gestapo in Lyon, who had been hiding under the name Klaus Altman in Bolivia, with the long-standing protection of the authorities. Thanks to many people's efforts, he was extradited in 1983. At the trial, numerous victims came forward to testify in detail about the abuses inflicted by Barbie and his men—crushing genitals, ripping off fingernails, administering electric shocks, slashing with knives, and beating with iron rods—allowing the French to examine the hell that Germans and their French allies had created for Jews and members of the resistance under the occupation. Barbie, who expressed no remorse, was found guilty of crimes against humanity and sentenced to life in prison.

❖　　❖　　❖

With the French public's renewed interest in this past, new historical work proliferated, taking on aspects that had previously been neglected, like the role of the army, the corporate sector, or the universities. The archives of the Second World War became more accessible, and the state made changes to the high school curriculum. It also constructed monuments in Paris such as The Shoah Memorial and a sculpture representing civilians in distress on the site of the Vélodrome d'Hiver, reminding France of her shame.

This fervor for illuminating and commemorating the past was also a reaction to a new mounting threat: the electoral breakthrough of a party led by a politician who cultivated an ambiguous relationship with Vichy. I remember Jean-Marie Le Pen's appearances on television in the eighties and nineties, when he was crowing over each of his electoral victories, his clenched fists brandished in the air like some boxing champion, with steel in his eye and a carnivorous smile. I can still see him, this charismatic, wily character, an unequaled master of the rebuttal, afraid of nothing, especially not the provocation and cliché he developed with devotion, since it was how he managed his success. In 1972, he had created the National Front, an assemblage of lost sheep from the extreme right who had been scattered at the end of the war. Some of the functionaries in the National Front had actively collaborated under the Vichy regime. One group had found its cause with the war in Algeria, defending until the end France's colonial domination over the land it had occupied since 1830. Le Pen had been stationed there as an intelligence officer and was later accused of resorting to torture, which he denied, all the while legitimizing the practice.

After a difficult start, Le Pen's electoral successes multiplied in the eighties, benefiting from the emergence of new worries: constantly rising unemployment, economic insecurity, and immigration in large urban areas. Over the course of the nineties, his party gained an increasingly important place in French political life, achieving breakthroughs in the popular electorate, where many felt orphaned by the decline of the Communist Party following the collapse of the Soviet Union.

Jean-Marie Le Pen never hid his historical parentage. He defended Marshal Pétain, whom he saw as a grand head of state, and whose portrait appeared at his party's rallies. He also seemed to take a certain pleasure in the ambiguity of his position on National Socialism and the Shoah. In September 1987, asked by journalists about Holocaust deniers who disputed the presence of gas chambers in the camps, Jean-Marie Le Pen replied: "I have not really studied the question, but I believe it's only one small point in the history of the Second World War." This statement created a shock wave, even amid members of his own party, which didn't stop him from repeating it.

This type of provocation had an audience in France, on the far right but also on the far left, where a certain theory was on the rise—the idea that the gas chambers were completely made up. The objective was to defame the eyewitnesses, to discredit serious works of historical scholarship, to considerably lower the estimated number of victims of this genocide, and ultimately to question the very scope of the Shoah. Unfortunately, until the 1990s, this completely unfounded theory found an outsized resonance with certain politicians and members of the media that consequently brought them more publicity.

In May 1990, thirty-four Jewish graves were defaced in the Carpentras cemetery in southeastern France, provoking a considerable outcry. Two months later, there was a vote on the so-called Gayssot Act to punish the denial of these crimes against humanity. It was the start of a series of these laws recognizing the enslavement and the genocide of Armenians as crimes against humanity.

French historians became concerned about the intervention of the state in the interpretation of the past, but also about the growing influence of eyewitnesses. They were afraid of confusing history, politics, and personal memories. The historian Pierre Nora even spoke of a "tyranny of memory" and accused the parliament of condemning the work of historians by "edicting official truths." The philosopher Paul Ricoeur, indispensable in this debate, theorized, "To make memory an imperative is the beginning of an abuse." He also says, "I'm cautious about the expression 'duty to remember' . . . I prefer 'the work of memory.' "

In my opinion, Ricoeur's formula is key to understanding a major difference between the ways France and Germany have confronted their pasts. In France, the terminology for describing the process is limited, and people mainly speak of a "duty to remember." In Germany, semantic variety is one measure of public interest in the task: *Geschichtsaufarbeitung* (historical work), *Erinnerungskultur* (remembrance culture), *Geschichtspolitik* (history policy), *Vergangenheitspolitik* (politics of the past). The most important German term, *Vergangenheitsbewältigung*, is even used in international academic circles to recognize a specific way of *coming to terms with the past* that has been developed in Germany.

In France, this work has mainly been the purview of the state, along with historians and victims' groups. "As sociologists, we doubt the force of the influence of political authorities on individual behavior," write Sarah Gensburger and Sandrine Lefranc in their 2017 treatise. The memory work should not be imposed from on high but needs "to be supported by many strong players," and target the shaping of individual critical thought.

One of the great achievements of this work in Germany is that it has not only involved large groups but has also managed to place an emphasis on how an individual might transform into an offender, or at least a *Mitläufer*. In most other European countries, including France, people were encouraged to identify with the victims or with those who resisted, but not with the perpetrators or with the mass who followed the current.

Of course, the people's responsibility in occupied countries was not comparable to the complicity of the Germans with an obviously criminal regime. France had many more members of the resistance and many more citizens who helped and concealed Jews than Germany did. Still, a majority supported Pétain and his collaborationist policy, at least until the German invasion of the free zone in November 1942, and allowed an antidemocratic, repressive, and anti-Semitic regime to move in. Denouncers and profiteers were numerous and many people were indifferent to the victims. Unfortunately, the attitude of the great majority—who were neither members of the resistance nor collaborators, but who contributed to the consolidation of criminal measures by remaining apathetic—has been largely ignored in the memory of France, as it has been in many European countries. The people have mainly identified themselves as victims, eluding individual and collective responsibility for the course of history. Most countries didn't ask the question that is central to Germany's work of memory: "How did it happen?" This question allows people to study the psychological and collective mechanisms that lead an individual or a society, often in the context of a crisis, to become complicit in crimes out of conformism, opportunism, indifference, blindness, and fear. It shows that people often have more choice than they think. History might not repeat itself, but these mechanisms do. So if people understand them, it helps them remain cautious about their own moral fallibility. More generally, making people aware of their role in the course of history offers a chance to reinforce their sense of individual responsibility in a democracy. Germany has fully exploited memory work to anchor democracy in its society and its institutions. Other countries have missed that chance.

✿   ✿   ✿

When I was in journalism school in Paris, a teacher took us on a field trip to Bonn, just before the government moved to Berlin. I remember being impressed by the ease with which we entered the Chancellery, a functional, no-frills steel-and-glass building, where a leading official received us without fuss, in an informal office. What a contrast with the décor of the president's and prime minister's Élysée and Matignon, palaces with gilded interiors, mirrors, and chandeliers all giving the state an aura of monarchical inaccessibility, where leading officials sit in lavish rooms and the visitor feels small under the distant ceilings.

This architectural disparity also reflects the institutional difference between the two countries. In France, the presidential system personalizes power, incarnated in the president of the republic, who sometimes tends to rule as a sovereign, while in Germany, power is much more spread out, with the central focus on the Bundestag, the body that controls executive action and serves as an arena for real, substantive, televised debates. France's centralization doesn't leave much room for its regions, while the German federal system leaves many prerogatives up to the states. The gathering of these diverse political elements constrains German political representatives to dialogue, argument, and search for compromise, preventing them from imposing a vision, as a president can do in France.

Another effective check on executive power is the German press. Its variety and quality are exceptional in Europe. Also because the relationship between journalists and power is quite transparent. Three times a week, in a large building dedicated to the press, the Bundespressekonferenz, the ministers' spokespeople, respond to questions from journalists until there are none left. Beyond these regular news conferences, German journalists can choose to invite politicians to come talk to them on particular occasions—and the politicians are the ones who make the trip and submit to the rules of journalism, not the other way around: a powerful symbol of the freedom of the press.

In Germany, democracy is also part of the life of big businesses. Union representatives sit on the board of directors and are therefore part of the decision-making process. A friend who coaches British and foreign executives stationed in Paris on how to understand the *French touch* in business told me how surprised they are when they encounter the marked sense of hierarchy that reigns in France and makes the chain of command endless. In the same post, these foreigners have more power than their French counterparts, who have to ask their boss, who has to ask his boss, who has to . . . I often feel this difference in restaurants, at a store, on the phone with customer service. In Germany, employees have significantly more room to maneuver, and can therefore take the initiative, with some flexibility, where the client is concerned. This difference always makes my mother say, "The Germans know how to do business."

From my adolescence onward, I had always experienced the healthy relationship Germans have with hierarchy as a great liberty, a source of inspiration for constructing good self-esteem. I think that Germany's honest confrontation with its past not only conveyed a certain sense of moral responsibility to its citizens, but also forged a mind-set that is critical of authority. These qualities are beneficial to democracy: prudence in the face of "providential" men who promise to fix every problem, suspicion of extremists on the right and the left, and understanding of the necessity for a strong civilian society. An entire education taken from careful observation of one of the most developed examples of state manipulation of crowds and collective blindness—the Third Reich.

In *Mein Kampf*, Adolf Hitler writes, "The receptive powers of the masses are very restricted, and their understanding is feeble. On the other hand, they quickly forget. Such being the case, an effective propaganda must be confined to a few bare essentials and those must be expressed as far as possible in stereotyped formulas. These slogans should be persistently repeated until the very last individual has come to grasp the idea that has been put forward." His minister of propaganda, Joseph Goebbels, recommended that "those whom the propaganda is aimed at must become completely saturated with the ideas it contains, without ever realizing they are becoming saturated." The mass rallies would, in Hitler's words, "burn into the small, wretched individual the proud conviction that, paltry worm that he was, he was nevertheless part of a great dragon."

One instigator of these rules of manipulation was the sociologist and psychologist Gustave Le Bon, whose book *The Psychology of Crowds* impressed and influenced the Italian dictator Benito Mussolini as well as Joseph Goebbels and most likely Hitler as well. The book—which created an uproar when it came out in 1895, and which has lost none of its relevance in today's world—describes the transformation of an individual when he dissolves into a crowd, considerably reducing his faculties of reflection and personal will: "the disappearance of the conscious personality, the predominance of the unconscious personality, the turning by means of suggestion and contagion of feelings and ideas in an identical direction, the tendency to immediately transform the suggested ideas into acts; these we see are the principal characteristics of an individual forming part of a crowd. He is no longer himself, but has become an automaton who has ceased to be guided by his will."

To manipulate a crowd, Le Bon emphasized that a leader must use terms that bring up strong, impressive images, flatter the passions and desires of his audience, satisfy the taste crowds have for what is legendary, confuse the line between the unbelievable and the real, and above all, renounce all reasoning. In this way, he will obtain deference, self-sacrifice, and a sense of duty, to the point that the crowd will renounce deeply anchored human values.

The Third Reich excelled in this exercise of inverting morality to the point that it was able to pass off the murder of old men, women, and children as heroic acts. In October 1943, at Posen, in Poland, Heinrich Himmler declared to the SS Führer: "Most of you will know what it means when a hundred bodies lie together, when five hundred are there or when there are a thousand. And . . . to have seen this through and—with the exception of human weakness—to have remained decent, has made us hard and is a page of glory never mentioned and never to be mentioned."

The story of my ties with Germany is the story of a feverish and ambiguous relationship in which exultation quarrels with annoyance, trust with misgivings, respect with boredom. For example, in Berlin I miss the French art of conversation, that "sort of electricity that gives off sparks," as the French writer Madame De Staël puts it in her book *Germany*, which she published in 1813 after traveling there. Despite the two centuries between us, I was amazed to find myself in agreement with her thinking, when she observes: "The integrity of the Germans permits them nothing of the sort . . . for they never hear a word without drawing a consequence from it, and do not conceive that speech can be treated as a liberal art, which has no other end or consequence than the pleasure which men find in it."

I am also nostalgic for a particularity of French identity called "general culture," that broad knowledge of classical humanities and arts, which is highly valued in French teaching and society, and perceived as a common foundation on which to build a "French spirit." It's hard to avoid being cultivated in France if you want to be part of the elite.

But lastly, if I've chosen to live in Germany, it is also because my admiration for the whole overrules my irritation about the particular, and I savor the peace of living in a country where discernment, collective responsibility, and intellectual honesty often take priority in society, media, and politics.

When I told my sister that I was writing this book, she wasn't that surprised. Nathalie and I went to the same school, she has read the same books, and had the same education. She replied, "That's Papa's influence." It's strange because I always believed myself to be more French than German, and when we were little, my father was often absent on business trips, and if he was with us, it was not to endlessly saturate us with the history of the Third Reich. The transmission happened in other ways. Perhaps because he never lectured us or judged us, and because he let us make our own choices very early, he made us want to follow his example of freethinking founded not on obliviousness but on the legacy of a dictatorship.

XII

The Wall Is Dead, Long Live the Wall

When the Berlin Wall came down on November 9, 1989, I was too young to ask my father to take me to Berlin. I regret that I wasn't there to witness this triumph of liberty, the crowds who embraced without knowing one another, crying and laughing, enthusiastically swinging picks to make holes in the wall that had separated them for decades. In the images and films of those elated days, I see neither bitterness on the faces of the East Germans, imprisoned for half a century in a country they didn't choose, nor hostility from the West Germans as they faced their new compatriots, with whom they would have to share everything.

Helmut Kohl must have been seized with such emotion when, a month later, during a speech in Dresden, tens of thousands of East Germans came to see him, crying, "Helmut, Helmut!" "Unite, Unite!" and waving West German flags. The chancellor later said that this was the moment he realized there could not be, should not be any other option but reunification. Margaret Thatcher, the British prime minister, and François Mitterrand, president of France, didn't share his opinion, fearing the return of a strong Germany in the center of Europe.

In West Germany, too, certain intellectuals were reticent. "Because of Auschwitz, no reunification" was their slogan. At their head was Günter Grass, who declared at the Berlin SPD party convention that a "unified state, whose changing leaders, in just forty-five years, have written the history book on suffering, rubble, defeats, millions of refugees, millions of dead, and the burden of unmanageable crimes, does not warrant a new edition." Would the Nazi past, already responsible for the division of Germany after the war, now be allowed to compromise the dream of unity? Kohl decided it would not, and followed through on his instinct.

On October 3, 1990, two countries that had evolved in diametrically opposite ways since the end of the Third Reich were reunified. On the one side, a democracy founded on economic success and critical confrontation of the Nazi past. On the other, a dictatorship founded on an antifascist mythology that had allowed it to avoid any moral responsibility for its history.

More than a half century after the end of the war, Germany found itself once again facing the prickly question of how to transform a dictatorship into a democracy. Taking inspiration from the positive experience of West Germany, the focus was put on economic development and confronting the past.

The day of reunification, as I walked out of a fevered speech by the headmaster of my international lycée, who addressed us, students from all nations, as a "new hope for peace in Europe," I suddenly realized that this was undoubtedly one of the most powerful historical events I would experience in my lifetime. So as a young girl carried by a new passion for the great odysseys of history, I traveled with my mother to East Berlin to visit my father.

For eight months, he worked for the Treuhandanstalt, an organization placed under the authority of the German finance ministry, which, after reunification, had inherited the estate of the GDR, where almost everything belonged to the state. The Treuhandanstalt had been charged with finding private investors for significant real estate assets and for about 8,500 businesses employing more than 4 million people. The West German state had asked prominent companies to temporarily "lend" experts to guide this vast conversion from a centrally planned economy to a social market economy.

We were living outside Paris, where my father worked for the French headquarters of Mercedes-Benz. As soon as the board offered him this mission, he immediately accepted the chance to participate in the reunification of his country, which he had known only in its divided state. "I got involved for different reasons, out of professional interest, patriotic feelings, and because I wanted to help the East Germans. It was clear to me there had been an injustice, that they had paid a much higher price than us for the Third Reich, since they had suffered under a dictatorship, politically and also economically. For me it was a kind of honor to help."

After the wall fell, the GDR continued to exist for almost one year. At the beginning the dictatorship regime continued to exist but it was losing control. The Communist SED party's authority vacillated, its membership changing in a flash from 2.3 million to 700,000, and many of its leaders were ousted.

The GDR police watched passively as anarchy spread. Nobody knew anymore what was legal and what was not, and everybody tried to exploit the situation. Bars, concerts, parties, theaters popped up anywhere and everywhere in wildly different spaces and apartments. People were unwinding, reveling in the freedom that had been denied them for forty years. Anarchy also became the seed of crime and violence. Political movements that had been strictly forbidden under the GDR broke out. Punks, skinheads, radical leftists, and above all neo-Nazis, engaged in street riots. Hardly anybody got arrested.

The GDR had become a lawless state. People wanted to get rid of the old regime and demonstrated in the streets, expressing their desire for democracy. Under pressure, delegates of the state agreed, for the first time, to meet with leaders of civilian and religious groups, dissidents whom they had persecuted until then, who had played an important role in the uprising.

From December 1989 on, together with eastern representatives of western political parties, they met regularly to debate the future of the GDR: economic and democratic reforms; the dissolution of the Stasi, the state security service; and free elections. Soon two camps formed, one for those who wanted a very quick reunification—such as Helmut Kohl's CDU party—and one for those who preferred to reform their country first in order to negotiate reunification at eye level. This question was settled in the first free parliamentary elections in the GDR, on March 18, 1990, when the very pro-reunification CDU came out ahead, with more than 40 percent of the votes.

The citizen groups didn't even reach the 5 percent of votes needed to enter parliament: those who had helped to bring down the dictatorship found themselves cut out of configuring their country's future. Over them, many people had chosen quick reunification, because they were sick of insecurity and above all of material privation. They wanted the deutsche mark.

In fall 1990, my father was among the first West Germans to go to East Berlin to help with the economic conversion of East Germany. He was project director, charged with the sale of very large businesses in the industrial sector. "When I arrived," my father says, "nearly everyone at the Treuhandanstalt was East German. Many large West German companies were unwilling to lend qualified experts. We would call them up and say, if you don't send anyone, we won't sell you anything. They ended up lending a hand." In addition to those difficulties, the German leadership in Bonn hadn't even put together a budget for office supplies, and the equipment was in a pretty terrible state. "We didn't have enough typewriters, or even pens. Worst of all, there were only six telephone lines, a ridiculous number in view of the enormity of the task that awaited the organization."

My father had a certain number of former high-ranking Party members on his team, even former ministers. Sometimes in the evening he would invite them for a glass of wine so that he could listen to them talk about their daily life under the GDR and their fears for the future. Despite the fundamental principles of a "state of workers and farmers," a privileged class had certainly existed in this Communist state, a political elite that frequently abused its power to gain privileges. For them, the end of the regime meant an inevitable fall in status. My father began to feel some sympathy for them. "In spite of everything, there was a certain coherence between their way of life and the socialist ideal—they lived relatively modestly for senior officials. They said that a master butcher in the West had a more beautiful house than the GDR head of state Erich Honecker! Their privileges were mainly to have power, not money, and the difference in lifestyle for a minister and his secretary was much less striking than in the West."

His East German team had a negative image of Western social conditions. "I said to them, 'You have a false image of us, go and see our businesses.' They came back very much astonished; the way workers were treated didn't correspond to what they'd had in mind. One of them was demoralized after visiting a West German factory and admitted: 'I knew you were ahead of us, but I didn't think it would be so far.'" These colleagues were a big help to Volker because they were very familiar with the internal structure of GDR companies. "On the other hand, they had no idea about marketing, productivity, competition, and little understanding of the value of things according to Western standards. For example," my father remembers, "some were ready to sell

a piece of land on an island in the Baltic for one deutsche mark
per square meter . . ."

In the East, as in the West, people counted on privatization to reap
large gains. But when my father discovered the disastrous state of
most companies in the GDR—the shoddy building materials, the
lack of organization, the low productivity, the polluting production
processes—he knew it would be difficult to find investors for many
of them. Especially since they had lost their main clients with the
collapse of the GDR and the Eastern bloc: nobody wanted Eastern
products anymore, and everyone was looking for Western goods.
The bell tolled for many products made in the GDR. The first
companies were liquidated. Four million jobs were threatened.

"The people were very disappointed, they had hoped that by
unifying with the rich West Germany, their jobs were guaranteed.
They had absolutely no idea of how a market economy works: when
a company is not competitive, it is liquidated," explains my father.

For East Germans, who had no experience of unemployment,
and considered it a Western phenomenon, it was a seismic shock.
The GDR had preferred to create nonproductive positions than to
recognize the failure of one of its claims: 100 percent employment.
Compared with his Western colleagues, an East German laborer
produced about a third of the value.

Despair and anger spread among the population. Employees of
threatened companies came to protest in front of the headquarters
of the Treuhandanstalt. Tensions ran high. "When we had several
candidates, the decisive criterion was not to choose the one that
offered most, but the one that would save the most jobs," says Volker.

Management errors and numerous internal cases of fraud and
corruption within the Treuhand itself didn't help with the finances.
The Treuhand was accused of grave negligence and of proceeding
too quickly with the sale of businesses. "It's true that we had to make

decisions rather promptly," my father acknowledges. "We didn't have the time to examine the files of each business in detail, and we couldn't ignore the possibility that the interested parties might be trying to cheat us or lie to us." To this day, my father believes that there really wasn't any alternative at that pace. "If we didn't move quickly, the economic activity of these companies could collapse to the point that they would become unsalable. If we couldn't manage to speedily convince the investor, all could be lost, including the jobs."

But if Bonn and West German businesses had supplied adequate means and numerous qualified officials from the start—at the beginning, they were only a couple of hundred!—fewer errors would probably have been made. "The situation was certainly very complicated, and Helmut Kohl was very much involved. But the West simply underestimated the challenge, and I also remember an indifference reigning in the West, and that truly shocked me."

Bonn's politicians let the Treuhand's managers do the dirty work. They became a scapegoat for all East German woes. On April 1, 1991, the president of the organization, Detlev Rohwedder, was assassinated at his house by a gunman from the Red Army Faction. His windows had been armored on the ground floor, but not upstairs. This was the last murderous attack carried out by the RAF before the organization fell apart in 1998.

For some people, Detlev Rohwedder was the symbol of an unbridled capitalism; in truth he mobilized energetically to reduce the social impact of the economic transformation.

By 1994, at the end of the Treuhandanstalt's mission, out of 4.1 million jobs, 1.5 were saved; one third of the companies had been liquidated, two thirds privatized; 85 percent of companies were sold to West German investors. Instead of bringing money, the privatizations cost the state 250 billion marks in aid for investors, social programs for workers, and the enormous cost of environmental cleanup. The German state had many other additional costs, especially to replace the disastrous infrastructure of the East.

In total, the cost of the reunification is estimated at 2,000 billion deutsche marks. But this is partly compensated by the fact that many West German companies largely profited from the opening of a new market in the East.

As a result, in the East, many felt as if they had been annexed by the West. And in the West, many thought the cost of reunification had been too high.

One of the clearest memories I have of visiting my father in East Berlin is of the hotel where we stayed, which housed numerous Treuhandanstalt employees. The Palasthotel was a legendary place under the GDR, a paroxysm of Communist luxury, exclusively reserved for foreign visitors, and located south of Alexanderplatz, on the banks of the Spree. The ground floor was an endless empty space, and at its edge was a large restaurant whose atmosphere was brown—that was the first qualifier that came into my head, so much had the color seemed to bleed onto everything—the floor, the walls, the windows, the staff uniforms, the menus, and even the contents of the plates, to the point that it was easy to lose your way in this monochromatic sea that absorbed landmarks like the Communist regime, diluting differences through the tyranny of the identical. To reach the more than 600 rooms in this colossus, you had to pass through a sort of intermediary mezzanine floor, an immense, intimidating hall leading to the labyrinths of corridors where a client, coming back late at night after a business dinner and plenty of schnapps (the only abundant commodity in the GDR), might experience a troubling moment of claustrophobia, before he was able to find the door of his room. Dozens of hidden cameras would be observing him as soon as he entered the hotel, sometimes all the way to his bed, if he was one of those distinguished guests whom the pretty receptionist had selected for a special chamber, one of the ones where the Stasi stuffed the upholstered wall hangings with microphones and cameras. The irony, in retrospect, is that many clients were aware of it, just as they were aware that the charming woman at the bar was a Stasi agent, as was the one who offered to accompany him back to his room.

With the exception of prostitutes and staff, the Palasthotel was forbidden to GDR citizens, to "protect" them from Western decadence—American cigarettes, scotch whisky, French cheese, West German limousine service, and above all, contact with the enemy. My room's decor was straight out of a James Bond film: seventies furniture, a radio built into the nightstand, an old television in a cube of white plastic, and an enormous bay window, in lead glass, which extended from floor to ceiling and gave the impression that you could reach out and touch the ample cupola of the snow-covered Dom, a neo-Renaissance-style church just opposite the hotel, on the other side of the Spree.

While my father worked, my mother and I toured the area around the hotel. The urban landscape was divided between old streets, bordered with elegant but dilapidated historic buildings, and large modern arteries, as oversized as the glacial, concrete-block buildings lining them. Taken together, they created a feeling of crushing emptiness, with cars that were ridiculously small and rare compared to the size of the streets, and stores appearing so infrequently that we didn't dare venture too far into this ghost city in subzero temperatures. There were a few restaurants and bars, but they smelled of either damp tobacco or boiled cabbage. Later, I would find much to like in this sparse black-and-white setting, but at the time, if I came across young East Germans on Alexanderplatz, I saw them as having escaped the worst, and the idea that they would soon have access to all the colors of the West, those of freedom and consumption, and the delirious offers of entertainments, gadgets, and cuisine, warmed the naïve heart of this capitalist child.

* * *

I didn't understand that this world had also known happiness. The emotions of youth, of falling in love, of having a first child, and other pleasures that sometimes felt as though they had disappeared in the West because abundance made us indifferent. There had been the excitement of flirting with the forbidden: reading Western newspapers, listening to hit songs in secret among friends, defying the police by riding a skateboard, a sport that was made in the USA, and therefore banned. It was only later that I understood, while reading this sentence from a former dissident, Roland Jahn, who is now president of the Stasi archives: "Even under a dictatorship, the sun shines—but not always for everyone."

After reunification, the East Germans had to relearn everything. Jana Hensel, who was an adolescent then, described this over-whelming change in her book *After the Wall: Confessions from an East German Childhood*: "In the first years after reunification I spent every spare minute I had studying the West, analyzing what I saw and trying to understand. The goal was a perfect copy. I didn't want to stick out anymore. I was tired of people in the supermar-ket making snide comments about my clothes, tired of going to restaurants and not recognizing half of what was on the menu. I wanted to know everything everyone else knew. My brain was a perpetual scanner, registering the body language, the behavior, the slang, the haircuts, and the wardrobes of my fellow citizens from the West."

Suddenly, West German norms were applied everywhere—in laws, systems for retirement, taxes, social security—you had to adapt very quickly. Losing your bearings was disconcerting, perhaps less for young people than for an older generation who watched, powerless, as the things that had kept them company for decades disappeared: a rhythm, a rhetoric, a decor, a type of clothing, a code of social and economic conduct, the TV programs, parades and celebrations, certain food items. The first posters advertising IKEA appeared, the first McDonald's opened. People had to adapt to new prices, marketing, performance, competition. Instead of waiting in line for a rare ration under communism, people had to learn how to choose from abundant offerings. "In the East, people were accustomed to functioning as a collective, where the individual didn't have to choose," my father explains. "One detail stood out to me: in many apartment buildings, it was impossible to regulate the heat individually, even to turn it off! If you were too hot, you opened the windows. Everything was a little bit like that, in social as well as professional life, there was very little room for individual responsibility to maneuver, the state organized almost everything. Then suddenly there was all this turmoil, people were asked to act, to choose, to give their opinions. It was hardest on the elderly. They were totally overwhelmed. Many panicked. There was a wave of suicides."

Part of the East German population experienced reunification as a humiliation, even as a colonization of the East by the West. This impression was strengthened by the fact that more than 85 percent of East German businesses were acquired by West Germans, and only 6 percent by their Eastern compatriots. The latter had neither the means to acquire big companies nor the experience to run them. Those who lost their jobs felt useless, as if all that they had learned was worthless. But they were not so much victims of the West as of the GDR regime, which had deceived all its people and kept them in ignorance and dependency. Still, "the West could have done more to accompany people from the beginning, to help them, to explain things to them, in order to make the transition less painful," my father says. For that, the indifference of West German society toward the fate of its new co-citizens was too great.

❖   ❖   ❖

The challenges of reunification didn't only lie in becoming a market economy, but also in reckoning with the past of the SED dictatorship. In contrast with the post–Third Reich era, a clear confrontation with the past quickly began, as an essential condition of democratization. Those who were most threatened by this process, like high-ranking members of the Party and the Stasi, clung desperately to the ruins of their power, hurrying to destroy their archives in secret after the Wall came down. Civil rights activists caught wind of it and occupied branches of the Stasi all across the country. When they arrived, the floors were covered with torn and burned papers, and tens of thousands of garbage bags were stuffed with files shredded into a thousand pieces, but miles of other archives remained intact. When the Wall came down, the Stasi had as many as 91,000 official agents, and 180,000 unofficial ones called IMs. In total, it had benefited for forty years from the collaboration of 620,000 East Germans recruited from within civil society. Stasi informers were everywhere—it could be your lover, your mother-in-law, your colleague, the grocer on the corner, the newspaper man, the pretty girl who makes eyes at you in the café, and sometimes even your spouse. Distrust reigned at work, between friends, in leisure activities, and even in the midst of family life. The Stasi condemned citizens to a state of permanent anxiety and interior isolation, even though most people were not politically motivated, and simply wanted more freedom. Whoever fell into the Stasi's clutches risked being mistreated and detained in a cold, solitary cell. The Stasi beat and tortured people to make them talk, prisoners were forced to denounce people, to collaborate with the agents, or to sign false confessions. They were also exploited for forced labor, in complete contradiction with the principles of Marxism and Leninism.

As so often happens after a dictatorship, opinions were torn between those who demanded that the past be brought to light, and those who wanted to make a clean break. The former wanted the Stasi archives opened, and the latter wanted them to remain closed, either to save their own skins or because they feared that the eventual settling of scores and acts of revenge would destabilize and divide society. Kohl's government was opposed to opening them, but after a hunger strike by militant social rights activists in September 1990, he gave in. The Bundestag voted in an overwhelming majority to approve the Stasi Records Act, and a new Federal Authority for Stasi Documents was created.

Its current president, Roland Jahn, who in 1983 was expelled from the GDR to the West, where he became a journalist for television, was there the first day the records were opened. It was January 2, 1992. "It was already a triumph to see," he said, "they no longer had the power to do whatever they wanted, you had your file in your hands . . . but it was also depressing, because everything you had feared, that they had infiltrated your privacy, that they wanted to destroy you, you could suddenly see it in black and white, it was terrifying." In his reporting, he encountered many Stasi victims who were in shock at discovering they had been betrayed by those they thought were their best friends.

Many people fell into traps the Stasi laid in order to force them to spy on targeted people, at work or among their friends. Others got involved with the Stasi voluntarily, moved by their ideological convictions. Such as Monika Haeger, a Party devotee who succeeded in infiltrating the most intimate circles of clandestine dissidents, making friends with them before reporting on them to a Stasi agent. In her interview with Roland Jahn, Monika provided rare testimony, describing how convinced she was to contribute to "the idea of socialism, of humanity, of the human." "I had simply refused to see things that should have been very clear: that they were everything but humans, that they were profoundly inhumane," she continued in tears.

Indoctrination began at the earliest possible age in school, where the professors taught history, geography, culture, and economics through the prism of ideology, while special courses were also devoted to promoting the Communist worldview. One of the most important grades in the school report card was the one for so-called ideological engagement. Mass organizations for young people did the rest, and almost everyone joined, or else they would risk discrimination later, at university and in the workplace.

Many acts committed under this system of oppression were very difficult to pursue under criminal law. It was impossible to have mass trials for everyone who had collaborated with the regime, and even among the leadership class, it wasn't simple to identify who was guilty. My father, who worked with former ministers and members of the Politburo, remained rather indulgent toward them: "I never compared them to Nazi leaders. They were not comparable. These men had not committed massacres, nor had they unleashed a war of aggression, and in the end, they accepted the political demands of their citizens in 1989 without spilling a drop of blood or sending in the army." Others in West Germany didn't hesitate to draw unflattering parallels between the Nazi and Communist dictatorships, and they continued to do so long after reunification, to the point that the former dissident Günter Nooke was obliged to say to the Bundestag in 2004: "There is no doubt about it—Bautzen"—a Stasi prison—"is not Auschwitz!"

The Republic of Germany was prudent in its judicial pursuits against high-ranking bureaucrats from the East German regime. It didn't want to create the impression of practicing "revenge justice."

Finally, in 1991, West German justice decided to open the first of a long series of trials that would run until 2004, against border guards accused of being responsible for the deaths of several hundred East Germans. These trials presented the same dilemma that had faced those who had served the Third Reich: How to condemn someone for acts that were legal at the moment they were executed, when they would have risked being sanctioned for disobedience? West German justice decided that the deliberate execution of fugitives was equal to murder and that it violated basic rights, universal standards of justice, and could not be abrogated by the laws of a state. The majority of border guards were condemned for "accessory to murder," but considering the enormous pressure the regime put on these soldiers to make them take up arms against fugitives, the judges pronounced penalties that were very light. Almost none of the accused were actually condemned to prison sentences.

In the trial for the victims of the Wall, the priority wasn't the border guards but the bigwigs of the regime who had given the order to fire and built the merciless machine of border security—a combination of mines in the ground, razor wire, and body-heat detectors capable of automatically unleashing machine guns at the slightest signal. On May 3, 1974, Erich Honecker, who led the GDR government from 1971 to 1989, spoke at a meeting of the National Defense Council: "Without exception, we must continue to fire on those who attempt forced passage across the border, and we must reward those comrades who have used their firepower with success." In total, some forty firm prison sentences were pronounced, including some for ministers and members of the Politburo. Egon Krenz, who had succeeded Erich Honecker just before the Wall came down, was condemned to six and a half years in prison. Honecker, who had fled to Moscow with his spouse, Margot, was handed over to the German police in July 1992 and placed in pretrial detention in Berlin, while his wife was exiled to Chile, where she remained until her death.

Erich Honecker's trial was never completed due to his poor health, and he was allowed to go into exile in Chile, where he died shortly after. As for Erich Mielke, who developed and oversaw the Stasi for thirty years, creating one of the most feared surveillance systems in the world, he was sentenced to six years in prison for a crime that went back to 1931, when, as a member of a paramilitary group associated with the German Communist Party, he had participated in the killing of two police officers. In the end, fixed prison sentences may have been limited in number, but they were generally rather severe.

The victims of the regime accused the justice system of only paying attention to the dead and ignoring many whose interior lives had been destroyed by the persecutions they had endured. It must have been hard for them to watch the reintegration of police officers into the Western state organization and the distribution of licenses to judges who had been pillars of the repressive GDR system. But as Minister of Justice Klaus Kinkel observed in a 1991 interview: "After a revolution or a change of government, it's not possible to change a whole people. And naturally, it's not possible to completely change the elites, the ruling class." In the following decades, a series of prominent leaders who were integrated into reunified Germany had their past involvement with the Stasi catch up to them, and some had to end their careers. These scandals also kept discussion of the GDR past alive.

The Bundestag also attempted to shed light on the past, creating an investigative commission for "Working Through the History and the Consequences of the SED Dictatorship in Germany." This body, made up of deputies and experts, was meant to contribute to the reconciliation of society and to engage in a dialogue with public opinion to reinforce a democratic conscience and the development of a common political culture.

The battle of memory also played out on another field. As often happens after a dictatorship, a hunt for symbols began. Emblems and statues were torn down, names of streets were changed, buildings were demolished. They had to remove the statues of

Lenin that had swarmed the country, including the most imposing example, a sixty-two-foot-high colossus erected in Berlin in
the center of a square bearing his name. Berliners were opposed
to demolition, postering it with signs: "We protest the offensive,
primitive iconoclast"; "You're in the FRG! Why are you still afraid
of a stone Lenin?" After being deified by nearly half the world, the
gigantic head of this icon of the Bolshevik revolution suddenly rose
up, lifted by a crane through the Berlin sky under a driving rain.

Names like Stalin and Lenin, bloody dictators who sowed terror, could not continue to be honored under a democracy without
great difficulty. But sometimes the great cleanup of history went
too far. Certain people sought, with an energy verging on hysteria, to wipe out all traces of the GDR, as if everything in that
country was cursed. Names like Marx and Engels narrowly missed
appearing on the blacklist. Not far from Berlin's TV tower, tall
sculptures representing the authors of *The Communist Manifesto*
were threatened for a time, but finally spared, thanks to stubborn
defenders who had graffitied "We are not guilty" at the feet of
the two bronze men. Someone else quickly erased the "not." The
legendary hotel on Alexanderplatz where I had visited my father
was torn down because it was contaminated with asbestos. The
war of symbols reached its peak with the Palace of the Republic,
a rectangular block with mirroring bronze-colored glass facades
built in the heart of East Berlin in the 1970s to entertain the people
with a Western-style temple to consumerism: an immense white
marble lobby lit by thousands of hanging lightbulbs. The space
offered boutiques, restaurants, a bowling alley, discos, bars . . . A
small betrayal of Communist dogma. In 1990, it was closed for a
long asbestos-removal process, raising the question of its ultimate
fate and unleashing a long, howling debate between those who
favored demolition and those who wanted to renovate.

An entire GDR generation associated part of its youth with
this leisure space. Finally, the Bundestag voted to demolish the

building in 2003. In its place, they decided to build a palace modeled on the baroque palace of the Hohenzollern, which had been bombed during the war and torn down by the GDR in 1950. For many East Germans, it was as if they were not allowed to have experienced moments of happiness under the dictatorship. Several years after reunification, a wave of nostalgia for the GDR appeared that was nicknamed "Eastalgia." Old products from the East returned to supermarket shelves, and furniture, lamps, and other everyday objects became cult items. Eastalgia parties were organized in spaces decorated with an abundance of GDR accessories and propaganda—portraits, flags, and banners. This overt detachment from Western lifestyles found its political expression in the federal elections of 1994, when the new Communist party PDS gained 4.4 percent. Some East Germans were reacting, among other things, to what they perceived as a demonization of their home country by the West. "Criticism of the GDR was perceived as a criticism of the individual. And that was especially unfortunate," Roland Jahn explains. "People tried to live under the GDR, then came the split with reunification. . . . They tried to bounce back on their own steam. And they were worried about losing what they had built all over again. The first victims of this fear were foreigners."

After the Wall fell, a new phenomenon appeared in eastern Germany: neo-Nazi groups started to emerge everywhere, and it became sadly routine for them to descend in packs and attack foreigners in the middle of the street.

The hate culminated at the end of August 1992, in Rostock on the Baltic Sea, when assailants attacked the home of Vietnamese refugees, shouting, "We'll get you all!" and "We'll roast you!" They tried to force open the doors of the home, breaking windows and throwing Molotov cocktails, while about three thousand spectators cheered them on. The house began to catch fire. Inside, where a camera team was filming the events, the refugees began to despair, caught in the trap of flames and smoke. The children screamed, women cried, others ran in every direction trying to force a way out, finally managing to open a door that led to the roof. The police on duty, though alerted, waited for hours before clearing a way for the firefighters.

These images seized Germany with fear. What shocked people most were the thousands of people who had come to cheer on or even help the assailants: normal citizens, of different ages. A coquettish woman in her sixties, with her white hair pulled back, earrings, and a necklace, told the camera: "Well, it's a disgusting business, Germans are afraid of losing their jobs, their apartments, they're in crisis, and here come these refugees, dirtying apartments, they have no culture, I mean not like Germans, who are known for their cleanliness and all that . . ." Another woman, in her thirties, agreed: "These are real gypsies, they made a campfire, they did all this . . ." It didn't interest these people that the burned-down building housed Vietnamese workers who had been "invited" by the GDR to do the very low-paid jobs that East Germans avoided.

Rostock had 1,640 foreigners and 240,000 residents.

In the West, xenophobic violence also increased after the fall of the Iron Curtain with the influx of refugees from the East. In 1992, the number of people requesting asylum reached its peak of more than 440,000. Even though the rate of admission was very low, the conservative and extreme right parties launched a very emotional campaign against the refugees.

This was the context when, in November 1992, in Mölln, two neo-Nazis set fire to a house where Turkish families were living: two little girls and their grandmother died in the flames. A few months later, once again in the West, at Solingen, four neo-

Nazis burned down a building that also housed Turkish families. A woman and her little boy died jumping out a window; a young man and two children were burned to death. Chancellor Helmut Kohl didn't bother to go to any of these funerals, contenting himself with sending his minister of foreign affairs, Klaus Kinkel. His spokesperson explained that the federal government did not want to get into "condolence tourism."

This indifference was not shared by the population. In total, more than a million took to the streets in the western part of the country to say "Never again!" In Mannheim, where I was a student at the time, I joined a long "chain of light"—thousands, tens of thousands of people linked arm-in-arm, with lights in their hands, standing together against racial violence. For two hours, as I stood between an old woman who held a candle in her trembling hands and a young guy with a punk hairdo, I felt the force of memory against hate.

In the East, however, demonstrations of solidarity with the numerous victims of xenophobia were rare. The scenes in Rostock had not provoked as much public indignation as they had in the West, where the images had been a reminder of the pogroms against Jews under Nazism. Unlike the murders in Mölln or Solingen, in the East several attacks had taken place openly, in broad daylight, and the perpetrators didn't hide when the cameras arrived, and an approving crowd often gathered to encourage the attacks.

They had to face the facts: the memory work of National Socialism, which was so central in constructing West German identity, had been ignored in the GDR, leaving reunified Germany with a heavy heritage. In its foundational myth, the GDR represented only German Communists, who had fought fascism beside the Soviet Union and created a new Germany. This was true for some of the founders, who had actively resisted and had been imprisoned in concentration camps. But they projected their experience onto the GDR population as a whole, when the majority had in fact supported the Nazi regime. In this way, the regime discharged all individual fault and responsibility under National Socialism. Since people were not antifascist by nature, it had to be imposed from above; the regime bombarded them with countless commemorative ceremonies, monuments, and rituals, at school and in their leisure time. The Communist resistance, the fallen soldiers of the Red Army, were at the heart of these commemorations, not the Jews or other victims, who disappeared from the country's collective memory. "In eighth grade, we had to go to Buchenwald, which had been transformed into an enormous memorial. We talked about the Communist heroes, but never about how fascism had functioned, or why so many people supported it," remembers Roland Jahn. Jana Hensel writes in her book *After the Wall*: "In the history lessons we got as children, everyone was part of the antifascist resistance movement. Grandparents, parents, neighbors, everyone."

The subject wasn't debated within families either, and the younger generation didn't rebel in 1968 like they did in the West. The GDR designated West Germany as the only depository of Nazi crimes, and West Germans as the ones who had to excuse and compensate for what had been done, especially to the Jews. An entire team was charged with digging through the Nazi past of prominent West Germans to blackmail them later or to discredit them by publicly revealing the ways they were implicated. This practice was the heart of their anti-West propaganda. The accusations were partly true. But while West German society slowly started to realize its contribution to the crimes of the Third Reich and to learn how to identify with the persecutor, the East Germans kept denying their historical responsibility and identifying with the victims.

Besides, the East Germans lived in a bubble. With the exception of West German television, none of the intellectual and cultural riches of the world could penetrate. They rarely left their country, and when they got the chance, it was to go to other Communist countries that functioned in the same way, on the Black Sea coast in Bulgaria, or to Lake Balaton in Hungary. Until retirement age, they basically didn't have the right to travel in the West, and never as a family or a couple for fear that they wouldn't come back. It was also very complicated for foreigners to enter the GDR, even if you had a visa. The number of foreigners didn't exceed 200,000, and they were cloistered: the unpopular Soviet soldiers lived in barracks, while workers recruited from Communist countries in Africa and Asia lived in separate homes, forbidden to mingle with the population.

The dictatorship controlled all forms of contact with foreigners. The lack of experience with other cultures and the absence of individual moral empowerment toward the Nazi past favored a vision of foreign countries that was loaded with clichés, prejudice, and fear.

Today, three decades after the Wall fell, the East has nothing in common with the East my father knew. Streets and facades have been renovated, scrubbed, polished, and billions invested in infrastructure. When I host foreign visitors in Berlin, I encourage them to visit these regions immortalized by the master of German romantic painting, Caspar David Friedrich. In the north, you can cross a great plateau of clear lakes, the refuge of an enormous variety of birds, historic towns, and many castles, before arriving at the coast of the Baltic Sea, where turn-of-the century bathing towns offer a journey back in time. In the south, the best way to admire the countryside is to take the train from Berlin to Prague, and to watch the forests and lakes unrolling, the Elbe swerving between the green hills where, just before the Czech border, a tall collection of rocky spires rises like something out of a fairy tale. In some areas, especially in Saxony and Thuringia, the economy is booming, industry is developing, and unemployment is continuously falling. The economic and social differences between the East and the West have lessened considerably over the last ten years, to the point that some parts of the former GDR surpass their Western counterparts.

However, if you visit Dresden or Leipzig on a day when citizens are demonstrating, it would be obvious that a significant number of East Germans are angry with the government, with traditional political parties, with journalists, with the West, with intellectuals, with the European Union, and especially with refugees. Xenophobia never disappeared from the East after reunification, but beginning with the arrival of large groups of refugees fleeing the war in Syria at the end of 2014, it has taken on another dimension. Violence against refugees exploded in the East, becoming four times more common, in proportion to the number of residents, in the East than in the West in 2014. This phenomenon was exacerbated in 2015. Communities in East Germany saw crowds brandishing the flag of the Third Reich and attacking the homes of refugees, foreigners, and politicians. Angela Merkel's decision to open the borders to refugees in September 2015 added even more fuel to this violence. It broke ground for the rapid rise of a new xenophobic party on the extreme right, the AfD.

In September 2017, two weeks before the federal elections, I went to Jena, a pretty university town in Thuringia, to write a report for a French magazine on the AfD electoral campaign. Several hundred people had gathered before a platform in the market square, encircled by barricades and guarded by a horde of police officers. On the podium, a leading candidate seized the microphone and began insulting all the parties in the Bundestag: "The Green Party," whose people in the street push the three Cs, "climate change, cocaine up their noses, and child abuse"; the FDP, "a sect for one man, a mix between a mannequin for underwear and an ad for cheap perfume"; the SPD, "that pile of trash, do you see their faces?" On the other side of the barricades, counterprotestors made an uproar to derail the meeting. Civil society in Jena had mobilized. They hoisted banners calling for people to "Resist Hate!" The AfD candidate shouted at them: "We hear that nine times out of ten, your parents were brother and sister, and when I catch sight of their faces, ladies and gentlemen, I also have the impression that the family pets were also involved . . ."

Then, after demanding that the sleepy public applaud him, he launched into a hate-filled tirade against Angela Merkel. "The main problem is this tyrant, whom we must elimin—" He stopped himself, proud of his wink at Nazi language, and demanded at least thirty-five years of "jail" for Merkel. A security forces helicopter appeared in the sky, momentarily drowning out the speaker with its whir. He pointed to it, and asked, "Can we take out the helicopter?" The violence and the vulgarity of these statements from the podium didn't seem to shock the mostly male public, who had none of the particular style of neo-Nazis. They were twenty, thirty, forty years old when the Wall came down.

On September 24, 2017, the AfD gained 12.7 percent of the votes—21.9 percent in the East as opposed to 10.7 percent in the West. It was the first time since the end of World War II that a far-right party entered the Bundestag.

In Jena, I ran into Roland Jahn, who was there by coincidence. He had been invited to a conference titled "Are We About to Forget the Stasi?" In the hall, which was filled with mainly retired citizens, an audience member said that people around him felt threatened by "political correctness," a bit like they were "under the GDR." Jahn replied, "Today, you don't end up in prison for voicing your opinion. You have to be careful: hate is not freedom of speech." In the audience, a woman stood up: "We were cowardly, most of us participated, in one way or another. Me, too, I didn't have the courage to oppose it." Jahn agreed. The *Mitläufer* of the GDR are one of his favorite subjects. In 2014, he published a book on them. "After reunification, the debate was marked by a confrontation between perpetrator and victims," he explains, "but many East Germans could not identify with either of these two roles. We didn't examine the aspects that would have allowed us to better understand how a conformist society contributed to stabilizing this dictatorship."

After the conference, he showed me around Jena, where he grew up. He knew every wall, every street, their hidden scars erased by a deluge of renovations. Here was the university where he had been kicked out after having criticized, in a seminar, the removal of the poet Wolf Biermann's citizenship. All his classmates except one voted to expel Roland, friends of his who had been afraid. He was deeply hurt. In his book he writes, "There are many forms of adaptation, from silence to servility. But adaptation also has a price; it has served to legitimize those who, in the name of the state, committed injustices." Of course, you can't ask someone to stand up to a dictatorship if the price is his own freedom, he allows, but "everyone who adapts also has room to maneuver."

The success of extremist parties like the AfD in the ex-GDR has many reasons, but Roland Jahn is convinced that it is also the result of a memory gap, and not just where the Nazis are concerned: "Many people refuse to ask themselves about their individual responsibility under the GDR, and this is still true today." Another memory gap concerns the meager attention West Germans paid to the suffering of their Eastern compatriots after the Wall came down—the cultural shock, the wave of unemployment, the feeling of being devalued.

The shortage of empathy in the West, and the lack of memory work in the East, divide Germany to this day.

Through hidden alleys and secret shortcuts, Roland Jahn moved through Jena with the ease of a kid who grew up in these streets and often had to run to escape from the police. "Each time I return, these old images come back to me, and I think, *What a road we've traveled, what freedom we've won!*"

XIII

Nazis Never Die

How I love the city of Berlin. Sometimes in the evening, on my way home through the deserted streets of Berlin after a late dinner, I circle by bike through the historic district, to pay homage to the sites with troubled pasts, whose wounds I know as if they were my own. Once, a hundred feet from my door in the Kreuzberg neighborhood, the Wall cut my street in half. Behind it, there was a militarized zone, then another wall, and on the other side, the GDR. At night, from my windows, you could have glimpsed silhouettes in the lighted apartments of East Germans. And those neighbors, what did they see when they looked toward the capitalist West? Freedom, probably, but also a suicidal deference to consumption.

One night in 1969, just at the end of my street, a young East German succeeded in sneaking into the militarized zone. But then he tripped a cable that set off the alarm. Eight border guards poured from their watchtowers, brandished their arms, and fired like madmen, 148 times. He was twenty-eight.

Today, there's a pretty garden walkway where the Wall used to be, and lilacs fill the air in springtime. And in my street, there are *Stolpersteine*, the square brass plaques embedded in the sidewalk to recall the tragedy of former residents who were deported for being Jewish.

✿   ✿   ✿

Europe was brought back to life twice—in 1945 and 1989. On
the ashes of dictatorships, people built democracy, liberty, and
peace through their own hard work. Once a land of ferocious wars,
genocide, and murderous divisions between brothers, Europe
has become an Eden in the eyes of many people at the mercy
of megalomaniacal leaders who dispose of human lives as if they
were playing a game of chess. For years, we've been following the
drama of people crossing the Mediterranean, taking unimaginable
risks to get from Africa to Europe. With eight hundred people in
a boat made for one hundred, they beg the heavens to stop the
wind from picking up at sea and turning their rickety vessel into
another giant coffin sinking under the cold water, to join the vast
cemetery of nameless refugees. We've also seen the exodus across
Turkey and the Balkans; the people fleeing wars in the Middle
East, the death that strikes anywhere, without warning. How many
times have these people dug through the ruins of a school, a house,
their temples pounding, in the hopes of finding a loved one alive?

In 2015, the number of refugees fleeing the war in Syria swelled.
Many ended up in Hungary, in hopes of getting to the West. The
country was quickly overwhelmed and images of the disgraceful conditions they were met with swept across the world. On September 4,
a long column of refugees left Budapest on foot, walking along the
highway toward Austria, hoping to reach Germany. Viktor Orbán,
the Hungarian prime minister, announced that he wouldn't do anything to stop them. The German chancellor, Angela Merkel, had
just a few moments to make up her mind. She pictured the panic,
the escalation of violence, the armed intervention of the Hungarian
police, the blood, the dead. Three days earlier, the sea had returned
the body of a three-year-old boy, washed up on a Turkish beach, and

the photo of his little lifeless body, his face turned into the sand, still resonated as the ferocious symbol of an indifferent Europe.

As someone who grew up in the former GDR and knew that borders could be prisons, Merkel must have seen images rise in her mind: the sight of tens of thousands of East Germans pouring west after the Wall came down. And the memory of another trauma as well: the long columns of 12 million German refugees who were chased from Germany's lost eastern territories after the war and terrorized by the Red Army. Each time, the Germans had been forced to make space and sacrifices for these brothers. This time, too, she was convinced *"wir schaffen das"*—we'll make it work. Merkel opened the border.

When I turned on my TV on September 5, 2015, I saw a train in the Munich station with a cloud of refugees disembarking—a few veiled women, some children, but mainly young, unaccompanied men. For a fraction of a second, I feared they would be unwelcome, and by the look on their faces, they must have been thinking the same thing. An instant later, the camera showed these words written on the ground, on posters, and banners: *Willkommen! Welcome! Bienvenue!* and you could hear clapping. Hundreds of German citizens had come to greet the refugees with balloons, teddy bears, water, sandwiches, cakes. The strangers' faces lit up— first with small, timid smiles, a moment of shock, then the frank joy of relief, some hands waving, making the victory sign, others pressing the German flag to their hearts.

My mind was racing as these images superimposed themselves on those packed trains of the Nazi Reichsbahn, unloading their human cargo on the platforms of camps where the guards welcomed the condemned with boot heels, shouting at them to hurry up on the way to their deaths. I saw the lines of Jews in the Mannheim train station, suitcase in one hand and child in the other; crowds of indoctrinated Germans making the Hitler salute in unison; the photo of Peter Fechter, the young East

German in a puddle of blood at the foot of the Wall, condemned to die alone by the border guards after an hour of agony, just because he'd wanted to be free. I realized that something historic was happening here: after long reflection, after trying to purge the poisonous inheritance of these ancestors—monstrous Nazis, Communist dictators, and the crowds of *Mitläufer* who had accompanied them—the German people were finally playing a major role on the side of right, the position of defenders of humanity, prophets of faith in humankind. In the weeks that followed, tens of thousands of German volunteers offered their support anywhere they could, to the extent that the authorities were overwhelmed not only by migrants, but also by those who wished to help them. The media quickly took up this new religion of doing good, calling it *Willkommenskultur*, welcome culture, and launched euphoric messages calling for the Germans to liberate the best parts of themselves following the example of the chancellor, that daughter of a Protestant pastor, who had known better than anyone how to bring morality back into politics. Across the world, voices praised this generosity that people thought had disappeared. A century after the start of the long damnation that was unleashed by World War I, the hour of German redemption had arrived.

Little by little, the enthusiasm of these beginnings became more measured, as border villages woke up one fine morning with more refugees than native residents in their streets, as overwhelmed volunteers sounded the alarm, and above all after New Year's Eve in Cologne, where more than six hundred women were sexually harassed in front of the train station, where a thousand young men, mainly from the Middle East and North Africa, had gathered. At the end of 2015, a million refugees had arrived on German soil. Angela Merkel's immigration policies were losing popularity. Hostilities increased even more when, in December 2016, an Islamist at the wheel of a truck crashed into a Christmas market in Berlin, killing twelve people and injuring more than fifty.

A mute, pervasive suspicion began to spread dangerously, concerning Muslims, refugees, Arabs. The change was visible in people's faces when a fully veiled woman passed by a café terrace, or in the tension that electrified metro passengers when a group of teenagers shouted in Arabic as they jostled one another on the platform.

The media was accused of providing ecstatic coverage of the arrival of refugees that didn't take into consideration the fears of part of the German population, especially in the east. Most news outlets adjusted their coverage, introducing a more critical perspective.

German optimism took another blow when Hungary, Poland, the Czech Republic, and Slovakia, eastern members of the European Union, refused to accept their quota of migrants foreseen by the EU—at most tens of thousands for the largest countries—or offer support to Italy and Greece, the principal doorways for refugees entering Europe. These countries from the former Soviet bloc had very few refugees, and yet the populations already felt "overwhelmed." The refugee crisis revealed a profound difference in attitude between east and west Europe. The latter, which was used to multiculturalism, was shocked by what it considered xenophobia. It realized that on the other side of the Iron Curtain, the inwardness imposed by the Communist dictatorships had created an image of the rest of the world that was full of negative assumptions. For forty years, these populations had lived cloistered lives, forbidden from leaving the Communist bloc and closed to all outside influence. They were accustomed to an extreme homogeneity, devoid of ethnic, cultural, political, and religious diversity. What's more, they had been deprived of the memory work that might have clarified the dangers of nationalism, racism, and anti-Semitism. The Soviet Union had imposed its own memory on these people—the commemoration of the fight of the Red Army and of the Communists against fascism—to obscure the reality that most of these countries had been seduced by fascism, had been allied with Nazi Germany against the Soviet Union, and had actively collaborated in the extermination of the Jews.

When the Iron Curtain fell, some people's first reflex was to commemorate the heroes who'd been forbidden under Soviet rule: the pro-Reich leaders, the militias who had supported the Reich against the Red Army. Under the influence of the European Union, countries such as Romania finally confronted their past responsibility. But in the past few years, others have sunk into a contagious fascist nostalgia—above all Hungary, where Admiral Miklós Horthy is celebrated as a hero, despite the fact that he allied his country with Nazi Germany during the war. The result of his politics was that Nazi Germany, with the help of Hungarian collaborators, deported more than 560,000 out of 825,000 Jews, as well as thousands of Sinti and Roma. Prime Minister Viktor Orbán calls Horthy "an exceptional statesman," and many places and streets in Hungary bear his name.

Since he openly defied the European Union over the refugee crisis, Orbán has become the chief practitioner in Europe of a nationalist rhetoric that is anti-EU and riddled with lies. He propagates the conspiracy theory that the European elites are voluntarily orchestrating the "great replacement" of the white population with Arab immigrants. He creates scapegoats such as the Hungarian-American Jewish billionaire George Soros, whose organization Open Society actively supports democracy in the former eastern bloc. Soros is an enemy of this Hungarian leader who, behind his new model of "illiberal democracy," is dismantling democratic institutions one by one—taking control of the media, muzzling civil society, obstructing justice, and harassing NGOs.

Orbán's authoritarianism influences the region, especially in Poland, where the Law and Justice party, or PiS, also attacks the foundations of democracy by controlling television, purging the army, and stifling justice. Xenophobia and anti-Semitism have increased to a dangerous extent in Polish society. After years of tolerance, in 2022, the European Commission froze post-pandemic recovery aid, insisting Poland adhere to the rulings of the European Court of Justice concerning the independence of the Polish judiciary.

It's an open question—should regimes that openly scorn the very foundations of the European Union, while benefitting from the advantages it confers, have a place in the community? But to exclude them would be an injustice to the political and civil opposition to these regimes that is still very much alive in these countries.

Forty years of deprivation of democracy and civil society and falsification of history under Soviet rule has probably played a role in Hungary's and Poland's autocratization. But in the West, too, nationalism and populism are threatening democracy. The European Union was created on the memory of wars and dictatorships, the promise of "never again." It succeeded in preserving a long period of peace. But still more memory work must be done to help citizens resist drifting toward nationalist and antidemocratic political parties and ideas. Two countries particularly involved in the crimes of the Second World War have been surprisingly light in their work of remembrance and are paying the consequences to this day: Italy and Austria.

In 2010, I met a German-Italian who was selling Italian wines in Germany. We barely knew each other when he invited me to visit him for a few days in Tuscany, in his house on a vine-dotted hill. In the living room, on the wall above an orangewood bench, I noticed a painting in the Surrealist style, a work by his father, an Italian painter and an "admirer of Germany." It was the portrait of a man wearing epaulettes and a soldier's helmet with a pair of shades for protection against sun or dust. Behind him, a desert landscape unfolded in the Quattrocento manner, with an Arab-style fortress in the background. When I came closer, I noticed two words that merged into the blackness of the sky: "Erwin Rommel." The Desert Fox, who served as field marshal in the Wehrmacht and became a legend during the North African campaign.

My host had that remarkable habit of waking up at dawn to go harvest porcini mushrooms, equipping himself with tall boots and a scythe for cutting a way through the insect-filled undergrowth. One morning, I woke up before he returned and went down to make coffee in the blue-tiled kitchen. My eyes wandered to a wooden bowl that served as a catchall, and I noticed a metallic object inside. It was a key chain shaped like a bundle of elongated sticks bound together by a cord that wrapped around a tiny hatchet. I picked it up and noticed an inscription on the hatchet: *Fascismo e libertà*. When the master of the house returned from his hunting, I asked him why he had a key chain with a Fascist symbol on it. Without seeming embarrassed or surprised, he replied, "Because I'm a Fascist."

One night when we were eating dinner with his friends at a local trattoria, I asked them what they thought about Silvio Berlusconi, who was the leader of Italy at the time. One of them said to me: "It's not Berlusconi we need, but a real statesman, a true one, a man like Mussolini." Seeing my alarmed face, his neighbor doubled down. "It's been more than sixty years since Italy became a democracy, and what's the result? A total failure. Democracy might work in Germany, but not here. Italians need a strong power, a strong man." The others agreed, and with three stabs of a fork, democracy was destroyed and fascism was celebrated as a golden age.

My Italian friend and I came from the same generation, both dual citizens with a German parent, and from similar social upbringings, including experiences abroad—how was such a discrepancy possible? I had never wondered if memory work existed in Italy, since it had seemed so evident—the country had created fascism and was allied with Nazi Germany from the start. I had been mistaken.

After the war, the anti-Fascist Italian parties that had just come to power wanted to avoid fostering divisions in society and giving the Allies a negative impression of their country. They chose amnesia. Most Fascists were pardoned and reintegrated into society; very few Italian war criminals were put on trial. The Allies supported that policy and didn't organize anything equivalent to the Nuremberg Trials. As a consequence, the enormous crimes committed abroad by Fascist Italy have been forgotten: the brutal occupation of Yugoslavia and Greece during the war, riddled with massacres of civilians and brutal internments; the bloody colonial wars in Libya and Ethiopia that caused hundreds of thousands of civilian deaths during the 1930s.

In Italy, there are almost no monuments to recall these crimes perpetrated in other countries. There has barely been an official apology, and almost zero reparations have been paid. Few people are aware that Fascist Italy built hundreds of concentration camps, where it interned "undesirables" including many Slavic peoples. What Italian has heard of Rab in Croatia, Gonars near Trieste, Renicci in Tuscany, or Chiesanuova in Padua?

Even the Nazi and Fascist violence on Italian soil against the Italian population wasn't the subject of serious research until very late, despite the fact that tens of thousands of Italians were executed, raped, tortured, and kidnapped.

Italy failed to carry out substantive reflection about the fact that fascism was born in Italy, that atrocious crimes were committed in its name, and that an overpowering majority of the population supported it as Italian *Mitläufer*. On the contrary, a very comfortable legend was perpetuated: that of the *Italiani, brava gente*, presenting the Italians, including those who supported fascism and went to war or colonized Africa in its name, as brave people, if a bit naïve, who wouldn't hurt a fly, manipulated by Benito Mussolini and Nazi Germany.

At the start of the 1990s, a huge judicial and political scandal was the death knell for Italian political parties that came out of the resistance to fascism. This shake-up favored the coming to power of new parties, such as Silvio Berlusconi's Forza Italia and Gianfranco Fini's Alleanza Nazionale, which distanced themselves from anti-Fascist references, even beginning to open the way for a partial rehabilitation of fascism. Since then, in Italy, to openly declare your Fascist penchant is no longer taboo, as I experienced in Tuscany. Even in the middle of society, it's no longer rare to hear people say "fascism is demonized," that "it has positive aspects." Facebook pages and websites advocating fascism proliferate with total impunity. Knickknacks in memory of Mussolini, and even Hitler, are freely sold. Some villages honor Fascists, naming an airport after them, or constructing a mausoleum.

Nostalgia for fascism has boosted the rise of the extreme right leader Matteo Salvini, who governed the country in 2018 for one year, supported by the populist left-wing Five Star Movement. The country plunged into Europhobia, racism, and a vulgar populism. Donald Trump's former strategist Steve Bannon praised this fusion of right and left populism as "a unique experiment" that "will change global politics." But it failed. Salvini was dismissed from the government one year later. Five Star still has some power in the government, but is weakened by the departure of an increasing number of parliamentarians and a decline in popularity. Nevertheless, too many Italians are still attracted to demagogic, manipulative speeches. According to polls, half of the Italians still don't believe fascism is dangerous.

❊   ❊   ❊

Italy isn't the only European country to struggle to come to terms with its past. Austria also hid for a long time behind Nazi Germany's crimes to escape the memory work that might have helped to prevent the rise of the extreme right.

In 2018, on the highway to Vienna, while vast snowy valleys bordered with crenelated peaks unfolded before my eyes, I heard an Austrian on the radio talking about his father, Otto von Wächter, an SS-Führer, governor of the district of Galicia while Poland was under Nazi rule, where 3 million Polish Jews were murdered. "He had nothing to do with the deportation of Jews because it doesn't fit with him, so to speak," said Horst von Wächter. The story of Otto von Wächter and the poisonous inheritance he left his family followed me for an hour. Over and over, Horst tried to find excuses for him: obeying orders, blindness, powerlessness. His daughter Magdalena, who, like me, never knew her grandfather, said, "I'd also very much like to believe it, I want to believe it, I believe some of it, I believe my father." Magdalena's fourteen-year-old daughter, Gwendolyn, put it in even stronger terms: "I heard he wasn't such a bad Nazi."

How is it possible that Horst defends his father, implicated as deeply as he was in the Nazi criminal machine, while my father firmly condemns Karl Schwarz, a simple *Mitläufer*? Later I learned that Magdalena had changed her mind about her grandfather and condemned his actions. Yet how is it possible that she, unlike me, chose to blind herself for so long in the name of family loyalty? How do you account for these differences? As for Karl and Otto and their different degrees of guilt, was the heavier burden too difficult for his descendants to accept? And did another element factor in—that they grew up in Austria while my father and I mainly had a German education?

The war was barely over when the Austrians rushed to inscribe, in the foundational text of the Second Austrian Republic, that they had been the first victims of Hitler's imperialism. In reality, when German troops invaded the country—the Anschluss of 1938—it didn't put up any resistance. The Viennese police had already donned Nazi armbands and started to arrest "undesirables." A few days later, Adolf Hitler, who was born in Austria, was welcomed as a hero by 250,000 people in Vienna. The will to draw closer to Germany was common in Austria, tracing back to the dissolution of the Hapsburg Empire in 1918, which had reduced Austria to a very small country. On top of that, National Socialism was already rooted in the country during the interwar period, and anti-Semitism was just as rife in Austria as it was in Germany.

The Austrians celebrated the arrival of German troops with anti-Semitic violence of rare intensity. Vienna, the star of Central Europe, once bursting with culture, became the theater of its own decline. The crowd began to pillage, beat, and kill those who had contributed so much to the brilliance of their city. How many Austrian citizens plunged into the sadistic pleasure of publicly humiliating Jews, making them crawl down the streets with bare hands, or forcing devout men to shout "Heil Hitler" at the top of their lungs? Of the 185,000 Jews still in Austria in 1938, 120,000 managed to leave and 65,000 were murdered. The near-totality of the Roma community, some tens of thousands of people, was exterminated.

In the chaos of the Anschluss, Austrian bureaucrats and soldiers were integrated into the Nazi apparatus. Those who refused to conform rarely risked more than losing their jobs or being forced into retirement. Even so, the majority collaborated. Historians still debate why so many Austrians were part of the staff involved in carrying out the Holocaust.

After the war, Austria plunged into a half-century of denial about its crimes, going so far as to deny the existence of anti-Semitism in its society. In the eighties, while the world was just beginning to understand the monstrous dimensions of the Holocaust, Austria continued to protect Nazi criminals, even celebrating them as heroes. After the election of Kurt Waldheim, a former Nazi, as Austrian president in 1986, it took the indignation of the international community for Austrians to finally feel some shame. In 1991, for the first time, a chancellor, Franz Vranitzky, recognized the shared Austrian responsibility for Nazi crimes. Many new measures followed to commemorate and compensate the victims of Nazism, and to shed light on this history. Didn't these measures arrive too late for the victims, long dead, and for Austrians, who had been cloistered for decades in a culture of denial?

It didn't prevent the FPÖ, the Freedom Party of Austria, a party that maintains an ambiguous relationship with the legacy of National Socialism, from becoming a junior coalition partner in Chancellor Sebastian Kurz's government in 2017. Its leader, Heinz-Christian Strache, was named vice-chancellor. Strache has historically cozied up to neo-Nazi and Holocaust-denying groups, and photos show him making the *Kühnengruß*, a sign with three raised fingers that's a variation on the Hitler salute. His party colleagues don't hesitate to collaborate with publications that contain anti-Semitic, racist, and neo-Nazi content, and more than half of the FPÖ deputies are members of student confederations, *Burschenschaften*, that support a *völkisch* worldview which defends the idea that only individuals from the same origins can constitute a people—a central tenet of Nazi ideology.

In 2000, when the FPÖ came to power for the first time as a junior coalition partner of the conservative People's Party, a vague indignation swept through Europe. For several months, members of the European Union reduced their bilateral and diplomatic relationships with Austria to a minimum. Seventeen years later, the FPÖ victory didn't make waves, forming part of the normalization of far-right ideology that had gained ground all over Europe in the last decade.

In 2019, a secretly recorded video showed that Strache had been receptive to a Russian national's offer to gain control of Austria's largest tabloid, *Kronen Zeitung*, and provide positive coverage for the FPÖ. Strache suggested he could offer lucrative public contracts in exchange. The scandal led to the collapse of the government and Strache's resignation. The decline of the FPÖ was immediate, but it is still the country's third-largest political force.

Poor track records have weakened the appeal of some populist and extremist parties. Unfortunately, others emerged unscathed from these repeated demonstrations of incompetence, corruption, and autocratic tendencies—especially in France. In April 2022, in the second round of the French presidential elections, the extreme right reached a historic record since WWII: the candidate Marine Le Pen received 41 percent of the votes. Though the incumbent president, the moderate and pro-Europe Emmanuel Macron, was reelected, some electors supported him only to prevent the extreme right from coming to power. In the first round of the two-round presidential elections, the traditional moderate left and moderate right parties collapsed. Far-right candidates like Marine Le Pen and Eric Zemmour and far-left candidates like Jean-Luc Mélenchon gained, all together, almost 55 percent of the vote—despite the fact that all three have sympathized with Putin's policies, including his brutal war in Syria and his annexation of Crimea in 2014. Mélenchon has expressed admiration for dictators like the Venezuelan Hugo Chavez, while Marine Le Pen has done the same for Hungary's autocrat Viktor Orbán. These results reveal how vulnerable the French have become to populist, anti-European and anti-democratic rhetoric. Even friends of mine have locked themselves into a left-wing ideological blindness that distances them more and more from democratic principles.

While Putin's Russia has sought for years to tear Europe apart by supporting antidemocratic leaders, interfering in elections, spreading fake news, and launching cyberattacks, the invasion of Ukraine triggered the opposite: a unified European front and the renewed consciousness of our shared commitment to peace and democracy. Many internal divisions have melted away, and the EU imposed broad financial and economic sanctions on Russia. An unprecedented sense of solidarity with the millions of Ukrainian refugees swept across Eastern Europe. Poland has taken in more than 2.5 million refugees. The invasion also helped discredit populist leaders, who, in recent years, had openly expressed their admiration for Vladimir Putin. The most dramatic political shift came from Germany, a country that traditionally embraces pacifism, which broke a historical taboo by announcing a massive investment in military defense and security. For the first time since the end of World War II, the continent's first economic power is paving the way to assume a military role in Europe.

The invasion also allowed NATO to put aside internal divisions, uniting Europe and America like nothing since the fall of the Berlin Wall. A relief after years of tensions under Trump's administration.

The United States is like the brother we've always admired in some ways, and in others like the one we've always felt suspicious of—for its blind veneration of capitalism and somewhat simplistic view of the world. Still, a brother and a powerful ally we can count on in the event of a major crisis. We value this alliance more than ever, as we now know that there is no guarantee of eternal friendship. This has been clear since the day the United States elected Donald Trump as president, a man who incarnates the opposite of the founding values of the European Union, and those of the United States. Seemingly unable or unwilling to deal with the demanding rules of democracy, which require reflection, argument, and nuance, he instead embraced an unexamined, authoritarian style; violent, vulgar rhetoric; and a dangerous incompetence. For many Europeans, the shock was brutal. "The End of the World as We Know It" was the headline in *Der Spiegel*, accompanied by an illustration of a fireball with Trump's features, his mouth wide open, ready to swallow the planet. In the days following his election, a flurry of racist and anti-Semitic acts seized the United States. During his campaign, Trump drew from the reservoir of the "alt-right," the far-right extremists who defend white supremacy and include neo-Nazis in their ranks. By flirting with this ideology, Trump activated a particular base and got elected. Fifty years after the Supreme Court's abolition of racial segregation in the United States, and seventy-one years after the victory over Nazism in Europe, a victory that was foundational for U.S. patriotism, what amnesia can claim Trump as its symptom? His election was part of the reason I decided to write *Those Who Forget*.

Donald Trump is not a Fascist—partly because he cannot commit to a cause other than himself. He is an opportunist who used the same methods of mass manipulation that the Fascists used a century ago in Europe—it's not for nothing that he chose Steve Bannon, an admirer of fascism, as his first propaganda adviser. The playbook is very simple: first, stoke fear. Create catastrophic scenarios and present oneself as a providential figure outside the system who will solve the problems his country faces: for Trump, it was the "invasion" of migrants and terrorists, the end of white supremacy, the sabotage of traditional familial structures, and the danger of Islamization. Demagogues like Trump offer a false and oversimplified vision of the world, putting their citizens in danger by ignoring the real, complex problems.

Second, blur the line between truth and lies. Much has been made about Trump's obsession with fake news, his attack on the American press and on scientific facts, and his denial of climate change, fatal for future generations. The efficiency of this method, already proven by the Nazi propaganda minister Joseph Goebbels, is now amplified by the rise of social media. The more these incendiary messages provoke interactions, the more the algorithms circulate them. Posts that appeal to reason and reflection don't generate as many emotional reactions and therefore are shared less.

The idea behind spreading lies and conspiracy theories was summarized by Hannah Arendt: "If everybody always lies to you, the consequence is not that you believe the lies, but rather that nobody believes anything any longer . . . And a people that no longer can believe anything cannot make up its mind. It is deprived not only of its capacity to act but also of its capacity to think and to judge. And with such a people you can then do what you please."

Third, give people a clear-cut identity. Trump offered: white, nationalist, Christian, sexist, conservative. He provided his voters with the flattering feeling of belonging to an exclusive community, like the *Volksgemeinschaft* (people's community) under Nazism, which can keep out so-called enemies because of their ethnicity, religion, sexual orientation, political opinions, intellectual background. Trump hypnotized his followers with the slogan "America First."

Trump's victory brought an alarming flaw to light: the susceptibility of Americans to manipulative tactics that undermine democracy. If the interference of Russia in favor of Trump's candidacy played a role, it only served to reinforce a preexisting tendency toward authoritarianism in American society, stoked by a group of Republicans and media companies such as Fox News, which spread a terrifying, simplistic vision of the world, sowing fear at every opportunity. Trump pushed the limit further and further, attacking the human rights and democratic norms that once made U.S. democracy great. While doing this, Trump and his administration tried to make hate speech look like a defense of freedom of speech and abuses of power like a resistance against political correctness. Fiddling with words, turning their meaning upside down, is an old technique that permitted the Nazis to invert morals and make crime acceptable: what was good yesterday becomes evil today, and what was evil becomes good; defending human rights is "weak," insulting and humiliating disabled people and racial minorities becomes "courageous."

When a mob of Trump supporters stormed the Capitol Building in Washington, D.C., on January 6, 2021, it should have at last become clear to the Republican Party and their electors that their leader was a real danger to democracy. Before the attack, Trump, who refused to recognize his electoral defeat against Joe Biden, had given a speech in which he encouraged a large crowd to violently resist Congress's certification of his opponent's victory. But the assault on the Capitol was only the tip of the iceberg. Tearing down democracy didn't happen through the force of one man, but because of the massive complicity of a significant part of the political class. Neither fear nor blindness are valid excuses for supporting Trump's ruthless assault on democracy. Loyalty is often a convenient alibi for cowardice, indifference, and opportunism. In the aftermath, many Republicans left the sinking ship and put the blame on Donald Trump. But getting rid of him and forgetting about his mandate will not help to heal America.

No unification, no democratic foundation will be sustainable without questioning what happened, and most of all how it *could* happen. This means, within the framework of a wide collective reflection, acknowledging the responsibility of Trump's aides and supporters, in the Republican Party, in the institutions, and in the media and the business world, and also the failures of the Democratic Party. But just facing up to the Trump era won't be enough. True healing is not possible without confronting the deep roots of the trauma and divisions in American society: the Civil War, the massacres of Native Americans, and the enslavement, segregation, and oppression of Black Americans, including the barbaric mob ritual of lynching, then photographing the victims for postcards sold as a souvenir. These shadows of the past won't disappear if they are ignored. They will continue to dig the nation's grave in silence.

The United States is not the only country that urgently needs to address its history of colonialism and slavery: the United Kingdom, which once ruled a fifth of the globe, has its own work to do. Until

2016, when I took a long trip to Cairo to make a documentary film, I had never wondered about how the British had confronted their colonial past. While I was interviewing primary sources and historians of twentieth-century Egypt, I was surprised at how often I encountered disparaging comments about Britain. Hostility was still fresh toward the British, who occupied Egypt in 1882 to control the Suez Canal, and then imposed their presence by force for seventy more years.

When I returned to Berlin, I met two English thirty-somethings at a birthday party, and I spoke to them about my experience in Egypt. They replied that Britain had nothing to be ashamed of: they were proud of their colonial past. I was taken aback. Perhaps because of where I come from, I have a tendency to project the memory work Germans have done onto other countries, and it seemed obvious to me that Britons would be apologetic about a colonial history fraught with massacres, slave trade, cultural annihilation, economic exploitation, oppression, and hasty redrawing of borders.

In fact, these two young men represented a widespread sentiment among British people. A 2019 poll by the British government's polling institute, YouGov, revealed that one third of the population believed colonies were better off as part of the British Empire, a higher proportion than any of the former colonial powers except the Netherlands. Britons are also more likely to say they would like their country to still have an empire. This poll stunned some British people, particularly those from former colonies. "If you grew up in Britain, like me, you probably would not be able to recall being taught anything substantial about British colonial history in school," says the British-Iraqi writer Ruqaya Izzidien in an article for *Al-Jazeera*. "The British curriculum dedicates plenty of attention to the violence of others—in Nazi Germany or during the American Civil War. . . . But a British school would not teach you anything about the brutality of British colonialism," she continues.

In 2010, the UK's secretary of state for education, the Conservative Party's Michael Gove, sought to bolster the teaching of colonial
history in schools. He turned to Niall Ferguson, a well-known
conservative historian and writer and producer of many television
documentary series, who presents the Empire as a "good thing"
globally, something that could have helped to spread free markets
and parliamentary democracy, in some ways redeeming its "sins."

The "good deeds" often cited in Britain include the construction of railroads in India and the economic prosperity it generated
for its colonies. The latter assumption might be viable in certain
regions, but elsewhere it is weakened by the facts. In India, British economic policies unleashed a famine that killed at least 30
million Indian people in the 1870s, three decades after they had
applied the same policies in Ireland, resulting in the deaths of a
million Irish people, or 12 percent of the population. The Indian
politician Shashi Tharoor argues in his book *Inglorious Empire:
What the British Did to India* that in 1700 India was a rich country,
producing 27 percent of global GDP, and that after two decades
of British occupation, it had become poor, stripped of national
industry, with 90 percent of the population living in poverty and
16 percent illiterate. On the other hand, the British share of global
GDP rose from 1.8 percent to 10 percent in two hundred years.
The aim of British colonialism was to get rich, not to distribute
prosperity.

The British certainly did bring peace, as well as infrastructure
and medical progress to some areas, and they behaved better than
other colonizers such as the Belgians and the Japanese. Britain had
a pioneering role in abolishing slavery in the nineteenth century,
after developing a notoriously effective slave trade. In its defense,
Britain also encouraged the rise of a native elite in India who were
educated and Anglicized. But in fact, the colonizers imposed an
apartheid society, racist and unequal, and marked by massacres.
At the end of the nineteenth century, the cult of Anglo-Saxon

superiority over all others, and particularly over Black people, translated into brutal colonial campaigns designed to dispossess local African populations of their raw-material-rich or strategically valuable lands.

A collective awareness of this painful reality has yet to emerge in Britain. It seems that neither the political leaders nor the schools or mass media have fulfilled their responsibilities to memory work, while there is a cruel lack of museums and memorials to remind people of the errors of the past. On the contrary: there are still statues and places celebrating imperial figures without mentioning their controversial dimension.

For decades, the former colonies of the Crown, regrouped under the auspices of the Commonwealth, generally respected the narrative of an exemplary empire, likely because of diplomatic and commercial concerns. In the 2000s, however, victims of British colonial abuses have begun to demand justice from the British state. For example, the former Kenyan insurgents from the anticolonial Mau Mau rebellion that began in 1952, which the authorities violently repressed, resorting to torture and to summary executions, and confining almost the entire Kikuyu population in detention camps and reserves where tens of thousands died. After a long struggle, the former foreign secretary William Hague finally announced a compensation package for the victims and expressed "sincere regret" but downplayed it: "We continue to deny liability on behalf of the Government . . . for the actions of the colonial administration." Other judicial proceedings concerned colonial crimes in Cyprus and in Malaysia. "These legal proceedings are an imperfect means for coming to terms with the colonial past. Even when the British government accepts to pay compensation to settle the claims, there is no real admission of responsibility," says Zachary Douglas, a lawyer who has worked on several of these cases. "As a matter of law, the British government considers that each colonial government was a separate legal entity for which it is not legally responsible. The reality, however, is that the governors appointed by the British government to head the colonial governments scrupulously followed instructions issued by ministers in London. The historical archives in each of the cases I was involved in are replete with examples. London was always calling the shots and the autonomy given to colonial governments was more a question of form than of substance."

Other European countries have faced much more openly the violence of their empire, like Belgium in the Congo or France in Algeria. In 2017 President Emmanuel Macron didn't hesitate to call French colonization a "crime against humanity."

Some British intellectuals have underlined a correlation between the vote to withdraw from the EU in 2016, Brexit, and the glorification of the British Empire. According to the Oxford professor Danny Darling, author of *Rule Britannia*, there is a British elite responsible for Brexit, an elite that was raised in the traditions of the British Empire and educated in schools where old-fashioned history ("we civilized the world") was taught. They are symptomatic of a Britain struggling to conceive of its place in the world post-empire. The inability to honestly face the past has fed the illusion that Britain still has enough influence to operate without the European Union, though in reality its influence is in decline. After the Brexit referendum a common slogan was "Now Let's Make Britain Great Again." So far, since its formal exit from the EU on January 31, 2020, Brexit has clearly done more harm than good to the United Kingdom, at least economically.

From all these observations, I deduce that countries that avoid confronting the past are especially vulnerable to the rise of nationalism and populism. But even Germany, a country that has learned from the errors of its past like no other in the world, succumbed to populism in 2017. For the first time since 1949, an extreme-right party, the Alternative für Deutschland (AfD), entered the Bundestag, with 12.6 percent of the vote. Plunging into the breech caused by the refugee crisis, its popularity continued to grow in the following years, especially in the ex-GDR, where AfD's popularity is two to three times higher than in the west—partly because of the fragility of a still-young democracy and a faulty memory. Thirty years after the Wall came down, a division persists.

People often ask me if this evolution is a sign of the inadequacy of memory work in Germany. Yet the energy the far right deploys to combat this process of reflection seems to indicate the opposite. Its leaders denounce a "propaganda of reeducation" and claim "a 180-degree turn" to put an end to the "culture of shame." They support "the right to be proud of German soldiers who fought during the Second World War" or affirm that "Hitler and the Nazis were only a speck in the thousand-year history of glorious Germany." If they mobilize this way, it's because memory work is an impediment to their success. But what most speaks for the effectiveness of memory work is the fact that in the 2022 federal elections, AfD gained only 10.3 percent of the vote: one of the weakest rates for the far-right in Europe. Collectively coming to terms with the past has given German democracy an unsuspected strength.

No society is immune, and learning from the past is a process that must be continually nourished and rethought, just like democracy. The populist and autocratic threat in Europe and the USA reveals the need to rethink memory work, to adapt it to new generations for whom the Second World War feels like a distant heritage, by establishing an emotional tie through family memory. It is also urgent to make room for another past: the history of slavery and colonialism. Facing up to these shadows shouldn't be done in a culture of guilt, nor should it be used to stir up hatred or sectarianism or to nourish an anachronistic, simplistic vision of the past. Tearing down statues, removing art pieces, and hindering independent thought and research in universities is not going to make the present better. Denouncing is not enough. Memory work is successful when it reminds each one of us of our present-day responsibilities and our own weaknesses and strengths. When it makes us empathize with the victims but also realize that we are not immune from failing, like all those *Mitläufer*, ordinary people who became complicit in crimes by following the current. Through indifference, opportunism, and blindness many of us already conform to unfair and fatal systems that destroy our planet, generate monstrous inequalities, and value money over humanity. Keeping the memory of the past alive helps us to live more consciously. To shape the future together, understand the world instead of suffer it, and identify priorities and avoid dangers—those that come from others, but, above all, those that come from ourselves.

We Europeans have come a long way. Our memories and our dreams are fragmented, and sometimes contradictory. But in this diversity, there is at least a common denominator: we have conquered murderous dictatorships and ideologies that crushed human identity, blinded people, and manipulated them into serving the madness of their leaders. We have built democracy and given citizens back their dignity and the right to choose their identity. Let us not abandon memory to autocrats like Vladimir Putin and to populists. Let us not allow them to transform Europe, once again, into an infamous beast that destroys civilizations, force-fed on national egotism and intolerance. Let us defend a continent where various religions and multiethnic cultures have bestowed an unparalleled richness. Let us give Europeans back their pride in this bright heritage, the heritage that caused them to fight against those who would extinguish it. We will no longer be victims of history. Each one of us will be indispensable.

Epilogue

Julius Löbmann is no longer living. In 1961, he joined little Fritz and his wife, Mathilde, somewhere in the universe. He had no children with his second wife. Irma Löbmann, Siegmund's wife and the mother of Lore and Hans, lived for a time in Strasbourg, then finally moved to be with her children in the United States. They have since died.

Lotte Kramer, who married another German Jewish exile in Great Britain, had a son and several grandchildren. Her wounds never healed. She kept the telegram her parents sent to her in England, from the Gurs camp, in March 1942: "We have to move house. Adieu." It was their last sign of life.

After the war, Lotte wanted to see Mainz once more. "The bombs had destroyed so much, it was very sad, but our house was still standing. I went to see Greta and Bertold, friends of my parents. Their daughter had something for me. Before she was deported, my mother had filled a big trunk with a pile of things, bed linens and tablecloths. It was a dowry for my marriage. She had guessed she would never return."

In the 1970s, Lotte Kramer began to write poems.

SILENCE

Today the river slinks like oil,
Hardly a current in its mud
As autumn leaves crawl on its face.

I left them in their blinding talk
To meet adopted path and sky,
And bend the grass for light and space.

Here I can hold the air with birds,
Still, solitary in their flight
Without men's calculated race.

Now only sun and water rule
Unchallenged over silent pain:
And the burst cry of a grey swan.

Lotte Kramer

Translator's Note

The text of this American edition of *Those Who Forget* has benefited from Valerie Steiker's editorial sensibility. I am grateful to Eva Gschwend for her help in translating some quotations from the original German, and to Alice Kaplan for her guidance on sources related to the trial of Robert Brasillach.

Whenever possible, I have used the existing English translations of quotations from other languages. The following list acknowledges the translators and English-language versions where these citations can be found, in the order in which they appear in the text.

For quotations from Freud's *Group Psychology and the Analysis of the Ego*, I have used the translation by James Strachey.

For de Gaulle's comments about the trial of Robert Brasillach, I used Alice Kaplan's excellent translation from her 2000 book *The Collaborator*. The full context of these quotations is also available in Richard Howard's translation of de Gaulle's *War Memoirs*, and the following quote about Pierre Laval is from Howard's translation.

The quotes from President Richard von Weizsäcker's speech about Nazi crimes are from *The New York Times*, May 9, 1985, as translated by the West German Foreign Ministry.

The quotations from Nolte about the *Historikerstreit* are based on James Knowlton and Truett Cates's *Forever in the Shadow of Hitler?: Original Documents of the Historikerstreit, the Controversy Concerning the Singularity of the Holocaust*. In this case, I have slightly revised the translations for style and accuracy.

The quotation from Stendhal's *On Love* is translated by Sophie Lewis.

The lines from Paul Celan's "Death Fugue" are from Jerome Rothenberg's excellent translation, collected in *Paul Celan: Selections* (University of California Press, 2005). The rest of the poem is also available at Poets.org. I have used Marco Roberto's translation of Hitler's *Mein Kampf*. The passages from *After the Wall: Confessions from an East German Childhood* are from the translation by Jefferson Chase.

About the Author

Géraldine Schwarz is a German-French journalist, author, and documentary filmmaker based in Berlin. *Those Who Forget* is her first book. It won the European Book Prize, Germany's Winfried Peace Prize, and Italy's NordSud International Prize for Literature and Science. First published in French as *Les Amnésiques* (Flammarion), then in German as *Die Gedächtnislosen* (Secession Verlag), the book is currently being translated into nine languages.

About the Translator

Laura Marris is a poet and translator. Her work has appeared in *The Yale Review*, *The Common*, *Asymptote*, *The Brooklyn Rail*, and elsewhere. She is a MacDowell Colony fellow and the winner of a Daniel Varoujan Prize. Her recent translations include Louis Guilloux's novel *Blood Dark*, which was shortlisted for the 2018 Oxford-Weidenfeld Translation Prize, and she is currently at work on a new translation of Albert Camus's *The Plague*.

THOSE
WHO FORGET

Géraldine
Schwarz

This reading group guide for Those Who Forget *includes an introduction, discussion questions, and ideas for enhancing your book club. The suggested questions are intended to help your reading group find new and interesting angles and topics for your discussion. We hope that these ideas will enrich your conversation and increase your enjoyment of the book.*

Introduction

During World War II, Géraldine Schwarz's German grandparents were neither heroes nor villains; they were merely *Mitläufer*— those who followed the current. Once the war ended, they wanted to bury the past under the wreckage of the Third Reich.

Decades later, while delving through filing cabinets in the basement of their apartment building in Mannheim, Schwarz discovers that in 1938, her paternal grandfather Karl took advantage of Nazi policies to buy a business from a Jewish family for a low price. She finds letters from the only survivor of this family (all the others perished in Auschwitz), demanding reparations. But Karl Schwarz refused to acknowledge his responsibility. Géraldine starts to question the past: How guilty were her grandparents? What makes us complicit? On her mother's side, she investigates the role of her French grandfather, a policeman under the Vichy regime.

Weaving together the threads of three generations of her family story with Europe's process of postwar reckoning, Schwarz explores how millions were seduced by ideology, overcome by a fog of denial after the war, and, in Germany at least, eventually managed to transform collective guilt into democratic responsibility. She asks: How can nations learn from history? And she observes that countries that avoid confronting the past are especially vulnerable to extremism. Searing and unforgettable, *Those Who Forget* is a riveting memoir, an illuminating history, and an urgent call for remembering.

Topics & Questions for Discussion

Nazi Germany

1. Schwarz defines her German grandparents as *Mitläufer*, ordinary people who, like the majority of the German population, "followed the current" (page 1) during World War II. She argues that without the cooperation of the *Mitläufer*, the Nazis could never have carried out the atrocities of the Holocaust. What does she mean by that?

2. How did Mannheim change during the 1930s and early 1940s, and how did this impact the city's Jewish community day by day? How did it impact Schwarz's grandparents?

3. How did opportunism motivate many Germans to support anti-Semitic measures? How did its citizens become accomplices in a criminal regime? What role did indifference, fear, and blindness, as well as the manipulative strategies of the Third Reich, play in society's transformation?

4. What parts of Hitler's regime were appealing to Lydia, Schwarz's paternal grandmother? How does Schwarz use her grandmother's example to convey a popular opinion of the time?

5. When did Schwarz herself become aware of the original owners of her grandfather's company, the *Mineralölgesellschaft*? How did she go about learning more about the Löbmanns' lives?

6. What did the first letter from Julius Löbmann ask for or demand? What did Schwarz's grandfather think of Julius Löbmann's lawsuit? Why? How did the Third Reich's strategy of legalizing crime impact Karl Schwarz's behavior?

7. To what extent are Schwarz's grandparents victims and perpetrators at the same time?

8. What's the story behind Oma's dining room furniture? Describe its provenance, and the likely fate of the people who originally owned it. When did Schwarz discover its origins? Why does she argue that popular attitudes about the looting and auctions of Jewish property are even more revealing than apathy about the deportations?

Germany after the War

9. What did Schwarz's father, Volker, learn in primary school about the Nazi regime? What does this say about where postwar Germany was in acknowledging its culpability?

10. Describe the antimilitary, antinuclear, and antifascist move-

ment that sprung up in Germany in the 1960s. What changes did that movement bring? How did this lead to the transformation in attitudes around who was responsible for the Nazis' crimes against humanity?

11. Schwarz describes a "normalization" (page 222) process in Germany's participation in international politics in the early 2000s. What did this process look like?

12. Why do Schwarz's father and her aunt Ingrid have differing understandings of the past? What does this tell us about the reliability of memory and the need to confront memory with historical fact? How does Schwarz solve the problem in her book?

13. Schwarz quotes the philosopher Paul Ricoeur, who says: "To make memory an imperative is the beginning of an abuse. . . . I'm cautious about the expression 'duty to remember' . . . I prefer 'the work of memory'" (page 247). How would Schwarz describe "the work of memory" in Germany? How did the reflection about the responsibility of the *Mitläufer* help Germany build its democracy? How did Germany build something positive from a terribly destructive legacy?

France

14. What was the political situation in France after its defeat by Nazi Germany in 1940? How did life change for French citizens? How far did the collaboration of France with Nazi Germany go?

15. What was Schwarz's maternal grandfather's role during the

occupation? How does Schwarz define the scope of his responsibility compared to that of her German grandfather?

16. What was the official story after the war of how French people resisted occupation, as told, for instance, to Schwarz's mother? What were the myths of "resistant France" and "victorious France" (page 162)? How does this encourage or prevent what Schwarz defines as "memory work"?

17. What difference does Schwarz sees between France's and Germany's democracies and how does she relate it to the way each country confronted its past?

Learning from History

18. What does Schwarz observe about the lack of memory work in many European countries? What connection does she make between memory work and far-right nationalism? What parallels does she see between today's demagogues and those of the 1930s?

19. Compare the experience of Jewish refugees on the *Saint Louis* being turned away by Cuba, the United States, and Canada with Angela Merkel's welcoming thousands of refugees to Germany in the 2010s.

20. Schwarz suggest that we can best learn from history by reflecting on the role of the people, not just focusing on the responsibility of the leaders. How can the question *What would I have done?* remind us of our present-day responsibilities and help us to protect democracy?

Europe after 1989

21. How did the fall of the Berlin Wall play into the political conversation around Germany's past? How did Eastern Europe confront their own fascist past under the domination of the Soviet Union during the Cold War?

22. Schwarz writes that "Europe was brought back to life twice—in 1945 and 1989" (page 282). She argues for the importance of a transnational European memory, one that would build bridges between countries and communities through the work of remembering the trauma of the Holocaust, crimes committed under Soviet domination, and the criminal colonial past. Describe what she means by this.

Enhance Your Book Club

1. How has the United States reckoned with or failed to reckon with the massive injustices of our past? How are we as ordinary citizens complicit now? Discuss.

2. How would you describe the current role of Germany in international politics? How do you think this change has been accomplished?

3. Read Günter Grass's *The Tin Drum* and compare Oskar's experiences in Danzig to Schwarz's family's experiences in Mannheim.